THE GRINDING WHEEL

A JEFF TRASK CRIME DRAMA (BOOK 7)

MARC RAINER

Rukia

Dedicated to the memory of
Jamie Elizabeth Ambrose
1960-2020
Beloved little sister and talented editor,
Without whom this series would never have been possible.

THE GRINDING WHEEL

A JEFF TRASK CRIME DRAMA: BOOK SEVEN

By

Marc Rainer

1

THE FIRST OF her senses to return was her sight, and she opened her eyes to a nightmare.

She was groggy and disoriented as the drugs started to wear off. She slowly realized she was lying on her back, and as her head cleared, she began trying to make some sense of what she saw above her.

What—who—is that?

She saw an image above her on the ceiling. A young woman was bound—*no those aren't ropes; they're leather belts, so she's not tied, she's strapped down*—to a table. The table looked like it was made of metal—stainless steel, maybe—with wings reaching out from the top so that the woman was positioned as if she was on a cross. The leather belts around her wrists, ankles, and forehead held her hands, head, and feet in position on the table.

Her head throbbed for a moment, and she tried to bring her right hand to her forehead. Her hand refused to move. She jerked her head from side to side, moving it only slightly, but just enough to confirm that *she* was the woman strapped to the table. The image above her was not a poster or a photograph, but a reflection in a large mirror suspended on steel chains that hung through the tiles of a suspended acoustic ceiling.

She stared at the edges of the mirror, started to panic, and looked for something she could use to understand her situation. She could see the sides of the room, but because the mirror was hung so that her head was at the top edge of the reflection, she had no view of the area behind her, past the head of the table. The reflection showed that she was in a long, narrow room. The walls were made of concrete cinder blocks, painted in a faint shade of green so long ago that more bare concrete than paint was now showing. There was a counter along the side to her left, with tools and machines mounted on a workbench. Something was hanging on a coat tree near the wall at the far end of the bench. Two large freezers lined the other side of the room. Between them was the door to a pen of some kind, big enough for a large dog.

A severed deer head was looking at her in the mirror from the top of one of the freezers. She smelled a dark, sweet odor, and decided it was the stale stench of blood. There were a couple of deer heads mounted on the walls, so she assumed that the odor was probably from the processing of venison.

She felt her pulse and her breathing racing.

Easy, girl. Probably just another kinky john. He must have slipped me something. Let him have his fun, keep your cool, and get out of this and go home. Don't worry about the money. Wait for your chance and just go. Give him what he wants and just get the hell out of here.

She scanned the mirror again.

Where is the creep, anyway?

She wondered whether she should call for help. She had no idea where she was. If he heard her, would it make him mad? Maybe he was close by and was waiting for her to wake up.

At least that would get this party started, she thought, *and then that would get it over with.*

"HEY!! HEY!! Anybody?!!"

Nothing.

"Is *anybody* there? *Please?!*"

The sound of unoiled hinges creaked at the end of the room past her feet.

She strained her neck to lift her head against the restraining belt to get a look at the lower edge of the mirror. It looked down on a pudgy man with long, stringy gray hair surrounding a bald spot. He was dressed in dirty bib overalls. She followed him as he walked the length of the metal table, disappearing as he passed her head and the top of the mirror image. She heard a door open and close on squeaking hinges at that end of the room, and a strong chemical odor filled her nostrils. Moments later, the door hinges creaked again.

He was suddenly leering at her over her left shoulder, looking down into her eyes. He said nothing, but just stood above her, studying her face. He turned away just as suddenly as he had appeared. She looked at the mirror again and saw him reappear by the counter on her left side. She heard some machinery start up—a high-pitched, whining sound—and she felt her breathing racing once more.

"Hey, now. You wanted some fun. Why don't we just do that and then you can take me home? Hell, you don't even have to drive me. Just let me give you what you want and then let me go, okay? Please?"

There was no response from him. Instead, she saw him grab something from the top of the workbench and she heard what she thought was the grinding of metal on another surface. He walked past her, disappearing once more from her view in the mirror.

He was suddenly by her head again, leaning over her and staring into her eyes.

"*WHAT DO YOU WANT FROM ME?!!*" she finally screamed.

She saw a light of excitement flash in his eyes as her cry echoed off the walls. His eyes narrowed as the corners of his mouth turned up a bit into a slimy smile.

I get it, she thought. *He wants me to show fear. That's not going to be a problem here ...*

She screamed again, involuntarily this time, as his right hand suddenly flashed close to her face. He was holding an enormous pair of shears. He pressed the flat edges of the blades into her cheek, still staring into her eyes and measuring her reaction.

"WHAT ARE YOU DOING?!! *WHY* ARE YOU DOING THIS TO ME?!!" she screamed, twisting her torso and pulling against the straps on her wrists.

She tried to turn her head so that she wouldn't have to look at his face, but the belt had her skull locked in position. He remained above her, looking intently into her eyes as he brought the shears back above her face. He began opening and closing the blades—slowly at first, then more rapidly—an angry clacking sound filling her ears as they slammed together. He lowered the blades close to her face, making her fear that she was about to lose her nose. She screamed again, a terrified wail this time.

He was out of view again for a second. She closed her eyes, sobbing.

When she opened them, he was by her feet, waiting for her to look at him. She strained her eyes down past her cheeks, pulling against the head strap, shifting her gaze first down her body then up to the mirror, trying to see what he was going to do next.

His eyes met hers in the mirror. He held up the shears again, clacking them open and shut. He approved of the terror he saw on her face with a nod, and then began cutting the right leg of her jeans, starting at the bottom seam, and working his way toward her waist. He worked methodically, cutting slowly through the denim, making sure that the bottom blade of the shears pressed into her leg with every snip, not cutting her, but *threatening* to puncture her skin with every movement.

A horrible realization hit her like a lightning bolt.

He's destroying my clothes. I'll have nothing to wear if I leave this place. That's because he has no plans of ever LETTING me leave this place!

She said a prayer. She couldn't remember the last time she had prayed, but she prayed now with every fiber that remained in her soul.

He reached the top of her jeans and cut through the waistband. He turned back toward the foot of the table and began repeating the process on the left side of her jeans.

"You don't have to do this. *Please,"* she begged, whimpering pitifully.

He looked at her eyes again in the reflection in the mirror above them, keeping his gaze fixed on her face as he cut another few inches of the jeans leg. Three more bites of the shears brought him back again to the waistband, and a final cut severed the band.

He laid the shears down on the table beside her for a moment and returned to her feet. He untied her sneakers and pulled them off, dropping them onto the floor. He pulled the cotton socks from her feet and dropped them before grabbing the inside seams of her severed jeans—one side in each hand—and jerking them from under her in a single motion.

She screamed again.

He went back to the bench. She strained to watch him and saw him hunched over a power tool. She recognized it as a bench grinder, a tool she had seen as a child in her grandfather's workshop. She heard the whine of metal on the stone. She screamed once more, and suddenly realized that the scream of the bench grinder was roughly matching her own. She strained her eyes toward the left of the mirror; he was looking at her reflection again.

She saw in the mirror that his right foot was on a pedal on the floor—a pedal with a wire running up to the bench grinder.

She screamed again, crying for help, and noticed that he was pressing the pedal, trying to elevate the pitch of the grinder to match the notes of her own cries. He saw that she had discovered his game, and smiled as he stared at her, revealing a set of brown, badly-formed teeth.

"YOU SICK BASTARD!" she shrieked.

He came back to the table with the sharpened shears and began cutting her blouse, bottom to top first, then each sleeve, still moving slowly, methodically. He pulled the dissected garment off of her, leaving her lying on the table in only her thong and bra. He took the shears back to the grinder.

He doesn't need to sharpen those damn things again for my underwear; he only wants me to scream some more. I'm not going to play that game. Two snips and I'm naked.

"I know what you're trying to get with that thing," she said, her voice as steady and even as she could make it. "I'm not going to give you the satisfaction. If you have to play a rape game to get your little rocks off, then I can play that with you. If you have something worse in mind, then just get it the hell over with. I'm done giving you anything else. You're just a pathetic, sick, disgusting LITTLE SHIT!"

His eyes darkened, burning with rage. Whatever rays of light that had shown in them, generated by her fear disappeared completely.

Oh, God! What have I done? Did I blow my last chance with him?

She tried another futile pull with each arm against the belts on her wrists, involuntarily whimpering again.

The grinder stopped and he disappeared again. She rolled her eyes back toward the top of her head and tried to shift her head from side to side.

He always comes from that direction ... where is he? God, please help me!

The shears were the first thing back in her view, plunging by her face and slicing her bra in two as he cut the fabric between the cups. The shoulder straps were next. He immediately walked to the center of the table and cut the side straps of her thong. He put the shears down again and pulled the bra and thong from under her in two violent jerks.

She whimpered, but fought back the impulse to scream again, staring at him instead with a glare of defiance.

He walked back to the head of the table, leaning over her head and peering once more into her eyes. She refused to meet his gaze, turning her eyes away from his.

He was suddenly gone again, then he was back at the bench grinder, hiding his work this time with his body. The grinder continued its wail for several minutes, and she saw him put something down behind it on the work bench. Then she saw him walk to the end of the bench and take something off the coat tree.

It hadn't had a discernible form before, but as he put the garment on, she could tell that it was a large apron—an apron covered in dark brown, dried stains.

Those are BLOOD stains!

He reached to the top of the coat tree and pulled off a set of goggles. He walked back past the grinder and picked up something before disappearing again beyond the head of the table.

She waited, whimpering involuntarily. Nothing happened. She heard nothing, saw nothing. She looked up again at her naked form stretched out on the table.

It can't end like this. Maybe he left. God, I hope he left.

She screamed again.

He was back above her, a hideous, hovering figure in the goggles and a dirty surgical mask. He was holding the biggest meat cleaver she had ever seen.

2

TRASK PULLED off East 21st Street into a parking lot in front of the office of the Medical Examiner for Jackson County, Missouri. He felt a slight smile cross his face as he read the sign on the door.

It's hardly just a county facility anymore, he thought. *The docs here may get their checks from Jackson County, but their cases also come from several other counties, too.*

Most rural counties couldn't afford their own MEs, so they elected coroners—often undertakers with little or no forensic training or experience—who had a built-in conflict of interest: they wanted to get bodies embalmed and buried and get paid for it instead of conscientiously investigating and determining a cause of death. That being the case, the rural counties sent a few bucks to the more populous jurisdictions where they could take advantage of a professional staff on an as-needed, subscription basis. This ME also serviced Cass, Clay, and Platte Counties, as well as Jackson County, the home of Kansas City, Missouri.

Trask stopped and thought for a minute before getting out of the car.

My cases always seem to begin here. The life of a prosecution and investigation starts where human lives end.

There was another body waiting for him inside, waiting to be dissected so that he could—with a little luck and a lot of work—prove the case against the killer.

A white Ford Expedition pulled into the slot beside Trask's. A tall, white-haired guy with a matching handlebar moustache got out. He saw Trask, smiled, and waved.

"Morning, John," Trask said as he joined the other man at the door to the morgue. "Here we go again."

"Jeff. Glad you said you'd take this one," he responded. Special Agent John Foote of the Kansas City Division of the Federal Bureau of Investigation was one of the best investigators that Trask had ever worked with. The fact that this was going to be Foote's case was a positive for Trask. At this point in his career, Trask got to pick and choose many of his cases, and this one had not been a hard call to make. A serial killer in the middle of a war between drug-dealing street gangs offered both a change from the usual workload, and a chance to make a real difference. The streets might actually be a little safer for a while after they put this guy away and kept him there.

"Happy to work with the pros again," Trask replied. "Is this going to be a Bureau case or a CCU matter?"

"CCU. Land's already inside with the doc. He's had us looking at the shooter for months."

The Career Criminal Unit of the Kansas City, Missouri Police Department was a task force made up of local cops and agents from all the usual federal alphabet soup agencies: FBI, DEA, ATF, ICE, and even the United States Marshals Service. Unlike most similar task forces which were paid for and run by the feds, this one was unique: it was supervised by a cop. Detective Sergeant Tommy Land of the Kansas City Missouri Police Department was the squad supervisor, and directed the federal agents assigned to his unit.

It's almost always the opposite arrangement, Trask thought. *Local and state cops federally deputized and working as Task Force Officers—TFOs—for some federal supervisory special agent. The federal agencies then have their turf wars, hide information and sources, won't cooperate with each other, and nothing gets accomplished. In the CCU, they're all forced to play in the same sandbox. It works. It's the most efficient model I've seen since the nine-eleven hijackings.*

"This latest vic is number five," Foote said. "Five that we know of. Our shooter—his street name is 'Gloomy'—got careless and did this one in broad daylight. The victim's a rival gang member who was walking down the street not paying attention, listening to tunes on his earbuds. Gloomy jumped out of his car and put two in the back of the victim's head.

"The vic's aunt saw it happen from her kitchen window. She called it in, and the locals had units in the area. They rolled and blocked Gloomy's car in before he even had a chance to ditch the gun. Jackson County filed on him yesterday. He's locked down, and the county judge set bail high enough that he won't be making it any time soon."

"At least he's off the street for now," Trask thought aloud.

"You got that right. I'm getting tired of coming over here."

Trask nodded in agreement. "Where's the preacher?" he asked Foote.

"Billy's inside, too, but on another case. Homicide called him back on a detail. They're swamped even more than normal, between the gang dustups and their regular workload. Some sicko's apparently been pulling hookers off Independence Avenue. We just find pieces of 'em later. Billy drew that mess off the homicide wheel."

Detective Billy Graham—tagged with the nickname "Preacher" for obvious reasons—was normally Foote's working partner within CCU. The "wheel" was the next-up, assignment-drawing mechanism used to assign cases to detectives in their various investigative units. The cops had a wheel. Prosecutors in Trask's office had a wheel. Even the federal judges had a wheel. The next judge up got the next case, even though the information as to who was next was a closely held secret in the judges' chambers. It supposedly kept the parties from judge shopping. As the United States Attorney's office's Senior Litigation Counsel—a fancy tag for the guy who worked the bigger prosecutions—Trask could select some of his cases without worrying about his own wheel.

They walked into the lobby together. Tommy Land met them with one of the assistant MEs. The new doc was someone Trask hadn't seen before. He was short, pale, and pudgy, but his handshake was surprisingly firm.

"Doctor Stan Carter, this is Jeff Trask, the U.S. Attorney's Senior—" Land tried to make the formal introduction, but he blanked on Trask's title.

"Senior Litigation Counsel," Trask finished for him. "It just means that I'm getting old and I've been around for a while."

"Nice to meet you," Carter said. "Come on back." He waved them through a set of double doors into the business end of the morgue.

They entered what would have looked like an operating room if the place had been a hospital for the living. Billy Graham was waiting for them inside and gave Trask a wave. He was standing beside a stainless-steel table. The body of a young, black male was lying on the examination table. The skull of the corpse had been split open; the skin on the skull had been pulled back.

"The doc pulled these out of his head," Graham said, holding up a plastic evidence bag. Two bullets with traces of blood were visible inside the bag. One had been a jacketed hollow point and was too fragmented for any meaningful ballistic analysis. The other slug was a full metal jacket. That bullet seemed to be in fairly good shape.

"Three-eighties?" Land asked.

"Yep." Graham nodded, looking at the baggie again. "The FMJ should be good enough for ballistics, and it'll match the Ruger we got out of Gloomy's car. I don't think he can dodge this one, especially with a good prosecutor on the case." He smiled and bowed in Trask's direction.

"I just work with what you guys give me," Trask said. "You make it easy for me."

"My other case is more of a challenge, Jeff," Graham said, the smile disappearing from his face. His head tilted toward Dr. Carter, who took the cue.

"I would say so." Carter nodded in agreement.

The doctor walked to the door of a refrigerated section and rolled out a gurney. Trask could tell from the lumps under the sheet on the gurney that there was less than a full corpse underneath the covering.

"We were looking at these before we started the autopsy on your shooting victim," Carter explained to Land.

He flipped the sheet aside, exposing two human legs. They were different in everything except general size. One was badly discolored, seemed to have decomposed, and had been obviously subjected to some damaging forces. The other looked more natural, and more preserved.

"Do these go together?" John Foote asked, beating Trask to the punch.

"The DNA matches," Carter answered, nodding.

"You're shitting me." Land was scowling, incredulous.

"Not at all," Carter said. "They came from the same person. I'm guessing a white female, mid-twenties."

"Any ID on the victim from the DNA?" Trask asked.

"Not yet," Billy said. "We plugged it into CODIS, but unless she had a prior arrest, we may never see a match."

Trask nodded. CODIS was the acronym for the FBI's Combined DNA Identification System; swabs taken after arrests turned into DNA profiles from participating states and cities.

If this is one of the missing hookers, it depends on how long the girl had been a "pro," Trask thought, *if, in fact, that's what she was. If she was new to the game, she may not have had arrests or a DNA profile in the system, and if she was new to town, there may not even be a missing person report.*

"One of the ME investigators had to go downriver to Lafayette County to pick up this one," Graham explained, pointing to the more decomposed limb. "It could have gone into the river here, but it washed up on a bank down there. Every catfish and carp between those points probably took a shot at it along the way."

"The condition didn't give me much to work with, other than the fact that the bone had been sawed just below the hip joint," Carter said.

"The other one came wrapped in a plastic garbage bag, and it was dropped in a dumpster at a gas station off Independence Avenue," Graham continued. "One of our local hungry homeless unwrapped it, then lost his lunch instead of finding a meal. The ME logged it in three days *after* they got the one from the river."

"It had been preserved before it was dumped, probably in a freezer," Carter explained. "The condition of this limb was obviously far superior to that of the one from the river. I was able to make some disturbing findings."

"Yeah." Graham nodded, almost involuntarily.

"I was able to determine, based upon the edges around the cuts on the upper leg," Carter began, "that the initial wounds to the top of the leg were made *antemortem*."

Carter looked at Trask as he recoiled.

"She was alive when that started?" Trask asked.

"Correct. The shallow cuts were begun while she was alive. There was clotting in the small blood vessels in the cuts on the surface of the leg. That would not have occurred if she was already deceased."

"Jesus!" Foote exclaimed.

Land shook his head. "Bad enough to be butchered like a steer, but while she was still breathing—"

"How long was she alive?" Trask asked. "Or can you tell?"

"Not to a certain point in time," Carter answered. "I would estimate a day or so."

"Sick bastard," Tommy Land remarked, still shaking his head.

Trask felt Billy Graham's gaze.

"Any chance you can take this one, too, Jeff?" Graham asked.

"Only if you find me a federal connection, Bill," Trask said. "We've got one in the dope-related turf war on Gloomy's gang shootings. I can't do local homicides without a federal nexus."

He nodded. "I'll keep my eyes open for that. You don't mind if I bounce things off you from time to time?"

"Do it on a private phone line," Trask told him. "I can't be openly stepping on a county prosecutor's toes."

Graham nodded, staring at the legs again. "Understood."

Trask left the morgue and headed through town on the way back to his office at the courthouse. He had a playlist open in the car to horn bands from the sixties and seventies. Blood Sweat & Tears' "Spinning Wheel" started playing.

Trask sang along with David Clayton-Thomas a little as he thought about the bodies in the morgue, and he was thinking more about the one that was *not* on his professional plate.

Someone had certainly had her share of troubles before her leg had been "dropped by the riverside."

Trask doubted that he would ever be working the matter, however, and he tried to put it out of his head—to just "let the spinning wheel ride."

He drove north on Grand Boulevard through the downtown section of Kansas City. Old-timers in the office had told him that this main artery had been essentially dead before it had been revived by the construction of the Sprint Center and a central entertainment area, now called the "Power and Light District."

"You could fire a cannon down Grand after dinner and not hurt anyone," was a familiar statement. The town was coming back now, full of new life with recent championships by the Royals and Chiefs. It could be a good, lively, exciting place to live. It could also be a place to die in the worst way.

3

After an obligatory appearance at his office (he had to let someone there know he was actually working and not just tooling around town), Trask took the elevator down to the underground garage and drove out again.

Something made him reflect on how he had arrived there. There had been law school at Ole Miss, where the Air Force sent him after it was clear that his knees would never let him be a pilot. They had too much invested in him after the Academy in Colorado Springs to see him just walk out the door after five years. A free ride through law school while drawing a captain's pay had been too good a deal to pass up, so he'd signed on for law school plus another six years of an Air Force service commitment.

The JAG Corps had him doing a circuit prosecutor's job less than three years later. It had been terrific professional training, trying major case after major case, and learning from some true trial dogs. As far as a personal life was concerned, however, it had sucked. Three-hundred days a year on the road—base to base and case to case—got very old after a five-year grind. They sent him to the headquarters in DC to write appeals for a couple of years, but the next set of orders would have put him back on the road.

"You did such a great job before, Jeff, we've decided to put you back in a circuit prosecutor's job."

Thank you, sir. Hell no, sir.

He had driven across the river and interviewed with Ross Eastman, the U.S. Attorney for the District of Columbia.

"How many cases have you tried?" Eastman had asked.

"Hundreds," Trask had answered.

"That's impossible," the U.S. Attorney had said.

"Not really." Trask explained his old job, the travel, and the experience.

He showed the older man the officer performance reports.

"When can you start?" Eastman asked.

"We're skipping something," Trask said.

"Sorry," Eastman said. "We'll double whatever the Air Force is paying—"

Trask's left eyebrow went up.

"—And you can stay home and try cases."

Trask signed on the dotted line, then resigned his regular commission in the Air Force and transferred to the reserves.

He had been in the Department of Justice's District of Columbia office for a few years before transferring to Kansas City. He'd tried all kinds of federal cases in the capital, everything from simple drug prosecutions to major conspiracies and homicides. He thought about his supervisor in the D.C. federal court division as he drove to his next meeting.

"Get out of the office every chance you have, Jeff," Bob Lassiter had told him. "Meet the cops and the agents on their turf. They'll appreciate that more than you'll ever know. They're all sick of the ivory tower princes and princesses in our office who sit behind their desks and expect perfect, bow-tied little packages to be delivered to them so that they have it as easy as possible in the courtroom. Then—when the inevitable conviction comes in after they present their perfect little case—they take all the glory after having done almost none of the work.

"Visit the crime scenes, too. Fields and walls talk to you if you're willing to listen to them. Photos are nice, but they're no substitute for being there. Seeing the scene in person changes perspective. Distances are more real. You see and hear and understand more than you ever could from a picture or a written report."

Lassiter's career ended when he was gunned down while giving a case post-mortem press conference on the front steps of the federal courthouse.

Trask reached down and patted the thick cell-phone case on his belt. There actually *was* a cell phone in the front compartment. The rear slot was just big enough for a subcompact 9mm Sig Sauer. It was always cocked and locked whenever he left the courthouse. Despite Lassiter's fate, Trask still took his advice. He left the courthouse whenever he could, but now he always carried the gun.

He headed east on Front Street—a main artery running along the south bank of the Missouri River—until he came to a collection of non-descript, single-story buildings. Most of them held the usual collection of small business offices and dispatch or shipping centers. One did not. Trask parked and punched in his four-digit code on a keypad before entering the home of the Kansas City, Missouri Police Department's Career Criminal Unit.

Tommy Land was waiting for him. Land stood in front of his assembled squad and began his introduction.

"For those of you who haven't yet had the pleasure of working with Jeff Trask, let me fill you in. He is the Senior Litigation Counsel for the U.S. Attorney's office here in Kansas City. I don't know if that means that he's the *oldest* prosecutor over there …"

Land paused as a few chuckles made their way through the room.

"But I do know that he's the *best* that his office could assign to this case. We had a big drug case last year, and we took him a file with sixty potential defendants in it. We expected to see about half of those charged. Jeff indicted and then convicted all sixty."

Land paused again for effect, and Trask saw several raised eyebrows among the new members of the squad. One of the new detectives caught his attention. She actually *surrounded* his attention, and it surrendered. The new detective had coal black hair, sitting atop big, dark eyes. She appeared to be the result of perfect gene splicing between a couple of cultures. Trask *guessed* that she was Eurasian. He *knew* that she was one of the prettiest cops he'd ever seen. He also saw that she was sitting next to Billy Graham, and that Billy was looking at Trask while Trask was looking at her. Trask gave Graham a knowing wink.

"That should tell you that he's not afraid to work to make *our* work pay off, and he'll be supervising and directing the investigation with me, since he knows the ins and outs of federal cases better than anyone else here," Tommy

Land continued. "If Jeff tells you he needs something, you can consider that to be an assignment from me. Understood?"

Heads nodded all around the room.

"Anything you want to say, Jeff?" Land asked Trask.

"Not yet. Let's see what you're throwing at me first," Trask replied.

"Fair enough," Land said, smiling. "We have a front row seat for you."

He pointed to an empty folding chair in the closest row facing a large, portable whiteboard that had been set up in the front of the room. Trask took the seat next to Billy, on the side away from the new detective.

"I believe you all know John Foote," Land said, motioning John to come forward. "He'll be the lead on this."

Foote had also been the lead investigator on the sixty-defendant drug case. That assignment had thrown Foote, his partner Billy Graham, and others in the unit—and Trask—together for almost eight months.

"I'd just like to first echo Tommy's remarks about Jeff," Foote said. "He's the best prosecutor I've ever worked with, and if anybody can get us where we need to go on this mess, he's our guy."

Trask nodded as humbly as he could, given the accolades. He had never been one to take compliments that well.

"You guys did the heavy lifting, John," Trask said. "I just get paid to write some stuff and talk about it in court."

"You did your job," Foote said. "A lot of the deadwood in that courthouse you work in wouldn't have done anything but *complain* about a case that size."

"So, tell me about this new one, already." Trask did his best to cut off the compliments.

"Sure thing." Foote flipped the white board over. There were four homicides listed vertically on the board, summarized in chronological order. Each included the date of the murder, the victim's name, the location, and what Trask recognized as a CRN—a criminal report number—the numerical designation for the main KCMOPD report for each incident. An arrest photograph of a young, black male was centered below the list of murders.

"There is a common denominator in each of these homicides," Foote explained. "It's this little thug: WaShaun Stewart, Jr. His friends call him 'Gloomy.' It's a fitting nickname, since he's been known to throw some permanent shadows over lots of local families. Our evidence says he's the killer in each of these cases."

"Nice young man," Trask observed. "And exactly how young is he? That photo makes him look like he just got his driver's license."

"He actually doesn't have one," Foote replied. "That doesn't stop him from driving, of course. To answer your question, though, he just turned eighteen."

Trask couldn't stop himself from flinching. "Are you telling me that all those murders were committed …"

"Yep. By a juvenile, under the laws of the United States," Foote answered. "That brings us to the latest development. We have witnesses who have identified Gloomy as the shooter of another victim, just last night."

"After he turned eighteen, I hope?" Trask asked.

"Yes, by three days."

"Then everything just got a lot clearer—at least my job did," Trask said. "He's now a federal adult for charging purposes."

"We were hoping you'd say that," Tommy Land added. "We've taken these cases to Jackson County several times, always getting the same answer. All the other murders except one were committed before Gloomy's *seventeenth* birthday, which made him a minor even for Missouri state purposes. The state prosecutors told us that he'd go to juvie hall for a little while, *if* we could make an iron-clad case. One murder was *after* he turned seventeen, but it wasn't the strongest, evidence-wise. We could never satisfy the county guys with our proof. The whole 'hood is terrified of Gloomy and his crew. Without guarantees that he'd be locked up for good, nobody has wanted to sign up to testify."

"Tell me about that 'hood, John," Trask requested. "What are the dynamics? With this latest murder, if the drug turf war is an ongoing conspiracy with a timeline overlapping the juvenile murders and then extending into the commission of this latest hit, then we have something called 'validation conduct,' making the *whole thing* chargeable as an adult offense since he continued his participation past his age of majority—his eighteenth birthday. Are all the murders related? A continuing course of conduct?"

"That's our theory," Foote replied, nodding. "Gloomy is second generation in the 51st Street Crips, and all the vics have been members of the 33rd Street Bloods, also known as the 'Trey Wall.' From everything we can put together, they've been at war for a couple of years, mostly over dope turf."

"Then we have a working theory to start," Trask said. "That is, if the facts support it. I can file a motion to get even the juvenile murders certified for adult prosecution with the adult homicide and conspiracy, but only if the evidence supports that theory. Otherwise, you have what used to be a juvenile serial killer who'll be looking at one adult state prosecution for the latest murder. If the dope turf war theory proves up, I have a federal case. Without it, I don't."

"We'll work that," Foote said. "What I meant to say is …" he shot a glance at Tommy Land, "we'll make it work."

Land nodded, smiling. "The evidence will support that approach," he assured Trask. "We've been tracking Gloomy for a while. What do you need from us, Jeff?"

Trask stood and walked to the white board. He studied it for a moment, then turned around.

"What I need, Tommy, is—in a word—everything. I need every report on every incident mentioning either Gloomy or his crew, and every report on this Trey Wall rival gang."

Trask turned so that the assembled squad could hear his explanation.

"Those of you who haven't worked federal conspiracy cases before will like what I'm about to say. Unlike most state jurisdictions, the federal criminal law *favors* the joining of related criminal cases in a single indictment and trial. We have a rule of evidence—Rule 404(b)—that is what lawyers like to call a "rule of inclusion," meaning that evidence is admissible if it shows part of a common scheme or plan. Tie that up with federal conspiracy law, which allows us to prove any act committed in furtherance of a conspiracy, and you have what I like to call the 'big old federal dump truck.' Our goal should be to fill that bad boy up and dump it on the heads of Gloomy and his little gang."

Trask noticed some smiles of approval on the cops' faces. A lawyer was saying something that sounded strangely like common sense.

"When I say 'everything,' that's exactly what I mean," Trask continued. "Don't hurt yourselves thinking about it too hard, or at all. If a report mentions Gloomy or one of his crew or their rivals, I want to see it. I don't care if it looks like a federal crime, or even a crime at all. If they borrowed a car that they used to do a lick—"

Trask used the street slang for a shooting.

"I want to know who loaned it to them. If they stole the car, I want those reports. Stealing a car usually isn't a federal offense—it's a state or local crime —and borrowing one is no crime at all, but remember what I said: if it's an act committed in furtherance of the charged conspiracy, we can use it. We can throw it into the back of the dump truck. Get me the reports, and we'll sort all that out."

"I used to ride patrol in that neighborhood." One of the guys in the back of the room was raising his hand. "You're asking for a lot of paper."

"I figured I might be," Trask said, nodding. "When you were riding patrol, and you saw Gloomy or one of his posse doing a hand-to-hand drug deal, did you write it as part of a federal conspiracy case?"

"No," the detective said. "How would I know that? I'd write it up as a one-time dope sale."

"That's exactly my point," Trask responded. "Our guys and gals on the street almost never have the satellite view. You roll up on something in progress, and deal with what you see. You don't know where that dope came from, or whether other mutts in the crew are selling the rest of it around the corner. You don't know if it's related to a drive-by shooting and robbery of someone in the Trey Wall the week before. Gloomy's crew might have stolen the dope you see them selling from the Trey Wall. We're going to throw all that into the big dump truck and see what sticks together."

"We do have someone who might be a big help to you with that data collection and analysis, Jeff," Land said. He motioned to the pretty detective sitting next to Billy Graham. She stood and walked to the front, offering her hand. Trask noticed that Graham had stood, too, and he was following her like a guard dog. Trask shook her hand as Land introduced them.

"Jeff, this is Rebecca Suzuki. She just came over from the Intelligence Division. She's hell on wheels on a computer, and she's a lot faster than the rest of us when it comes to pulling stuff out of our various report systems. When I saw what you were dealing with on our sixty-defendant case last year, I thought of her, so I asked her to help with this. She can do a lot of the cross-referencing that you'll want."

"I'm sure that I'll need the help, and I'm happy to have it," Trask said. "Nice to meet you. Do you go by Rebecca?"

"That, or 'Becky,' or 'Beck,' whatever works for you," she said.

"Suzuki," Trask said. "Japanese, I assume?"

"She's actually Joplinese," Graham quipped over her shoulder.

"Billy and I went through the police academy together," Suzuki explained, pushing Graham back with an elbow. "My dad's family is from Japan; Mom is from Joplin, a couple of hours south of here."

"I'll talk to the guys who patrol Gloomy's neighborhood," she continued, "get their perspective on this, past and present. See where his relatives and friends stay, that sort of thing. I can run and cross-reference names, addresses, vehicles, license plates, all that. I just need to know how you want the info: thumb drive, disc, or email?"

"None of those," Trask said. "I never want an email. They're discoverable by the defense, and it's too tempting to put opinions, jokes, and non-pertinent stuff like that online. If you want to talk, call me. As for the reports, I want paper."

"Paper?" Suzuki asked. "Are you that old school?"

"Come see me after I get your paper," Trask said. "We'll link your new school up with what you think is old school and see how it works."

"Okay." Suzuki shrugged. "Anything else?"

"Yeah," Trask said. "I'll need about four big boxes of push pins."

"Push pins?" she asked, incredulous.

"You know," Graham said. "Those thumbtack things with the plastic handles on them."

"I *know* what they *are,* Billy," she said. "I just never had anyone else ask for them before."

"They take off less paint than tape," Trask said. "We're about to do some wallpapering."

It had been weeks since his last kill.

He drove the old truck along the avenue, looking for just the right target.

He finally saw her, standing on a dark corner, alone. He checked the area to see if the corner would be covered by any storefront security cameras. There was a gas station across the street from her, but it had been closed for months.

He looked to see if she was wearing gloves, since the temperature had been dropping lately. She was not. He was.

He pulled the truck to the corner.

"Hi," she said, forcing a smile when she saw him.

He showed her the card and a hundred-dollar bill.

"Can't talk, huh?" she said, reading the card.

He nodded, watching her lips.

She looked past the card at the numbers on the bill.

"Sure, honey, why not?" She faked the smile again and climbed in beside him, holding the card in front of her for a closer look.

"A deaf-mute? Oh, that means, you can't hear *or* talk, doesn't it?"

She looked at him but got no response. His eyes were fixed on the road as he drove.

"Guess I should have known better than to ask," she whispered to herself.

He checked on her every minute or so as they drove eastward. By the time he'd reached the intersection for I-435 North, she was unconscious. When he reached the building twenty minutes later, he carried her inside and dumped her into the pen between the two freezers. He locked the cage and checked his watch. He figured she'd be fully awake in about four hours.

4

It was Saturday, but Trask climbed out of bed at 6:00 a.m., just like he did on every other day of the week. He patted Lynn on the shoulder as she slept. The pups bounced off the foot of the bed as he headed toward the bathroom. They were waiting by the door to the walk-in closet when he came out. He smiled at them.

"Yes, ladies, it's almost time. Let me get dressed."

He pulled on some jeans and a sweatshirt and grabbed a jacket. He had the dogs harnessed and leashed a moment later.

Koko, the full-blooded Siberian Husky, walked on his left. Kodi, half Border Collie and half Jack Russell Terrier—a hybrid breed now recognized as a "Border Jack" by most kennel clubs—walked on his right. Both the dogs were rescues. Koko had been pulled from one of Missouri's infamous puppy mills when she was a few months old, rescued first by a society that had bought her away from the puppy mill, then transferred to Trask and his wife for a donation that covered her purchase price, plus medical expenses.

There had been two senior rescues in the house when Koko arrived as a puppy, but the older dogs had both died within a year. It had quickly become apparent that Koko needed another playmate. She had grown lethargic and depressed, wondering where her older sisters had gone. A trip to a local Humane Society shelter brought Kodi into the pack.

She was a transfer from a kill shelter in California, arriving at the Humane Society at about a year-and-a-half old. She had been fostered, adopted, returned, and then fostered again before coming for her audition with the Trasks. One of the shelter volunteers had brought her to the house to check out the home and how she got along with Koko. When the two pups didn't stop playing for two hours, the volunteer, Trask, and Lynn all agreed that Kodi had found a new "forever home." Although half the size of her younger sister, the little Border Jack was all muscle, and she was as fast and as strong as the Husky.

Trask glanced down at Kodi as they crossed Raintree Boulevard. Her backside was as ripped as an Olympic speed skater, the reason Trask had nicknamed the little dog "muscle butt." Kodi felt Trask's eyes on her and glanced up at him with a smile on her face.

"You know you're home now, don't you, squirt?" he said to her.

Their walking course was about a mile-and-a-half, twice a day: one walk early in the morning, another late in the afternoon. The sessions kept the dogs' energy levels manageable. Trask smiled to himself as he shook his head.

Next time do your breed research in advance, dummy.

He'd recently seen an article on the web listing all three of the breeds represented by his two dogs as those to be avoided by seniors or people who had little time to spend with them. Both dogs were highly intelligent, high energy to a fault, and easily bored. So far, Trask and Lynn had been lucky: no damage inside the house, and they'd only had the occasional crater to fill in the backyard.

Lynn was an early retiree now. She had done twenty years in the Air Force herself: a few as an emergency room medical technician, followed by more than a dozen years as a Special Agent with the Air Force Office of Special Investigations. Trask had met her while he was riding the Air Force prosecution circuit. One of her undercover operations had generated fifteen courts-martial. Trask had prosecuted all of them, and she had been the star witness in each one. The attraction had been immediate, as had been the mutual respect for the way they did their jobs.

Lynn's cases as an undercover agent had been airtight, with military dope dealers hopelessly trapped after taking her into their confidence and schemes. Rather than pleading those cases down to minimal charges and sentences,

Trask had taken them all to the wall, convicting all defendants of all charges and securing lengthy prison sentences for each defendant. They had married two years later.

After her military time, Lynn had served as a Medical Examiner's Investigator, and then signed on with the FBI as an analyst in the capital's Joint Terrorism Task Force. After a few years of that grind, she now took pride in being a "stay-at-home dog mom."

Trask turned the dogs around and headed back for the entrance to Hidden Cove Drive, crossing the road over the spillway that led from the cove to the main portion of Raintree Lake. The pups were finally getting leash trained. Their heads were perfectly lined up at his heels, walking on two slack leashes as they turned the corner for home.

The dogs bounced into the house after Trask opened the door for them. Lynn had their special, after-walk biscuits waiting for them.

"How'd they do today?" she asked.

"Two A-pluses," Trask replied. "Of course, we didn't meet anybody on the sidewalk today—too early—so there was no one for Kodi to growl at or charge."

"She's just trying to protect her new daddy," Lynn said. "She knows she's finally got a home, and anything that threatens that—or her new humans—has to be dealt with."

"We'll keep working on that with her. We can't have her biting people, or we'll get sued by some turkey and have to put her down."

"The e-collars should be here soon," Lynn said. "They have a beep, a vibration, and a mild shock setting. We'll start with the lowest step, and then try and redirect her focus when she gets fixated on one of those nasty threats."

"Sounds like a plan," Trask agreed. "She's a smart girl. It shouldn't take long, and we'll never use the shock button."

"She just needs a little more time," Lynn said, nodding. "It's good that we can split the walking duties with them. It helps with the bonding process, both for them bonding with each other, and to us."

Trask pointed to the dogs. Koko was lying on a pillow across the room, and Kodi was sitting so close to her that she was almost sitting on top of the bigger dog.

"*That* bonding process?" he asked. "You can't separate them *now* without explosive charges."

"Okay, with *us* then. And especially with you. If this new case goes capital, I'm not sure we'll see much of you for a while."

"It won't be a death penalty case," Trask said.

"Really? I thought this little thug had killed five people!"

"He has—five that we know of and can prove—and probably more," Trask said. "The *problem* is that he committed all his murders but the last one before his eighteenth birthday, and that makes him ineligible for any capital consideration on all except for the last one. I looked at the federal death statute all day yesterday, and I couldn't find any statutory aggravating factors that would qualify for the death penalty on the last murder. He just walked up behind the victim and put two in the guy's brain before the vic knew what hit him. No prolonged suffering, no especially heinous means of inflicting death, probably only a moment of premeditation. Gloomy just saw a chance to pop a rival gang member and took it."

"So, because he killed on impulse, we can't execute him." Lynn shook her head. "Like they say, 'The law is an ass.' What about the fact that he's killed so many others?"

"Can't consider those because he was a minor—at least for federal purposes—when those occurred. It's doubly ironic in this case because the age of majority in Missouri isn't eighteen, it's *seventeen*. He was a state adult for two murders, but a federal child when he gunned down the first four, and under federal law and Supreme Court precedent, we can't even sentence him to life imprisonment for any of the first four because that would be an Eighth Amendment violation. It's cruel and unusual punishment to execute a federal adult, or to give him a life sentence, because he executed four others while he was a federal child."

Lynn shook her head. "Sometimes the law is a complete and total ass."

Trask nodded. "Can't make this stuff up."

"Can you prosecute him at all for the pre-eighteen stuff?"

"Yeah. Since he committed the last one in furtherance of the same ongoing conspiracy—at least that's our working theory—we can ask the court to 'certify' the juvenile offenses for adult prosecution and treat them as actions committed in the conspiracy. The entire conspiracy can be prosecuted as an adult offense since he acted within the scope of the conspiracy after he turned eighteen. We can ask for a life sentence for the last murder *and* for the conspiracy, just not for the first four murders. He can only get something less than life for those. The certification process will take a little more time, but we'll get there."

"Better you than me," she said, shaking her head again. "My job was simpler: identify and arrest."

Trask nodded. "Sometimes the law *is* an ass."

"Who are your investigators?"

"Foote and Graham. CCU."

Lynn smiled. "I *told* you this would happen. They saw what you did on their last case. You'll never get rid of them now."

"Not sure I'd ever want to. They do good work."

"So, you get all of CCU again?"

"Yep. As required. John and Billy are the lead pair, but Billy's got a lot more on his plate. Some psycho has been dissecting women—probably hookers—and leaving their body parts strewn all over this half of Missouri. The morgue has a pair of legs in the cooler: one from a dumpster, the other pulled out of the river."

"Is that a federal case?"

"Not for now. Probably never."

"Good. I worry about you. Sickos like that scare me, and I don't scare that easily."

Trask smiled. "I know. That's one of the reasons why I love you." He started to say something else but paused. She noticed.

"What?" she asked.

"There's a third member on the lead team from CCU that I'll be spending time with at the office."

"Who is she?" Lynn asked.

Trask laughed. "Was it that obvious?"

"Hell, yes."

"Her name is Becky Suzuki. Originally from Joplin. I think she and Billy Graham may be an item. If they're not one already, they probably will be, soon enough."

"What does she look like?"

"Like she could step out of a Victoria's Secret display window."

"That ugly, huh?"

"Yeah. She's hideous."

She woke in the pen feeling strangely relaxed, groggy, almost numb. She wasn't bound, but she was afraid to move at first.

She finally decided to lift her head slowly to look around. There were white walls on either side of the cage. The back of the pen rested against light green concrete cinder blocks. The room was narrow, and she could see a work bench across the room from where she was confined. She quietly pushed herself to the front, trying to look beyond the corners of the white structures on either side, trying to see what was at the ends of the room, but her view was blocked by the walls on either side. The electric hums from both sides told her that the white walls were probably the sides of freezers.

She didn't see the metal water bowl before her foot kicked it, making a noise as it rattled against the edges of the pen. She recoiled in fear against the back of the cage.

"Hello? Can you help me? *Can you please help me?*" A female voice whimpered from somewhere to her left.

She was about to reply when she heard a door open and close. His head suddenly appeared at the front of the cage. She pressed harder against the grates behind her, swallowing half the air in the room in a shocked gulp. He leered at her for a moment, saying nothing, expressionless, but with a strange look of calm in his eyes. He disappeared, moving in the direction of the other voice in the room.

She heard a bench grinder whirring against metal. Then the screaming started.

5

"MR. BARRETT WANTS to see you, Jeff."

The receptionist behind the glass smiled as Trask nodded and opened the main doors to the office of The United States Attorney for the Western District of Missouri. Instead of turning right toward his own office, Trask crossed the hall and opened another door.

J. P. Barrett was standing beside his secretary's desk, holding a cup of coffee. He saw Trask and waved him into the conference room to the left, closing the door behind them.

"Want a cup?" Barrett asked, pointing to a coffee maker on a counter along the wall.

"No thanks, already had a couple."

They sat down across from each other at one end of the big table.

"How's the CCU case look?" Barrett asked.

"Time consuming," Trask said. "We'll have to certify the first four murders for adult prosecution. Gloomy was seventeen when he did number four, so he was an adult for state purposes, but still a minor for ours. That'll take a month or so, even if there's no appeal of the certification order, but Tommy Land says the county can keep Gloomy locked down for another three weeks before any hearing. We already have a grand jury in session, so I can file on the conspiracy and the last murder by then, and supersede later, adding in the other counts after we get the adult certification. Land and John Foote tell me there's a good basis for the conspiracy charge. The county is willing to transfer him to us as soon as we get an indictment."

"Good," Barrett said. "Good." He nodded and looked at Trask, hesitating before he continued.

"What?" Trask asked.

"Yeah, there's something else, and I'm not happy about it," Barrett said. "We're getting a new chief for our criminal division, and I didn't get a vote in the selection. If I had one, I'd be combining that title with the senior litigation counsel slot, and you'd be wearing both hats."

"That's flattering," Trask said, "so, thank you. Who's the new guy—or gal—and why didn't you get to make the selection?"

"To answer both questions, it's a favor to—and a favorite of—Senator Burke's."

Trask nodded. Burke was the senior senator from Missouri and a power player in Washington. Trask figured that Burke had called in some favor from either the president or the attorney general.

"Name?" Trask asked.

"I think you know him. It's Raymond Marsh."

"Oh, shit!" Trask exclaimed involuntarily. "You have to be kidding."

"I wish I were, Jeff. The AG called me Friday and told me this was how it was going to be."

"It's good for the AG, 'cause he doesn't have to deal with Marsh anymore," Trask said, "and good for Burke, because he'll get a fat check for his next campaign. Marsh is old money from St. Louis, and he's married to Burke's niece, if I remember correctly, so it's probably good for Marsh because he wanted to come home to Missouri for some reason. It's just not going to be good for you, or me, or the office."

"I know you had some run-ins with him in D.C.," Barrett said. "Is he really that bad?"

"Not if you're the kind of prosecutor who likes press conferences and doing as little real work as possible," Trask said. "If you like intra-office backstabbing politics and Ivy League elitism, you'll love him. He looks for ways to demean the cops rather than working with them.

"My problem with him—and his problem with me—started when I was in the appellate section in D.C. We handled all the appeals for the office, whether those cases came from the local court or the federal courts. Marsh was in the local felony trial section at the time, and he had withheld some exculpatory evidence in a rape trial. I discovered it going through the case file and had to confess error on behalf of the office, which resulted in the conviction being tossed on appeal. It also got Marsh's promotion to the federal side of the office cancelled. In the meantime, *I* got promoted to the federal side. Ray always thought I had torpedoed him to get my own advancement. He's never forgiven me for that."

"Doesn't sound like there was anything to forgive."

"I agree; he doesn't. I just followed the United States Attorneys' Manual and the canons of ethics. I don't know if Marsh has ever read either one. His family background and Yale Law degree seem to come with big connections and zero common sense."

Trask took a long, slow breath.

"Sorry. I just thought I'd gotten away from all the D.C. nonsense. Didn't know it would follow me out here. At least I get final word on my own cases, right? I still report directly to you on those?"

"That's right," Barrett said. "Anything you're working on in your capacity as senior litigation counsel is between you and me. There is, however, something else I need you to shoulder."

Uh-oh, Trask thought. *He said, "Need."* Trask had learned this was Barrett's gentle way of issuing an order. Trask would have no choice but to accept the boss's "request."

"Gary Garland's not working out as supervisor of our drug unit, Jeff," Barrett continued. "Instead of the crim chief hat, that's the other hat I need you to wear. The folks in the drug shop all respect you, and they could use some adult supervision."

"That means I'll be managing the wheel for case assignments down there?"

"It does."

"Which means that I—and my folks in the unit—will be working for Marsh on all those matters."

"That's true."

"What if we—Marsh and myself—have major disagreements on methods and policy?"

"Come to me on the down-low if it's anything you can't work out between yourselves. It's my job to referee those disputes. Just realize that I'll have to give him some deference in order to satisfy the AG and Senator Burke."

Trask exhaled. "I understand. I'll be happy to try and help with the drug unit. It actually saves me having to ask you for something else."

"Really? Like what?"

"I was going to ask you for control of the drug unit's trial preparation room to get ready for the trial on Gloomy. Now, I can assign it to myself."

Barrett laughed. "That you can. Let me know if you need anything else. Thanks, Jeff."

Trask shook Barrett's hand and opened the conference room door leading into Barrett's waiting room. He saw Raymond Marsh sitting in one of the chairs.

"Jeff," Marsh said, coldly.

"Ray."

He shut the door to muffle the hysterics and whimpering which came from the adjoining, larger room in alternating waves. It was normally a satisfying sound, but not when he had to concentrate.

He pulled one of the cards from the stack. Like the others, it simply read, "I am a deaf mute." He pulled a pair of the latex gloves from a box at the back of the work bench and put them on. A surgical mask came next; he could not afford to inhale any of the powder.

Opening the plastic baggie, he used a swab to extract a few grains of the pinkish-gray grit. He took the card and used the swab to coat one end of the card before dropping it into a sandwich bag. Next came the small glass jar. He unscrewed the metal lid—in which he had cut a slender slot just wide enough for an end of the card to slip through—and grimaced at the odor of the liquid inside. He needed a little more, so he reached for a larger plastic container of the stuff, pouring about an inch into the bottom of the jar before replacing the lid.

Still wearing the gloves, he carried both the card and the jar out to the garage. He entered through a windowless side door and climbed into the cab of the old Ford pickup. He lowered the jar into the cupholder end of an aftermarket device that fit between the driver's seat and the console, and placed the sandwich bag with the card inside onto the console tray.

Trask found three visitors waiting by his office door. John Foote and Billy Graham were standing behind Becky Suzuki, who was holding a huge stack of paper. On top of the paper were four large boxes of pushpins.

Trask chuckled as he unlocked the door and waved them inside.

"Ask and ye shall receive," Foote said, nodding in Becky's direction as he held the door for her. Graham followed her in, while Foote grinned like he was a chaperone at a junior prom.

Suzuki ceremoniously laid her burden on the front of Trask's desk.

"I'm not sure why you needed all this old-school method stuff," she said.

"*I'm* sure you shouldn't have said that," Graham told her.

"We'll see," Becky shot back at him. "I've been at the intel division for a while, you know. I don't think we missed anything, Billy."

"I'm *really* sure you shouldn't have said *that,*" Graham said.

"Like, I said. We'll see." Suzuki looked at Trask. "We touched base with the patrol guys who've handled that district for the last couple of years, cross-referenced all of Gloomy's gang-banging buddies, his cousins, his grandmother, aunts and uncles, anyone who might have anything to do with him. I included reports based on names, addresses, cars and plates, incident reports that just happened in the area. Then I ran anything having to do with drive-by shootings in which the Trey Wall gang was targeted. Did I miss anything?"

"Yes." Graham threw his hands in front of his face to guard against any assault.

"Like what, Billy?" Suzuki challenged, her hands on her hips.

"I don't know *what*. I just *know*." Graham still had his hands up. "We've worked with Jeff before. You haven't."

Trask laughed. "We'll see. Good work. Sounds like a very thorough head start."

"What else do you need?" Becky asked Trask.

"Two days," Trask said. "See me Wednesday morning."

At 10:39 p.m., Officer Dennis Welsh recognized her from two blocks away as she approached the cab of an older pickup on a corner of the avenue.

Same old game. Same old ratty Chiefs jacket. I never liked the ones with that much yellow on them. Looks cheap. They ought to do what the Rams did while they were in St. Louis: ditch the yellow and go to a true gold. The gear would sure as hell look better.

He called in the stop as he activated the lights on the marked unit. The pickup driver saw the lights and was gone before Welsh could pull into the curb. He had not been able to get the plate or a make on the truck. It didn't matter. He knew the hooker and he was focused on her.

Welsh got out of the cruiser and walked up to the woman, who was glaring at him.

"At it again, Sally?" Welsh asked. "I gave you a break last time, but I told you I wouldn't give you another one."

The woman started to speak, but an unintelligible moan was all Welsh heard. He caught her just as she started to collapse. He lowered her gently to the curb as he called for an ambulance.

He saw that she was clutching some sort of card in her right hand. He took the card and read it to himself. *I am a deaf mute.* A wave of dizziness hit him hard. He managed to call for backup just before he collapsed on top of the woman.

6

TRASK SAT at the head of the table in the small conference room. The seven other attorneys assigned to the drug unit had spread out in the other chairs around the table.

"Didn't you know this guy in D.C.?" Cam Turner asked Trask.

"Yes." Trask abbreviated his response with a subtle warning glance at his old friend. Cam—like Trask—was a product and graduate of the Air Force's Circuit Trial Counsel program, another JAG officer who had hit the road for years doing nothing but trying courts-martial, another former Air Force asset who was now working for the Department of Justice.

Cam took the hint and let the matter drop.

"Ray Marsh from Washington has been selected as the new crim chief," Trask continued. "He's moving into his new home this week, and he'll be in the office on Monday. He has directed that all proposed indictments and prosecutive memoranda supporting those proposed indictments will now be subjected to two levels of review before approval. I will be the first level, and he will be the second. Please make sure they are professionally accomplished."

"We've never had to have the crim chief review our pros memos before," one of the other lawyers protested. "At least not for approval—the unit chief has always had approval authority."

"We do now," Trask said. "That goes for me as well if the case comes off the wheel. Anything I handle in my capacity as senior litigation counsel may get different treatment, but otherwise, we're all in the same boat. That requirement may get relaxed at a future date. Marsh may just want to get a feel for the quality of everybody's work as he gets started. I can't imagine he'll want to keep that reading load on his desk forever. Let's just work through this and make the best of it, folks. Okay?"

The nods and shrugs around the table answered his question. The troops weren't happy with the changes, but they understood.

"Thank you, everyone," Trask said, dismissing them.

He crossed the hall back to his office. As he had expected, Cam Turner followed him in, shutting the door behind him. Trask motioned him to sit in one of the chairs in front of the desk. Trask sat behind the desk. Turner started to speak but saw Trask's hands held up in a stop sign.

"A couple of things, Cam," Trask began. "Three or four, actually. One: you and I are ex-military. We trust each other, and we can bitch to each other in private about our idiot bosses without any fear of being ratted out about that bitching to the same idiot bosses. We've had to do that before, haven't we?"

"That we have, chief."

"Don't call me 'chief.' We've known each other too long."

"Okay, hero."

Trask looked at Cam and shook his head, smiling. "Hero" had always been Turner's nickname for his friend, deserved or not.

"Anyway, Cam, we can't afford to assume that every one of those civilian attorneys in that room will appreciate the need for the same discretion. If they don't, and they see fit to try and leapfrog you or me by reporting some supposed insubordination to Marsh, it is my well-informed opinion that Marsh will try to have our heads on a plate. If he can't do it through J.P. Barrett, he'll call in another favor from Senator Burke, who will then put pressure on Barrett—"

"Point taken. Understood. We'll bitch in here." Cam nodded. "I should've thought of that myself."

"Thanks," Trask said. "Second point: I'm naming you as my deputy chief for the unit. If I'm out for any reason, you're it. I'm also naming you as second chair on the Gloomy Stewart case. It's going to be too time-consuming for one attorney, and I need someone I can trust."

"Okay, hero. Happy to help."

"Thanks again. Third: I didn't want to get into it in the first meeting with the unit, but I expect Marshmallow to send out some more imperial edicts about how we do our jobs. If he operates the same way he ran his trial team in D.C., he'll try and prohibit any attorney from leaving the building to do any investigative work. He thinks that's a job for the cops and agents."

"Moron," Turner muttered. "You called him 'Marshmallow.' That fits. What is he anyway? Six feet and 250? A big, soft puff-ball."

"We are again in agreement," Trask said, "and we will be looking for work-arounds when required. Fortunately, we won't be governed by Marshmallow's methods when we're working on Gloomy. I've already gotten a promise from Barrett that I can run SLC cases as I see fit."

"Then I'm happy to be on board, Captain," Turner said, smiling.

"I'll take that instead of 'hero'," Trask said.

A knock on the door interrupted them.

"Come in," Trask said.

The door opened, and John Foote, Billy Graham, and Becky Suzuki stood in the doorway.

"Yes?" Trask asked.

"This is Wednesday," Suzuki said.

"That it is," Trask said. "If you would all be so good as to follow me, please? You, too, Cam."

Trask led them down a hallway to the left, turned right, and opened the door to the unit trial prep room, a windowless area with each wall about fifteen feet long.

"Holy hell!" exclaimed Graham.

Sheets of typed paper were attached to the walls by push pins. The pages were arranged in numerically headed vertical columns. The columns began to the left inside the door and continued—without any space of bare wall between them—clockwise around all four walls.

Foote shook his head. "Almost ran out of wall, didn't you?"

"Actually, I did," Trask said, closing the door behind Foote. Trask pointed. Two more columns were taped to the inside of the door.

"And you papered the room … because?" inquired Suzuki.

"Here we go," Graham muttered, earning a playful shove from Becky.

"I did this with a major case I had in D.C.," Trask explained. "I found that it gave me a different perspective than the one I got sitting behind a computer terminal and trying to analyze a series of individual screens. As you can see, each of these columns represents an incident tied either to our man Gloomy, or to some of his family or friends. Detective Suzuki," Trask nodded at her and smiled, "did a very thorough job of collecting all these related reports. They're arranged in chronological order. Under each police report, I've included a list of persons on the scene—witnesses or defendants—the date, time, address, an event summary, and vehicles and plates, and evidence seized, whether it's dope, guns, a decedent's bloody shirt, shell casings, whatever."

"Anything he reads, he doesn't forget," Turner said, standing behind Trask. "If he types or writes it down, he can recite it five years from now."

"I wish that were true," Trask said, shaking his head. "It *does* help reinforce the memory, of course. It also raises a lot of questions."

"Such as?" Suzuki challenged again.

"Here we go," Graham said again.

"Okay," Trask said. "Let's look at event number 6 here."

He pointed to a column of pages.

"This was a drive-by shooting of some Trey Wall gang bangers on March 21, two years ago. One died. It's one of the homicides you wanted me to charge."

"Correct," Becky said. "A witness made Gloomy as the shooter, and the homicide guys flipped a Trey Wall member, who backed up the witness. Since we had corroboration, we recommended charging it."

"Fine," Trask said, nodding. "Murder weapon?"

"All we know is a .223 rifle," Suzuki answered. "Shell casings on the scene and bullets recovered from the corpse. No weapon recovered at the scene. It was a drive-by—like you said—and Gloomy and his boys drove off with the weapon."

"Look at number 24," Trask said.

Suzuki walked down the wall to another column of papers.

"This is fourteen weeks later," she said.

"That is true." Trask nodded as he spoke. "It is also true that on this date, about fourteen weeks later, different officers on patrol in Gloomy's neighborhood pulled over a vehicle driven by one Jimmy Norman. We know Jimmy Norman to be—?" he paused.

"Gloomy's number one lieutenant in the 51st Street Crips," Foote volunteered.

"Yes, and a search of the trunk of the car during the stop revealed three firearms," Trask said, "one of which was a .223 Bushmaster rifle. I've been through all the lab reports you gave me, and I couldn't seem to find one showing that the bullets or shell casings from the drive-by in column number 6 were submitted to the ballistics lab with a request to see if they were fired by the rifle from column number 24."

"It was three months—three-and-a-half months—later, Gloomy wasn't on the scene," Suzuki protested, "and—"

"And you owe us all dinner," Graham said, gloating. "That was the bet."

"And *shit*!" Suzuki said, shaking her head.

"Told ya," Graham said, grinning.

"As I was saying earlier, I've found that having this all on the wall allows us to check each event against all the others without having our eyes and heads locked on a single page on a computer screen," Trask explained. He smiled.

"Where do you want to eat?" Becky asked.

"I vote for barbecue," Trask said. "How does Friday night work, and can I invite my wife?"

"Why not?" Suzuki said, still shaking her head. "I'm kicking myself. I can't *believe* I missed that."

"Don't beat yourself up for a single mistake," Trask said, giving her a friendly pat on the shoulder. He winked at Billy Graham. "There are others."

7

SHE CLIMBED into the Toyota Corolla and shivered. The snow was starting earlier than the weatherman had predicted. It would be a slow drive back to Kansas City.

She pulled her cell phone from her purse and called home. Her mother answered.

"Be careful, Bev. It's snowing pretty hard here."

"I will, Mom. It'll just take a little longer."

"Take it as slowly as you need to. We'll hold dinner for you. Your Dad will probably be a little late getting home from work, too, so don't push it."

"I won't, Mom. See you in a bit. Love you."

"I love you, too."

She pulled out of the dormitory parking lot and headed for the highway. Even on the main road, she found herself slowing to a crawl. The wind was blowing the heavy snow straight into her windshield, and the car's lights turned the blizzard into a white curtain. She could barely see five feet in front of the little sedan.

She remembered a trick her Dad had taught her, and switched the headlights off, using just her daytime running lights. The less powerful beams didn't reflect the snow as much.

That's better. At least I can see a few feet farther now. Thanks, Dad.

She was able to do about thirty now, and she was grateful that there was almost no traffic.

I think *my taillights are on when I use the running lights, but I'm not sure. Hope I don't get rear-ended.*

She checked the rearview mirror. There was a single pair of headlights behind her, but it was a good distance back.

I'll keep an eye on that. May have to switch the headlights back on if he gets any closer, make sure he knows I'm here.

Her eyes returned to the road. A few seconds later, she felt her car lurching to the right.

Wonderful! Now what?

She pulled to the right shoulder of the highway and turned on her emergency flashers. She zipped up her coat and got out, walking around the front of the car. The snow reflecting off her headlamps and flashers provided enough illumination for her to see that her right front tire was almost completely flat.

"Not *now*. Why tonight? That's why I have triple-A, I guess," she said aloud to herself. *Wonder how long it'll take them to get here in this mess.*

The lights from the vehicle that had been following her slowed, and she saw the pickup truck pull to the shoulder behind her.

Maybe I won't have to call them.

She waited as an older man got out of the pickup. He held a flashlight in his right hand, and scanned the side of her car, halting the light on her deflated tire. He didn't speak, but he nodded when he saw the tire and then headed back to the rear of the truck. A moment later, he reappeared holding a tire iron.

"Thank you so much, sir," she said. "I'm sorry to be needing help in this weather."

He didn't speak. He nodded again, and then handed her a card.

"I love this place!" Lynn exclaimed as she stepped in front of the seat that Trask had pulled out from the table for her. "Who picked it?"

"That would be your loving husband," Cam answered. "And now we know why."

"I like it, too," Trask said. "Cam brought me here for my first dinner in town when I flew in for my interview with the U.S. Attorney. It was the first place I brought Lynn after we moved in. The food's great, and the view's interesting as well: Union Station, the old rail yard, Hallmark headquarters behind the train station. Interesting place."

Trask touched Lynn's arm. "Before you sit down, let me introduce someone. I think you remember John and Billy, and you certainly know Cam, but I don't think you've met the newest member of the team. This is Becky Suzuki. Becky, my wife Lynn."

The ladies reached across the table to shake hands.

"Very nice to meet you, Becky," Lynn said. "Jeff says that you've done a wonderful job pulling all the reports together on this case."

"It's nice to meet you, too," Becky said. "At least I did *something* right. If I'd done *everything* right, I wouldn't be footing the bill for this shindig."

"Told ya," Billy Graham quipped.

"Yeah, at least a hundred times." Suzuki gave him a playful elbow in the ribs.

Trask gave Lynn a quick glance. Her return nod told him she understood. Billy and Becky *were* an item.

"Have *you* eaten here before?" Lynn asked Becky.

"Only once or twice. It *is* great food."

"I agree completely," John Foote said. "If we can get a server over here, we can get some on the table."

He turned around to summon someone, almost turning the chair into a waiter who had walked up behind him.

"Hungry, are we?" the young man asked.

"Starving," Foote responded. "Please hurry and ask the ladies what they're having so that I can order the crown ribs, a crock of beans, a house salad, and a bottle of that merlot they're drinking at the next table over."

"Gotcha," the server laughed as he wrote down Foote's order. "I'll be right back with you after I speak to the ladies."

He took Lynn's order, then Becky's, then turned back to Foote.

"And what will you be having, sir?" the waiter asked, playing along.

Foote buried his head in a menu and pretended to study it.

"I might need a minute. Ask the others first."

"He's in rare form tonight," Graham said, chuckling, and speaking to Trask. "He hitched a ride with us so he wouldn't have to drive home."

"He seems to have ordered the most expensive thing on the menu, too," Suzuki said, scowling.

"We learn the most from our costliest mistakes," Foote said. "I have the luxury of a designated driver—whichever one of you assumes that role—and it's becoming ever more apparent that you two need a chaperone."

"What exactly was your mistake?" Lynn asked Becky, ignoring Foote.

"Oh, Billy bet me that Jeff would find something that I missed. I made the mistake of taking the bet, so here we are."

"You said 'something,'" Graham quipped.

"All right, *several* somethings," Becky shot back. She turned back to Lynn. "Jeff pointed out some ballistics tests that hadn't been done yet. Some were guns that were recovered weeks or months after shootings in the case. So far, we've matched three—"

"And the case is much stronger," Foote noted.

"Don't blame yourself," Lynn told Suzuki. "He did that to me, and he does it to everybody. Like John said, though, the case gets stronger, and that helps put the perps where they belong."

"He did it to you?" Becky asked, confused.

"Lynn was a special agent in Air Force OSI, then an investigator for a medical examiner's office, and then an analyst for one of the Bureau's Joint Terrorism Task Forces," Cam explained. "She knows her stuff, and shoots pretty well, too."

"Sorry," Becky apologized to Lynn. "I had no idea. What are you doing now?"

"No apology required," Lynn said. "I did what I could do, and I could never do what you do. I wouldn't have made it as a street cop in a city like this. Not enough strength or patience. Anyway, like I was saying, don't feel bad about being double-checked by Jeff. He sees things others don't. I've always said he's more of a detective than a prosecutor, and he's a hell of a prosecutor. As for your question, right now I'm a stay-at-home dog mom. It's my favorite job so far."

"Thanks, I think," Becky said, shooting a look at Trask. "No pressure, huh?"

"I'll tell you when there is," Trask said, smiling. "Don't worry about it. You'll probably catch something I missed before we're done with this case."

"I'll look for that, then," Becky said, smiling at Lynn.

"Side bet?" Billy asked.

"Oh, shut up!" Becky flicked her napkin in his face. She turned back to Lynn. "Cam said that you shoot. What do you like to carry?"

"We carried Glocks in OSI," Lynn said. "Jeff bought me a real nice little hand cannon for Christmas. That's what I carry now. It's a Springfield XD-S, a tiny little .45. Easy to conceal."

"It makes a helluva noise for such a little gun," Trask added. "She gets some funny looks when we go to the range." He shrugged. "She still shoots a lot better than I do."

"I've had a lot more practice," Lynn said, patting Trask's hand. "You're getting better all the time."

"You carry, too?" Becky asked Trask.

"Yeah, when I'm outside the courthouse, mostly in an inside-the-waistband holster. I have it on now. It's a Sig 938, a little single-stack nine. My favorite is a little bigger—but not much—a Sig 239."

"Nice gun," Billy noted. "I used to carry one as a backup. Loved it. Wore it out."

"It's a shame they don't make them anymore," Trask said, nodding. "Sweet trigger."

Their conversation paused as the meal was brought to their table. Becky noticed that the servers had delivered two bottles of the merlot to Foote.

"John?" she asked.

"It would be unseemly for me not to share," Foote said. He swirled the sample pour in his glass, then took a sip. "Excellent," he said, nodding to the waiter. "One bottle for the table, and one for me."

"I'll have one glass," Becky said as the server offered to pour the wine. "I have the short straw all around tonight, so I'll be driving."

"Fill 'er up," Billy said, lifting his glass to the waiter.

Foote turned to Trask.

"Jeff, my friend, we simply cannot have you being outscored at the range by your wife. It's just not done."

"Like I said, John, she's had years of practice. I just picked a gun up a little while back." Trask tasted his own glass of wine. "Nice choice. Excellent."

"Thank you." Foote nodded. "At any rate, we need to fix this problem. My partner here," he pointed across the table to Graham, "is a former instructor at the police academy range. I'm sure he can give you a few pointers."

"I'll take him up on that, then," Trask said.

"How about tomorrow?" Billy asked. "Squad time at the range. You're both invited."

"Okay," Trask said, checking with Lynn, who nodded. "We can crate the pups for a while."

"I'm curious, John," Becky said. "Why does it offend you that Lynn shoots better than Jeff?"

"I'd like to know that, too," Lynn chimed in.

They waited for a response as Foote emptied his first glass of wine and poured another.

"It's simply an insult to our gender's long-standing superiority in hand-eye coordination," Foote explained, taking another sip of wine. "Much of that superiority is genetic, of course, but much is also taught at a very early age, ironically, by women."

"What the hell are you talking about?" Suzuki demanded. "Are you really that much of a sexist?"

"Oh, no," moaned Graham. "I know where he's going with this now."

"It's a simple matter of fact and experience," Foote responded. "Biology. You see, it all starts with potty training."

"That's where I was afraid this was going," Graham said, shaking his head. "He has this theory—"

Cam Turner was starting to laugh. Trask just stared at Foote in disbelief.

"We—those of us who are males—start life with this attachment that we have to be trained to use, you see," Foote began. "Without training, we just spray our liquid ammunition all over the room, and the ones who usually train us are our mothers. I say 'train,' but there really isn't much hands-on training at all, because the moms don't have any idea how to tell us what we're doing;

they just get mad when we miss because they're the ones who usually have to clean it up."

Graham leaned back in his chair, laughing hard. "No 'hands-on' training, huh?"

"Perhaps a poor choice of words, partner," Foote said. "But you other gentlemen can back me up on this. We start with those little potty chair plastic bowls because we're too short to use a regular toilet. It takes a little while to master hitting the center of that little plastic bowl, but with enough nagging about it from our moms, we get there, right?"

"Okay," Trask said, laughing.

"Then, as we grow a bit in height," Foote continued, "we are suddenly confronted with the standard size toilet bowl. It is hardly a challenge, given the fact that it's six times the size of the kiddie toilet, yet we males love a challenge, and the standard toilet bowl accommodates us in that fashion."

"What?" Lynn asked. "How?"

Trask looked at Graham, who was looking down at his plate and giggling, and Turner, who seemed to know where Foote was going. Cam was looking away, staring out a window, getting more red-faced by the second.

"What, my dear, does a standard toilet bowl have that a kiddie toilet does not have?" Foote asked Lynn.

"A flush mechanism?" Becky Suzuki guessed.

"A correct response, but not relevant to the issue," Foote answered. "We're dealing here with target creation and acquisition."

"I have no idea what you're talking about," Lynn said.

"That's quite alright." Foote held up a hand as if to excuse her. "I wouldn't expect you to know, because you've literally never been in a position to know." He paused. "The answer, of course, is water in the bottom of the bowl."

Graham was now hiding his face in his hands. Cam was turned completely away from the table.

Foote pointed to Turner. "See? Cam knows where I'm going, and he's never heard this before."

"Water?" Lynn asked. "You aim for the water? How is that a challenge?"

Trask suddenly realized what was coming and broke up.

"See?" Foote pointed at Trask. "It's universal. No, Lynn, it's not the water itself that poses a challenge. The water in the bottom of a standard bowl is larger in diameter than a kiddie potty, so there's no challenge there at all. It's what happens after we start firing and hit the water. It's the bubbles: big bubbles, little bubbles, lots of bubbles. I always start with the big ones and work my way down. Of course, sometimes when you hit the big ones, you create more big ones, and then you have to fire on those. But you'd never know this as a female, because you're never in a position to see your bubbles, assuming you make any. I don't know myself, because I've never checked. That would be strange."

"Oh yeah. *That* would be strange," Lynn muttered.

Cam Turner was howling and had to catch himself to prevent falling out of his chair.

"As I said at the beginning," Foote explained, "it's target creation and acquisition. If you can't see the targets you're creating, you can't acquire them, and you can't practice hand-eye coordination by controlling your weapon and destroying those targets. That's where the male's superior hand-eye coordination begins to take form."

Suzuki shook her head. "Unbelievable," was all she could muster.

"Try hours in a car with him," Graham said.

"I just have one question," Suzuki asked Graham.

"What?" he asked in return.

"Is all that true?"

Graham turned to the window and tried to ignore the question. "Look," he said. "It's snowing pretty hard out there."

8

TRASK HELD up the harnesses so the dogs could see them, a visual cue letting them know that it was time for their morning walk. He got the usual, opposite responses. Kodi, who loved to be chased, led him on a couple of laps around the sectional couch before he cornered her and got the rig around her neck. Koko stretched out her front legs and bowed like an elephant before her mahout, making it easy for Trask to slip the harness over her head. She then stood, allowing him to click the buckle closed on the strap that ran across her chest and behind her front legs.

We never taught her that, Trask thought. *She came up with that all on her own. Smart girl. She knows it snowed last night and she can't wait to get out in it.*

He fastened the leashes to the harnesses and walked them out through the garage door and onto the driveway, which was seven inches deep in a wet, heavy snow.

Glad I bought the snow blower this season. If I had to shovel this stuff it would take hours. Got to get the snow off the deck in back, too. There's more weight there than the wood needs to support any longer than necessary. He sighed. *The joys of home ownership.*

A hard tug from Koko against his left hand shook him out of his thoughts.

"Okay, sorry girls. Let's go. Not too fast, Koko, heel up."

He might as well have been praying for rain. The little Husky wanted to run, and it was only after a few jumps and strong pulls on her lead that she settled into Trask's deliberate pace as his boots crunched through the snow. Koko fell back beside him on his left as Kodi walked on his right.

They trudged about a mile before turning back for home, cutting the usual morning trek off early due to the un-shoveled sidewalks. Kodi the Border Jack was struggling, her shorter legs barely keeping her chest above the snow.

"You may like this stuff, little wolf," Trask said to Koko, "but your little sister isn't as tall, and she wasn't bred to pull sleds."

He punched in the code to open the garage door when they got home, closed the door to keep the blowing snow out, and wiped the pups down with a towel hanging from a hook on the wall. Lynn opened the door that led from the garage to the house.

"It looks like you collected some Koko puffs."

Trask looked at his coat. Several large tufts of white Husky hair had used static electricity to attach themselves to his black coat.

"The good news is that she only sheds once a year," he said. "The bad news is that it lasts 365 days."

"We're about to wear out another vacuum cleaner," Lynn said, nodding in agreement. "I'll feed them while you do the driveway."

"The driveway and the deck," Trask muttered.

"Right. And the deck. What time is your squad getting here?"

"About 11:00," Trask answered. "I'll have time to shower and change, if you can get your shower after the girls eat their breakfast. Is your range bag ready?"

"Yep. I'm all cleaned, locked, and loaded."

"Good. Foote's driving his Expedition, so we can all fit inside and just take one vehicle out through the slush."

The driveway took twenty minutes. Using a smaller, electric snow blower, Trask was able to get most of the weight off the deck in another thirty. He looked back at the stretch of planks after he turned off the blower.

Seventy feet across the back of the house, and another eighty along the side, all for the view of the lake. It's a nice view, but when I have to replace this deck, I'll need another mortgage. Next house—if there is one—will have a concrete slab porch. I'm never pulling another pop-up nail or sinking another deck screw.

"John," Lynn asked from the seat behind Foote. "You're not married or currently seeing anyone? You don't have kids or even a dog?"

"None of the above," Foote said as he steered the big Ford onto the bypass and headed east.

"Then why is it that you're driving an automotive version of Moby Dick?"

Foote chuckled. "I actually thought about getting a personalized plate with 'MobyD' on it," he said, "but a set of vanity plates for a cop has always been a bad idea. If the word gets out on the street, you've just painted a target on your own vehicle. To answer your question: I'm a large guy, I'm more comfortable in a large vehicle like this, and—for some reason—I always seem to be hauling a lot of stuff or people, like a bunch of folks and their ammo bags going to a firing range."

"Chicken or the egg," quipped Billy Graham. "If you didn't drive the whale, people wouldn't ask you to haul them around."

"Don't be taunting Moby," Foote responded. "He could get temperamental and strand us out here."

"Really?" Becky Suzuki asked. "You've had trouble with this thing?"

"Not really," Foote said. "Just one flat tire, and I called AAA for that."

"For a flat?" Trask inquired. He was in the shotgun seat.

"You see the size of the tires on this beast, Jeff?" Graham asked. "Even bigfoot up there would have trouble lifting one onto the wheel studs by himself."

"And I would have gotten filthy in the process, detracting from my appearance as a poster boy for the Bureau," Foote added.

"Maybe thirty years ago," Lynn said.

"Billy will be your shooting instructor today, then, young lady," Foote responded, feigning wounded feelings. "I'll be assisting Becky."

"Lynn doesn't need any help, John," Trask said.

"And neither does Becky," said Becky.

"And why are we doing this, then?" Foote asked.

"To give some instruction to your friendly AUSA," Trask answered. "I'm deadly, but not that accurate."

"Scary combination," Foote said laughing. He turned north, heading through Independence, Missouri as they passed over I-70.

They drove past the businesses that lined the state highway in north Independence. The buildings lining the road gave way to farmland before Foote took an exit that led them around an LDS temple. Just south of the temple, they pulled into the grounds of the Kansas City, Missouri Police Academy.

"You've been here before, haven't you, Jeff?" Foote asked.

"You know he has," Billy Graham said. "The chief gave him that baton in the auditorium for our big dope case."

Trask felt himself smiling. The Chief of Police rarely bestowed ceremonial batons on prosecutors. The baton was now sitting in a glass display case in the Trasks' living room, nicely decorated with a blue and gold cord and a gold plaque thanking Trask for "outstanding assistance to the Kansas City, Missouri Police Department." Lynn reached up from the back seat and squeezed his arm. He smiled back at her, acknowledging the gesture and her pride in him.

"For anyone who cares," Trask said, "J.P. Barrett is jealous as hell of that thing. If the opportunity arises—"

"We'll see if he ever deserves a nomination," Billy said, laughing.

"J.P. at least knows his way around a courtroom," Trask thought aloud. "He's been a line AUSA and knows the biz, not like some of his predecessors, from what I've heard."

"That's for sure." Foote was nodding in agreement. "Who was that knucklehead we had for a while under Bush the younger?" He paused before answering his own question. "John Greenleaf. One of the 'in crowd' in Washington before somebody made him the U.S. Attorney here. He demanded to handle a trial so he could show he was one of the guys and a real prosecutor. Your first assistant handed him the surest thing of surest things—a felon-in-possession-of-a-firearm case with a fingerprint confirmation and a confession—and he managed to get a mistrial instead of a conviction."

"*What?*" Lynn asked. "I could try a case like that, and I'm not an attorney."

"And you probably wouldn't have left a college librarian and a sociology professor on the jury," Foote added.

"Incredible." Trask shook his head. "God spare us from politicians."

They circled around the main building to a smaller structure that housed the firing range. Trask retrieved Lynn's range bag from the back of the Expedition and handed it to her before grabbing his own and following the group inside. The range was empty except for their group.

Trask put his bag on a table along the back of the hallway outside the firing area. He pulled his "eyes and ears"—goggles and noise-cancelling earphones—from his bag and put them on before reaching for the four magazines that he had loaded at home. He turned and saw through an observation window that Billy was hanging targets for each of them—the usual paper poster of the chest and head of an ugly, armed thug, stapled to a cardboard backing.

Trask entered the firing area and took the lane to the left. Fifty rounds later, he pushed buttons returning the target from the twenty-foot distance where he had set it. It showed a familiar pattern: a clustered set of holes, about two inches in diameter, but three inches left and three inches down from his point of aim. He felt a tap on his shoulder and turned to see Billy Graham.

"Clear your weapon and let's talk," Billy said, pointing to the hallway in the back of the firing area.

Trask punched the magazine eject button, racked the slide back to make sure the Sig was clear, grabbed his target, and then followed Billy out of the range.

"That's a good, close grouping. We've got a good foundation to work from," Graham said. "A couple of adjustments and we'll have that down-and-left drift fixed."

He took the Sig from Trask and held it so that the barrel pointed toward the ceiling.

"Watch as I pull the trigger."

Trask looked at the barrel. Graham pulled the trigger, re-racked the pistol, pointed it skyward again, and pulled the trigger. The barrel remained perfectly still.

"You try it," Billy said, returning the pistol to Trask.

Trask took the gun in his usual grip and pointed it upward. When he pulled the trigger, the gun moved noticeably to the left.

"It's two things, Jeff: your grip and your trigger pull. Let me show you a couple of things."

Graham took the pistol back from Trask.

"This isn't a big gun; it's a compact. That means it's going to move more with every mistake you make. The first thing you need to do is grip it as high as you can along the backstrap without putting your hand behind the slide. It'll hurt and bleed if you set it too high back there."

Trask nodded. He had done that—once.

"Your grip has to be balanced, too," Graham said. "Look." Billy stood so that Trask could look over his shoulder as he held the pistol, again pointing it at the ceiling. "Look at both of my index fingers. I have the webbing of my right hand high on the backstrap, and my index fingers along either side of the gun. The left finger from my support hand is the same length on that side as the right finger is on that side. Now that the grip is balanced, I can drop my trigger finger down inside the trigger guard, and when I squeeze it, the barrel doesn't move."

"I was working with one of those trigger diagrams," Trask said. "I thought I had to get the pad of my trigger finger in just the right spot—"

"Maybe on a different gun," Billy explained, but that 239 is a compact. Let the grip hold it in place and determine the correct point for your trigger pull. Leave those trigger diagnostics targets on the shelf."

Trask imitated Billy's grip and felt his trigger finger fall on the trigger exactly at the joint between the tip and center pad of his finger. He pointed the gun at the ceiling and squeezed. The barrel didn't move.

"See?" Billy said, smiling. "An easy fix. The way you were firing before, you were pushing the gun to the left every time you pulled the trigger. One more thing: breathe normally while you're shooting; don't try to hold your breath before every shot. Stay calm and relaxed, in control, and breathe normal breaths. Your eyes and arm need oxygen to work properly."

"Should I try that now?"

"Sure. Just don't expect everything to be suddenly perfect. You'll need time for the corrections to get recorded into your muscle memory, and to get completely away from what were some minor bad habits. You were right about what you said in the car. You're lethal—good center mass groups—but you could be more accurate. Just really focus on the front sight and try the grip and trigger corrections. If I had to bet, this next target will show a wider grouping, but it will be more centered."

Trask went back inside the range, hung another target, and fired another fifty rounds. Just as Billy had predicted, the pattern on the center of the thug's chest was wider—about six inches in diameter—but it *was* centered around the bullseye, and eight of the rounds had punched holes through the center ring.

Trask also noticed that the noise on the range had ended with his last shot. He turned and saw the rest of the group applauding when he turned around. He took a mock bow.

He pulled his ear coverings down around his neck.

"Thanks, coach," he said to Billy.

"No more left and low," Billy said, smiling. "Nice job. It'll get even better with practice."

"How'd *I* do, coach?" Becky was holding her target. There was a tight grouping around the bullseye, and another in the center of the target thug's head. There were also holes perfectly placed in what had been the cartoon's eyeballs.

"How'd you do that?" John Foote asked, pointing at the eye holes.

"I have you to thank for that, John," she answered. "I just pretended they were bubbles."

Lynn's target showed an even tighter pattern around the center.

"Nice work, lady," Graham said admiringly.

"Thanks. Only trouble I had was some jams."

Billy frowned. "Let me see your grip, Lynn."

She double-checked to make sure the gun was unloaded, then pointed it downrange.

"You learned to shoot firing a revolver, didn't you?" Billy asked.

"Yeah. How'd you know?"

"You're tea-cupping that thing—your support hand is under the magazine. You do that with a semi-auto—especially a subcompact like that XD-S—and you're putting extra tension on the feeding mechanism. That could cause a jam. What did you carry while you were in OSI?"

"A standard size Glock."

"So, your left hand was on the *side* of the weapon because it had a full-sized grip."

"Yeah, I think so."

"Now you've got a little gun again—a very nice one—but that old muscle memory thinks you moved back to a revolver. Move your grip to the side and out from under the mag, and I'll bet your jams disappear."

"I'll be damned," she said.

"Probably," Trask said, earning himself an elbow in the ribs.

"You have time for me to ask *you* some questions before we drive you back to your place?" Billy asked him.

"Sure."

"We'll need to stop at the office for a few minutes."

Instead of heading south toward Lee's Summit when they hit I-70, they turned west toward Kansas City. They stopped about fifteen minutes later.

Trask was the first out of the Expedition when it pulled in front of the CCU offices. He went to the key punch panel and entered his code to open the front door. He held it open. Lynn was the first to reach the door.

"They gave you their own code here?" she asked.

"I know," Foote quipped from behind her. "Incredibly lax security, especially for such a Secret Squirrel operation."

"We'll be in the conference room," Billy said as he and Becky walked past.

Trask followed the rest of the group down a hallway to the right, turning left into a small room. He chuckled when he saw the walls.

"This looks strangely familiar," he said.

Along one wall, someone had posted numbered vertical columns of typed paper, the sheets fixed to the wall with pushpins. There were only five columns so far. Trask walked up to one and saw that it contained all the known details for the corpse with two sawed-off legs—the legs he had seen in the morgue.

"I've seen this before," Lynn said, looking at Jeff. "You did this for the MS-13 case we had in D.C."

"And for the Gloomy thing here," Foote noted. "Billy thought it might help with our saw-happy serial killer."

Trask shot a glance at Becky Suzuki.

"I'm not betting on anything *this* time," she said.

"See anything?" Billy asked Trask. "Or see anything that's missing? We overlook any details?"

Details. The word sent Trask's mind wandering for a moment. "Take care of your details," had been his high school band director's favorite saying. Every member had learned to do it, and they had gone on to win perfect ratings from every judge that had rated them in competition.

There had been an upperclassman at the Air Force Academy who was also big on details.

"The devil is in the details, like they say. We just call it 'evidence' in this line of work." Bob Lassiter, his boss in the D.C. United States Attorney's office had lectured the new hires with Trask looking over his shoulder.

"Jeff?" Billy was looking at him.

"Sorry," Trask responded, returning to the moment.

"He was in trial head mode," Lynn muttered. "The impenetrable wall."

"See anything?" Billy asked again.

"What's this last one?" Trask asked, moving to the column on the far right.

"We're not sure," Becky said. "We think it might be connected, but it's different."

Trask read the notes and details on the wall.

"It's different because we have a survivor," he said. "More than one."

"Yeah." Billy nodded in agreement. "Denny Walsh, one of our patrol unit guys, interrupts a pickup of a working girl on the west end of Independence Avenue. The would-be john pulls off when he sees the patrol car, and Denny didn't make the plates. He gets out to talk to the hooker, and the next thing he remembers is waking up next to her on the sidewalk."

"The john was already gone?" Trask asked.

"Yep."

"Any security cams in the area?"

"None that picked up anything. We did check." Billy shrugged.

"Both Walsh and the hooker passed out. Were they checked out at the hospital?" Trask frowned as he re-read the notes.

"Not the hooker. We didn't have enough to hold her, and she was back on her feet when our second unit pulled up a few minutes later. She declined any medical assistance. Walsh went to get checked out and they ran a tox scan for the usual drug suspects, but nothing turned up." Graham shrugged again.

"If they did a blood draw, they should do a comprehensive scan, not just for the usual stuff." Trask offered. "If it was some kind of drug that knocked them out, how was it transmitted? Your guy certainly didn't knowingly swallow something at the scene. No drug dart wounds or anything weird like that?"

"No." Becky shook her head. "No taser wounds either."

"Did your CSI folks process the scene?" Trask asked.

"Yes." Billy nodded this time. "Once I heard about it the next morning. I thought it might be connected to this whole mess, so I had them look it over, but it was a few hours later."

"I'd go over their inventory and list everything they found and stick that on the wall. Every *detail.*" Trask thought for a moment. "If they were drugged, and it was a skin contact transfer of the dope, there's no telling what the stuff could have been on."

"Okay." Billy wrote an entry in a small notebook.

Trask went back to the other columns.

"We still have no IDs on the victims?"

"Not yet. No DNA matches for any of 'em," Billy answered.

"We have two torsos. Any sexual evidence?" Trask asked.

"No." Becky responded this time.

"And our connection between the murders appears to be the signature manner of dissection?"

"It's pretty singular," John Foote offered.

"Enough to be handed to a single county prosecutor as part of a series of related cases?" Trask asked.

"Not yet," Billy said. "The county bosses don't think we have enough to draw that conclusion."

"So, they think they have more than one killer out there using the same tools to butcher women in exactly the same fashion, huh?" Trask shook his head. "The county prosecutor's up for re-election this year, isn't she?"

"Just a few months away," Billy said.

"She doesn't want the words 'serial killer' in the papers while she's campaigning."

"I think you hit the nail on the head," Foote said.

"Well, let's assume she's wrong, since we know that already," Becky said. "Jeff, what should we be looking for in a serial killer suspect? You've worked these kinds of cases before."

"I'm not a qualified profiler," Trask protested.

"But you *have worked* with them," Lynn said. "And since you never forget anything besides what I ask you to get at a grocery store, run down the list for us."

Trask smirked at her.

"Okay," he said, "Here goes: abandoned by birth mother, history of substance abuse, bed-wetting as a kid, childhood abuse of some sort—psychological or physical—or both, growing up lonely and isolated, a history of violent fantasies, animal abuse, possible head trauma, sometimes a high IQ. They tend to keep some sort of trophies from their victims. Basically, we're talking about things we might see in any narcissistic, anti-social sociopath or psychopath, also known as criminals to those of us who didn't major in psychology. Any serial killer might have some or none of those bees buzzing around in his noggin. It doesn't hurt to look for these traits or to notice them, but don't hurt yourselves concentrating on them."

Billy looked up from his notebook.

"Anything else?"

"The lack of sexual motives strikes me as someone who really hates women," Trask said. "This isn't about sex; it's about hate. He saws them into pieces while they're still alive. It's the torture and pain he enjoys, the control, even to the point of a prolonged and agonizing death." He inhaled slowly. "You guys have got to understand something else."

"What's that?" Foote inquired.

"This is not—and probably will never be—my case," Trask said, glancing at each of them in turn. "There's no federal crime here, at least not one that I can identify yet. These are state matters. The kidnappings don't cross state lines, as far as we know. We *may* have drug distributions—we don't know that yet, either—but unlike the situation with Gloomy and his crew, the distributions—if they occurred—are there to facilitate state homicides. Gloomy's murders happened to further a federal dope conspiracy, and that makes them federally chargeable crimes.

"Your best bet is to get the best guys or gals in the Jackson County prosecutor's office assigned to this thing, put a task force together, and hope for some breaks. Remember that I now have a not-too-friendly new crim chief looking over my shoulder, and he's just looking for a reason to throw me into the nearest cauldron. I can't afford to be accused of playing in a park where I don't have jurisdiction. Feel free to call or come by and shoot the breeze for ideas—again, no emails or paper trails—and I'll be glad to bounce things off the wall, but that's the extent of what I can do."

Trask took another long breath.

"You know I'd love to help more if I could. I don't want to see any more paper on that wall than you do."

"I'm hoping to hell we don't have another one." The voice came from behind them.

They turned to see Sgt. Tommy Land standing in the doorway of the conference room.

"What's up, boss?" Billy asked.

"You know Captain Brown at South Patrol?" Land asked.

"Of course," Becky said. "He was running courses at the Academy when Billy and I went through it."

"His daughter Beverly was driving home from school last night. She's a sophomore at William Jewell in Liberty. She never made it, and her car was found on the side of the highway. Her phone was on the passenger seat. I was about to see if anyone wanted to ride up to the scene with me."

"We're all in," Billy said.

"I just need to run Jeff and Lynn home," Foote reminded them.

"Understood," Land said. "Jeff, any last thing you can think of?"

"See if anything from that scene matches this one," Trask said, pointing to the last column of paper on the wall.

It was three hours later when the tow truck pulled Beverly Brown's car onto the flatbed. Two teams of crime scene investigators had been summoned instead of one. They had combed and re-combed the area around the car. One of their department's own was missing, one of their family. The leader of the first CSI team waited until the car was completely off the roadway before he did a final sweep of the ground. He noticed a small paper card lying on the road.

I can't believe we didn't see this before. It IS flat paper, and it WAS in the dark under the vehicle. Probably nothing, but you never know. At least the car protected it from the snow.

He put a small yellow cone on top of the card, both to mark the location and to keep it from blowing away. He photographed the card as it lay on the road, then he took several other shots to show the relationship of the location to the side of the highway. He returned the camera to the trunk of his van, then retrieved a pair of long tweezers from a toolbox in the back of the truck. It was the second time he had taken them out that day.

Thought I was done with these.

He walked back to the yellow cone, pulled the card off the asphalt with the tweezers, and—using hands protected by plastic gloves—placed the card into a clear plastic evidence envelope.

"*I am a deaf mute,*" *he read to himself.*

9

THE WHITE EXPEDITION was parked in front of the house when Trask and Lynn pulled into their driveway. Trask hit the button for the garage door and waved as he pulled inside. Foote, Graham, and Suzuki got out and walked up the drive toward the house.

Trask came out of the garage to meet them while Lynn went inside to check on the pups. He was about to ask them what they were all doing working on a Sunday, but he caught himself before speaking.

The daughter of a cop is missing, one of their own. There's no such thing as a weekend or a day off at times like this.

"Just got back from church," he said instead. "Hope you haven't been waiting long."

"Just about five minutes," Billy Graham said, handing Trask a sheet of paper.

Trask looked it over. It was a photocopy of two personal cards, business size, one above the other. Someone had placed them on a copy machine for comparison. The cards were the same except for spots of dirt and some moisture stains on different sections. Each read, "I am a deaf mute." Trask looked up at Graham.

"The first was from the scene where our patrol guy and the hooker both passed out," Billy explained. "The one below it was found by the crime scene guys last night underneath Beverly Brown's car. She had a flat trying to drive home in the snow from William Jewell."

Trask fought back the urge to think out loud.

These are experienced detectives. Don't insult them by suggesting what they already know to do.

He turned when he saw Lynn walking down the driveway from the house. He handed her the paper, before turning back to Billy.

"We just wanted to see if you had any ideas," Graham said.

"What have you done with these so far?" Trask asked.

"Nothing," Foote offered. "They're at the lab, but we wanted to see what you thought before we had them checked for latents."

"You've probably had the same ideas that I'm working through now, then," Trask said. "You didn't want any fingerprinting processes to possibly taint a chemical analysis if these cards were used as the transfer medium to knock out the victims?"

"Exactly," Becky said, with an assertive tone.

"And," Trask continued, "if our guy *did* use the cards to dose the victims, he would have had to wear gloves to avoid dosing himself by handling the cards?"

"Yep." Foote nodded in agreement. "Our esteemed sergeant still thinks we should have the cards printed."

"I do, too," Trask said, surprising them for a moment, "but only *after* your chemistry whizzes at the lab have the first shot. If we don't, the defense counsel at any trial will beat the lack of a print test like a dead horse. You'll never hear the end of it."

"Tommy said the same thing." Billy was nodding now.

"I don't think we'll ever see a latent print because of the gloves," Trask said. "But we'll need to try just the same. Maybe the lab guys can cut some corners off the edges to run through a GC/Mass-Spec machine. It won't take much of the card to test. Odds are our perp soaked the whole thing down pretty well, and any liquid should have been absorbed by the paper. I'd ask them to run a complete chemical spectrum analysis. Don't just try for the common knockout drugs. Anyway, they'd still have some main pieces of the cards to try and print. Ask the chemists; they're the experts."

Trask paused.

"Any of you get close to the cards? Anything unusual about them, other than the words on them and the fact that they were found at two different crime scenes?"

"I did," Billy said. "The crime scene techs had them in plastic evidence sleeves, of course, and I opened one to get a better look at it. The thing stunk like hell."

"What did it smell like?" Trask asked.

"Ever have kimchi?" Graham asked him back.

"Couldn't get close enough to try it," Trask said. "The only cabbage I eat is in coleslaw. Lynn was stationed in Korea for a year with the Air Force. She's had some."

"Jeff has a weak gut and likes a narrow menu," Lynn offered.

"I have three requirements for food," Trask responded, shooting a glance at his wife. "It's cheap and it's quick and it won't make me sick. Meals are just pit stops on the racetrack of life."

"Except for bar-be-que at the old freight yard?" Foote asked.

"A rare exception," Trask agreed.

"Think kimchi and garlic," Graham said, trying to get back to the subject.

Trask nodded. "Make sure they test for DMSO."

"For what?" Billy was scowling.

"DMSO. Dimethyl sulfoxide. It's a super solvent that was discovered as a by-product of pulpwood processing. The NFL and college football teams won't admit it, but they couldn't operate without the stuff. It penetrates the skin and can pass through cell membranes like the speed of light."

Becky Suzuki looked at Lynn, who shrugged. Becky turned to Trask. "And you know this because? You're a chemistry whiz, too?"

"Oh God, no!" Trask laughed. "I did have to take a few courses at the Academy—part of the core engineering curriculum—but I got out of those classes by the skin of my teeth. Low Cs for grades. This knowledge comes more from personal experience.

"I grew up in Hattiesburg, Mississippi. Hattiesburg is smack in the middle of a southern pine forest, which means that they process a lot of pulp wood, which means that they have a lot of DMSO. The town also has a college football team—Southern Miss—think Brett Favre—and my dad was a professor at the university. We used to play a lot of pickup football on the campus when I was in high school. I sprained the hell out of an ankle in one game, and it swelled up like a melon. Instead of taking me to the doctor, Dad took me to the football team trainer.

"The doc hauled out what looked like a bucket of hot water—turns out it was melted wax—and grabbed my ankle and held it in that stuff until just before my skin came off. Then he takes a bottle of this really smelly liquid—"

"That would be DMSO," Foote observed.

"The FBI grasps the obvious," Graham noted.

"That *would* be DMSO," Trask said. "He took a cotton swab and rubbed the stuff on my ankle. I could *taste* it seconds later. Horrible. Had to be what garlic kimchi *would* taste like if someone ever force fed me with it. Anyway, by the next morning, I was walking on that ankle with an ace wrap. No swelling at all. If I'd gone to a regular doctor, I'd have been in a walking cast for weeks. The stuff is really magic for some things. They've used it in a couple of states to treat arthritis."

"If it's that good, why aren't they using it everywhere?" Becky asked.

"You can order it in diluted form online now," Trask said. "The problem with the stuff is that it's such a powerful solvent that it passes through cell membranes like lightning, and if it's contaminated with anything, it carries the contaminating substance with it. Like I said: this trainer put it on my ankle, and I tasted it in about three seconds."

"So, it could be used to transport other drugs," Becky observed.

"We'll make sure they check for that at the lab," Billy said. "I knew there was a reason we bothered you today, Jeff."

"No bother at all," Trask said. "Any word at all on the Brown girl?"

"Just those damn cards," Foote said. "Not much to work with. We've been talking to all the state agencies—getting them out on a weekend has been a real joy—to see what they can give us on the deaf-mute community in the area. That's been a dry hole so far."

"What was the vehicle description again on the incident with the hooker?" Trask asked.

"Older pickup. That's all the patrol officer got," Becky responded. "He wasn't close enough to make the tags or even the make of the truck. The handful of deaf-mutes in the area don't link to old pickups. We nearly had to waterboard some local health department supervisor to get some names. Privacy Act concerns, you know?"

"Yeah, I know." Trask nodded. "Don't you hate lawyers?"

"Most of 'em," Foote said, laughing. "Thanks, Jeff."

"One last thought," Trask said, "that just came to me. We believe that the prior victims were hookers walking the track on Independence Avenue, right?"

"That's been the working theory," Billy Graham answered. "Nothing to change it yet."

Trask nodded. "In that case, the scenes where those vics were grabbed don't necessarily tell us anything about where our bad guy lives or works. Duck hunters go to lakes to hunt; they don't live there. Our hooker hunter has to go where the hookers hang out to find them. Beverly Brown wasn't a hooker, and she wasn't on the track. She was probably a target of opportunity, meaning that our perp was on that road for a reason when he found her. He might live or work near that crime scene."

"I had the same thought," Foote said. "I hadn't said it yet. Glad we agree. We'll plug that into the equation. Thanks again."

"No sweat. Just remember," Trask said. "This isn't my case, guys."

"Got it," Becky said, smiling over her shoulder as the detectives walked back toward Foote's Expedition.

Lynn waited until the Expedition pulled away.

"I'm proud of you," she said, squeezing Trask's hand.

"For?"

"You have no idea how much those guys respect you, to drive here on a Sunday to pick your brain. Not about a court presentation, Jeff, *about an investigation!* I know plenty of investigators—I used to be one—and most of 'em wouldn't ask a lawyer for the time of day about the investigation phase of a case. They guard their turf, and they think of *themselves* as the experts on building the case."

"That's pretty flattering." Trask was almost blushing.

"DMSO, huh?"

"Yeah. I think big pharma has been scared of the stuff for years. It's scary good for sprains, and it's scary bad if you have to taste it."

"You're scary good sometimes."

"Thanks, babe. Did I miss anything there?"

"Just the way Becky Suzuki was looking at you when they left."

"I did miss that." He smiled. "There was another song playing in my head."

"It had better be the right one."

"'I Only Have Eyes for You.' The Flamingos. 1959."

She squeezed his hand again. "Good answer."

10

TRASK STOOD in his trial prep room looking at all the paper pinned to the walls. He'd done it dozens of times before, but he made himself go through the process again.

He started with the earliest incident, then worked the walls clockwise, forcing himself to go through each vertical row of papers, analyzing each event to make sure no more questions came to mind. He had come to the last event—the one on the back of the closed door to the room—when that door opened.

"Thought I might find you in here," Cam Turner said. "Got a second?"

"Sure. I just finished my review."

"What's this? Review number seventy-seven?"

Trask chuckled. "Yeah. Something like that."

"Find anything you missed in review seventy-six?"

"Doesn't look like it."

"So, is this the last one?"

"Maybe." Trask smiled. "Just checking my details, Cam."

"Sometimes I think you're obsessed with details."

"I had it drummed into me enough. I had an element sergeant at the Academy who was actually a teacher, not just a hazer. My first semester as a 'doolie'—you know, a freshman—I had a room to myself because my roommate washed out. The good news there was that I had some privacy; the bad news was that I had to get the whole room ready for inspections by myself: both lockers, both beds, both desks, had to wax and buff the entire floor.

"I thought I finally had the room perfect one Saturday morning. The upperclass guy's name was Brett Donald. He walks around the room doing white glove dust tests, nodding with approval, then tells me the room is 'almost acceptable.' He handed me a stopwatch, told me to time him, and then pushed my chair under the desk where it was supposed to be. He asked how long that took. I told him less than a second. He nodded, and just said, 'details.' For less than a second's effort and that oversight I lost the element's best doolie room award—being able to eat like a normal humanoid the next meal—and I never forgot it."

"Sounds like a good training sergeant."

"He was. He also knew how to dress someone down the *right* way. I saw lots of other upperclassmen screaming at doolies during what they called, 'special inspections.' Those 'inspections' were really just hazing sessions. Most of the upperclassmen worked so hard yelling and getting riled up that they worked harder than the doolies who were running in place or holding their rifles over their heads. Donald would walk up to you while you were doing the work and almost whisper into your brain. He never lost control, you had to work harder just to hear what he was telling you, and that calmness would scare the crap out of you."

Turner nodded. "I think I've seen you use that technique in interrogating some of our defendants and witnesses."

Trask nodded. "I have. I talked to Donald about that after my freshman year was over. He told me that you had to exercise self-control—especially over emotions like anger—before you could *be in control* of any situation. More than that, he said there had to be a *reason* to be in control of any situation, and that his reason with us was always to teach us something.

"Donald was also my coach when I had to box in intramurals one year. He taught me how to read the other guy's shoulder twitches to counterpunch. It really helped with one fight. I drew a sadistic upperclassman who'd hazed the hell out of me during basic training. He was a lefty, so he was always trying to jab with his right. I just kept my own right up to protect against his left, and any time I saw that right shoulder start to move, I'd throw my own left jab in his face. I worked him over pretty well for a couple of rounds before he figured it out and knocked me flat. It felt good for a while, anyway. Controlled anger *can* be useful sometimes."

He paused and took a breath.

"So, Cam, what brings you in even earlier than normal?"

"I thought you might need a heads-up before staff meeting this morning."

"About?"

"You have your police sources, and I have my own."

"Friends are a good thing to have."

"They are. At any rate, my friend tells me that someone on Tommy Land's Career Criminal Unit put in a call to Ms. Bonita Baylor, our county prosecutor, over the weekend, complaining about you working on one of her county cases —you know—the serial killer. Do you think you have a rat on that investigation team?"

Trask shook his head. "Not on the *real* team. That's John Foote, Billy Graham, and Becky Suzuki. I went to the range with them Saturday—missed you there, by the way—"

"I came down with a severe case of the honey-dos."

"I see. We stopped at CCU afterward because Billy wanted me to see a room much like this one. He'd papered the wall with incidents concerning our poor, butchered women, and wanted my thoughts. I told them then that unless some additional jurisdictional facts came out, this was going to be a county matter and not a federal case. I told them the same thing the next morning when they came out to the house."

"The next morning?"

"Yep. There was some common evidence between one of the attempted hooker grabs and Beverly Brown's crime scene."

"I really feel for her dad. Sam's a great cop. They were still pumping you about the case on Sunday?"

"Just picking my brain. I *again* told them I was happy to brainstorm evidence, but that it wasn't going to be my case."

Turner nodded. "Figures. Tommy Land had the whole squad working the thing all weekend. One of your guys probably mentioned that you'd looked at Billy's wall room, and then somebody else on the squad who thinks they've got a plug in with Bonita Baylor called her on the sly. Anyhow, I think you should assume that she has had time to call our new crim chief."

"Does she know Marsh?"

"She knows Senator Burke, and so does Marsh."

Trask nodded. "Yeah, you're probably right. Thanks. At least I won't get caught flat-footed." He checked his watch. "Speaking of staff meetings ..."

11

TRASK MANAGED to make the staff meeting's start time of 8:30 a.m. He walked into the United States Attorney's conference room and took his seat to the left of J.P. Barrett, who sat at the head of the table. He noticed that Ray Marsh was sitting directly across from him, to Barrett's right. The rest of the seats at the table were occupied by the various chieftains of the various divisions: General Crimes (bank robberies, fraud, and miscellaneous felonies), the firearms unit (felons in possession of guns, the most common violation for the district), the Civil Division (collecting debts owed to the government and defending the United States against civil lawsuits), and Administration (the manager in charge of staff personnel).

The meeting ran through the usual mundane agenda items—budget, personnel matters (which secretary was moving where, retirements and who would fill in for whom while that whom was on leave), and judges' concerns (which federal judge had complained about what)—before getting to updates on significant cases. Barrett saved the office's biggest current case for last.

"Where are you on Gloomy?" Barrett asked Trask.

"We go to the grand jury tomorrow afternoon. We have the certification to proceed on all the charges as adult prosecutions. He's looking at three life terms plus about three-hundred years if he's convicted on all counts."

"I saw the indictment in the office read-file on Friday," Marsh said. "I've never seen a drug indictment like that before."

Because you always took the lazy way out, Ray, Trask thought to himself. He remembered his conversation with Cam in the trial prep room and felt himself fighting back a flash of temper. *Marsh knows that the indictment was properly drafted; he's just firing his first torpedo of the morning.*

"It's a 'speaking' conspiracy indictment, Ray," Trask said as evenly and patiently as he could. He was responding for the benefit of the rest of the room, answering the challenge that Marsh had made in public, instead of private.

"Most drug conspiracy indictments aren't drafted with all the overt acts listed, because unlike general conspiracies, section 846 in the drug code doesn't require that overt acts be included. With a conspiracy this large in scope, and including several murders, we chose to write a speaking indictment to illustrate for the court and the jury the connections between the defendants' acts and the actual crimes charged. If they stole a car to do a drive-by shooting on a rival drug gang, the indictment explains why we're proving the car theft, which would otherwise be just a state charge. This approach also shoots down any defense motions for a bill of particulars that the defense would otherwise file. All the particulars are already in the indictment."

"That's why you're the SLC," Barrett said, smiling.

Trask nodded deferentially. *The boss just told you to shut up, Ray. Let's see if you have the smarts to do that.*

"I do have one other matter that I need to discuss with you and Jeff when the meeting's over," Marsh added.

There it is, as Cam suspected, Trask thought. *At least it won't be a surprise for me.*

He felt his temper rising again. *This snake had every chance to call me over the weekend, or to talk to me about these things this morning before the staff meeting, but NO, rather than act like a man, he wants to rat me out to the boss without even hearing my side of the story.* He took a couple of deep breaths. *Control. Control.*

"I think we're done with everyone else anyway," Barrett said. "Can you stay behind for a few minutes, Jeff?"

"Of course."

They waited until the others had left the room.

"What's up?" Barrett asked Marsh.

"I'm sorry to have to bring this up—"

Like hell you are, Ray.

"—but I got a phone call at home last night from Bonita Baylor at Jackson County. She said that she was advised by one of the Kansas City officers at the Career Criminal Unit that Jeff had been supervising the investigation into the slasher serial killer. She was pretty upset about it since that's a county case and not a federal matter. I felt that I had no choice but to bring that to your attention."

"Of course." Barrett nodded. "I would have expected nothing less." He turned to Trask, saying nothing, but raising a questioning eyebrow.

"A misunderstanding on that officer's part, whoever he or she may be," Trask said, calmly dismissing the matter. "I went shooting with three members of the CCU on Saturday morning at their invitation. They took us—Lynn and me—out to the police academy firing range for some pointers. On the way back we stopped at CCU because one of the detectives wanted to show me something.

"The lead detective on the serial killer case—the bad guy's not a 'slasher' by the way; he dissects his victims with saws—had seen what we've done in our trial prep room with the evidence against Gloomy. He liked the system and has started to use the same technique in his case. I took it as a compliment, as I believe it was intended, and I took some time to remind them that their other case was and will remain a county matter unless and until evidence is revealed that might give us jurisdiction.

"By the way, they came by the house yesterday with evidence connecting one of the prior attempted kidnappings with the disappearance of Captain Brown's daughter."

"A horrible shame," Barrett said.

"Yes, it is. They were just asking what I thought about some chemical analysis going forward. I gave them some ideas, but I reminded them again that it was a county case. I was in no way supervising anything. I can't supervise a case that's not assigned to me."

"That's not how the Jackson County Attorney took it!" Marsh blurted, falling back into his chair in evident frustration.

Trask looked to see if Barrett was going to respond. Barrett gave him the eyebrow again. A barely concealed smile appeared underneath it this time.

"I have no control over how Ms. Baylor *takes* things, Ray," Trask said calmly. "Nor do I have any control—and neither do you, by the way—over what investigators may do and what sources they may consult in a case not assigned to this office. As I indicated, all this happened as a matter of professional courtesy over the weekend, *in my spare time, and with repeated reminders to the officers involved that it was NOT my case, and that they should hook up with an assigned county prosecutor.* Per the guidance given to us earlier by Mr. Barrett here, I'll continue to make the calls on my SLC cases. I will *also* make the calls on what I do in my spare time. I'll be happy to consult with you on anything I pull off the wheel."

"Ray?" Barrett asked.

Marsh nodded but said nothing. He stood up and walked out of the room.

Barrett looked back at Trask.

"He'll be calling Bonita Baylor about now," Trask said.

"I know. I'll expect her call." Barrett shook his head. "Thank you, Senator Burke."

Trask nodded. "I thought I was leaving most of this crap back in D.C."

"At least you learned how to deal with it. Be careful with him, Jeff. Normally, I'd ask you two to kiss and make up, but that's obviously not how Ray wants to play it. He'll take every shot at you he can."

"I'll watch my six, and I'll try and give you some advance notice next time. Cam and I saw this coming, but we didn't have time to tip you off."

Barrett nodded. "That would help. You handled it this time. No harm done. Thanks."

Trask caught the attention of the secretary who sat across the hallway from his office door. He made a throat-slashing gesture. She nodded. No calls or interruptions.

He knew the rest of the morning would be filled with the curses of being a supervisor, and with feeding the gods of the bureaucracy their weekly ration of paperwork—some real, some virtual.

The most annoying—and ironic—of the morning's annoyances was Trask's annual financial disclosure form. It was required of anyone in a supervisory position in the United States Attorney's office and was designed to make sure that the position holders' finances were transparent in order to prevent any financial conflicts of interests. The disclosures were, of course, required by those in Congress who lived, breathed, and benefitted from every form of financial conflict of interest imaginable, from insider trading information to lobbyist handouts.

They write laws for the rest of us, not for themselves, Trask thought.

He knew that the only investment he would reveal with the form this morning would be an hour of his time, filling in blank after blank with indications of no change in his financial status. He had no stocks or bonds, other than those managed by whatever guru happened to be in charge of this year's thrift savings plan, the government-allowed 401k. Unlike those in the halls of Congress, Trask had his salary, and that was it. He could have saved himself and the system a lot of time if some rational humanoid upstream had simply provided a "no change" option for the entire filing, but no such person apparently existed, or—if they did—their entirely reasonable suggestion had been overruled as a dangerous affront to the system.

When he was finished filling out the form with non-information, Trask took a deep breath and made a third trip to the Keurig coffee maker he had brought from home. He stirred the cup when it finished brewing and returned to his computer terminal. The next task was an annual survey on internet security, mandated by the bureaucrats in the department's central office, the same office responsible for repeated and horrendous internet security breaches which had recently sent the private and personal information of every Department of Justice employee to hackers in China. Trask finished the survey, convinced that—based upon some of the nanny state supervision obvious in the design of the survey—he himself now qualified as a domestic security threat.

The next supervisory duty on the list was the filling out of one of Ray Marsh's micro-management forms, something called the "Weekly Unit Case

Status Report." It was usually due by noon on Monday, so that Marsh could take all the various units' data and plug that information into something he called the "Weekly Criminal Division Case Status Report," so he could brief J.P. Barrett on the Criminal Division's efficiency on Tuesday morning. The "Weekly Criminal Division Case Status Report" was not something that Barrett had tasked Marsh to do; it was something that Marsh thought Barrett would like to see every week, and so Marsh had tasked *himself* with the creation and the maintenance of the report. The unit reports had to be in by noon so Marsh would not be rushed in the preparation of the division report, and so that he had the time to call the unit chiefs on the carpet to explain any problems. That way, he would have answers for those problems when he spoke to Mr. Barrett on Tuesday morning.

A knock on his door interrupted Trask's compilation of case statistics. Cam Turner stuck his head through the door.

"Sorry to bother you. My curiosity got the best of me."

Trask waved him inside. "Just shut the door behind you." He took a long breath and turned to gaze out the long, narrow, vertical excuse for a window that had been built into his office. It was snowing hard again outside. He shook his head.

"If it wasn't for days like this, Cam, I'd hand both this supervisory gig and the SLC position back to Barrett and take the pay cut. That parking slot in the basement garage is a helluva perk when it's ten below outside."

"Wish I had one. How'd the staff meeting go?"

"You pegged it. Bonita Baylor called Marsh over the weekend to squawk about my 'supervising' the serial killer case. Thanks to you, I was prepared and was able to calmly laugh it off, which caused Marsh to uncalmly throw a hissy fit and storm out of Barrett's office."

"Great! I hate that little worm."

"I hate his forms even worse. The passive-aggressive side of me wants to be very late with his precious report today just to drive his blood pressure up. He might blow a gasket, and then we wouldn't have to deal with him anymore."

"Sounds like a plan to me."

"Yeah, except that if the blown gasket wasn't fatal, he'd hold it against you and anyone else who works for me in this unit. Barrett has my back, but I don't know if I can deflect the shitstorms away from everyone else indefinitely. I'll be a good little serf and pay the lord of the manor his tribute, so that my own vassals don't suffer. Give me about forty-five and we'll head down to the slop shoot for lunch. I'm not leaving the building in this blizzard, and I didn't bring anything from home today."

"Gotcha. In the meantime, my lord, I shall inform all the other varlets in the realm of your sacrifice, so that they—like I—shall be happy to die on their shields for you."

"Forty-five, Cam," Trask said, chuckling.

The modest little café in the basement offered a hot daily special, burgers, and made-to-order cold cut sandwiches. The weather outside meant that the café was full when Trask and Cam got in line. They both opted for the hot special, lasagna.

As they stood in line waiting to pay, Cam whispered over Trask's left shoulder.

"Ten o'clock."

Trask glanced in that direction and saw Ray Marsh seated at a table with one of the district's magistrate judges, Richard Horney.

"The Honorable *Reeshard HorNAY* is violating his own rule. He is now hobnobbing with one of the advocates who might appear before him," Cam whispered.

Trask chuckled. Judge Horney's name had been the subject of obvious and crude jokes from the moment he had been appointed to the bench. Many believed that the judge had manufactured a French heritage and pronunciation of his last name just to avoid the "Dick Horny" and "Horny, Dick" quips that were certain to follow him in perpetuity. Cam had adopted the habit of pronouncing Horney's first name as if it were French so that it was consistent with his last.

"No juries in today, so the appearance of impropriety is minimal," Trask said quietly. "Besides, you assume that Marsh will actually be appearing in court at some point, instead of hiding in his lair with his reports."

"*Oui, mon capitan.*" Cam nodded deferentially.

"I do wonder what they might be discussing," Trask said.

"They're probably discussing their *alma mater*," Cam responded. "They're both Yale grads, don't ya know."

"I knew Marsh was; didn't know about the judge."

"Yep. Methinks something's afoot, *mon capitan*."

12

At 1:30 p.m., Trask shoved a thick stack of papers into his briefcase. He closed his office door and locked it before turning to face the secretary across the hall.

"Sheila, if anyone asks, I'll be at the CCU this afternoon. I'll probably head home from there."

She smiled knowingly and nodded. "What if it's Mr. Marsh who's doing the asking?"

Trask laughed. *There are no secrets from secretaries.*

"If Mr. Marsh asks, you have my permission to lie. Tell him I've been down there all day."

She laughed in return.

"Be careful driving home," Trask said to her. "It's pretty brutal out there."

He made a stop in his trial prep room and took a final look around the papered walls before heading for the elevator. As he got out in the basement parking garage, his mind was racing.

I need to give John Foote this stack of cheat sheets for the grand jury session tomorrow, so I have a legitimate reason for going to CCU. It'll put me a few miles farther east, and I can just hit 435 south so that I'll have a head start on the commute when it's time to head home. I'll have a chance to see if Billy got anything back from the lab as well. Finally, I've had enough of Marsh and his games for the day. I hope he hears where I've gone and does blow that gasket.

He drove the Jeep slowly over the icy roads, grateful to have an all-wheel drive vehicle. Some of the other drivers on the road did not, and he gave them a wide berth when he could, watching them fishtailing or spinning their wheels when they accelerated too quickly.

You live here, folks; you ought to know how to drive in this stuff. I was born and raised in Mississippi, for God's sake. Of course, there were those four years in Colorado.

Trask got out of the Jeep and entered his code on the CCU keypad.

As he opened the door, a tall figure in a police uniform was coming out.

"You're Trask, right?"

"Yes." Trask saw the nametag and the rank insignia and realized he was speaking with Captain Sam Brown. The man understandably looked like he hadn't slept in days.

"I want to thank you for trying to help Graham with this," the captain said. "I know it's not your case, and I hear you've caught some flak for it."

"Happy to do what I can," Trask said. "Wish I could do more."

I'd say that I'm sorry for your loss, but we're not 100% sure yet that it IS a loss, and you might not have crossed that bridge yet. No words can really matter at this point, anyway.

Captain Brown nodded solemnly. "We all do." He started for his car.

"Sir?" Trask called after him.

Brown turned back toward him.

"You've probably considered this already, but it looks like your daughter was probably a target of opportunity. We don't see any connection between your job and this incident. She had a flat at the wrong time and place."

In other words, don't look for any reason to blame yourself. Bad things happen to good people.

Brown nodded again. "Thanks for that." He paused. "I had just put new tires on her car, too. She probably picked up a nail someplace."

It was Trask's turn to nod.

He'll make it. Don't know that I would if I were in his shoes.

Trask walked inside and saw Tommy Land waving him into the sergeant's office.

"Captain Brown?" Trask asked, nodding back toward the outer door.

"Yeah. He wanted to see if we were getting anywhere, wanted the truth. Unfiltered. Billy gave it to him. Sam Brown's a realist. We all know that it's a 99% done deal that Bev is gone and gone in the worst way. It really sucks. Sam's a strong guy mentally. His wife is not. Sam said she's been sedated now for a couple of days. After Billy gave him the rundown on the case, he let us know that Bev had a small butterfly tattoo on her left shoulder and a birthmark on the inside of her right calf. He also brought in buccal swabs from himself and his wife in case we need to test anything for DNA."

"You're right, Tommy. This sucks."

"One other thing before I forget it," Land said. "I found out who tried to rat you out to Bonita Baylor. New kid who just got here. He's been reassigned. I'm not having political moles digging in my yard here."

Trask nodded. "They didn't land any punches. Don't give me his name yet. Let's give him the benefit of the doubt and see if he learns his lesson. I don't want to prejudge any cases he might bring us from his new assignment."

"Fair enough. You here to see Billy?"

"John first. I've got a stack of papers for him to cram on tonight. We have Gloomy's grand jury session tomorrow."

"He should be back any minute. I know he's in the building. When you're done with him, Billy's in the conference room hanging more paper. He'll want you to stop in."

"Thanks. I'll do that."

Trask walked out of Land's office just as John Foote walked into the bullpen from a door at the opposite corner. Foote saw Trask and waved him over.

"Come into my office," Foote said.

Trask smiled. Foote didn't have an office. Like all the other agents and detectives assigned to CCU, he had a desk pushed up against the wall of the open bullpen. Trask sat down in a chair beside the desk and pulled the stack of paper out of his briefcase.

"These are essentially condensed versions of the incident reports hanging on the walls of our prep room. They're in chronological order, and that's how we'll present them tomorrow. Every incident has an event description, witness and defendants involved, evidence taken at the scene, and I've added any connections between the evidence at one scene and the evidence at another. You know: rifle from this one matches bullets from another."

"Got it."

"We have more than sixty of these to go through, but it shouldn't be a problem. You can refer to these as necessary while you're testifying. They're all based on your unit's reports anyway."

"I appreciate this. You made it easy."

"No sweat. It's an experienced grand jury, in session almost a full term, so we won't have to explain the basics for them."

"Great. We start at 1:30?"

"Yep. I have the whole afternoon blocked out in case we need it, but I don't think we will."

"We won't. I'll do my homework tonight. Billy wants to see you."

"That's what your fearless leader just told me."

They got up and headed for the staff room. Billy Graham and Becky Suzuki were seated at the table in the center of the room reviewing some files.

"Have a seat," Billy said when he saw them walk in.

Trask took a chair across the table from him. Graham slid a folder across the table.

"You were right about DMSO being the transfer agent—the solvent," Graham said.

Trask opened the file and saw the usual graph of spikes generated by a GC/Mass-Spec (Gas Chromatography/Mass Spectrometer) analysis. He studied the printed summary at the bottom of the page, looking for an explanation in English.

"Need a translation?" Graham asked.

"Please."

"The nasty stuff carried by the DMSO is a new designer drug called 'pink,' or U-47700. It's a synthetic opioid. Think fentanyl light. Almost as deadly, but not quite. We contacted DEA headquarters for a run-down on it. They've usually seen it as a pinkish powder—"

"Hence the name, 'pink.'" Foote was smiling.

"Thanks, bubbles," Suzuki said, shaking her head.

"It was originally developed in the U.S. as a pain reliever for use in surgery and cancer patients," Graham continued. "Now it comes from China. There's one more thing about this little cocktail. DEA said that some of their recent studies on fentanyl have shown it can produce short term amnesia. This pink stuff may have some of the same side effects, especially when it's carried through the cells by something like DMSO."

Trask nodded. "That would explain Officer Welsh's lack of recollection about the attempt on Independence Avenue."

"It *could,*" Becky corrected. "DEA said it was fairly likely that pink could have those effects like fentanyl, but they can't confirm that yet. Too little data."

"While you were on the phone with DEA," Trask wondered, "did you happen to ask whether or not they had put 'pink' on the controlled substance lists?"

"I did," Becky said. "Schedule I since 2016. Does that make this a federal case?"

"It *could,*" Trask answered. "Every distribution—by whatever means—of a controlled substance could be a federal violation. Let me think about that and talk to my boss."

"Marsh?" Billy asked.

"*Jesus*, word gets around, doesn't it?" Trask exclaimed. "NO! Not Marsh, J. P. Barrett. This isn't like Gloomy's case, where he kills in order to be able to sell dope. There, the dope sale is the goal, and the murders are tools used for and connected to the drug deals. This is the flip side, guys. The drug distributions, through the handing out of those damned cards, are a tool toward the murders. There are policy considerations and turf wars at play in this already, and the calls have to be made above my pay grade."

"How do you think that will play with Barrett?" Foote asked.

"I have no idea," Trask answered. "Let me think about it tonight."

13

TRASK SMILED as he looked around the grand jury room.

To those who've never seen the inside of one of these things, it's a mysterious star chamber, where any corrupt prosecutor can literally indict a ham sandwich. To those of us who take our jobs seriously, it's one of several hats we have to wear in the course of a criminal proceeding. First, we're investigators, riding along with and sometimes supervising the cops or agents. Then we're strategists, crafting an indictment to give us the best shot at a conviction, maximizing the strongest charges while minimizing any weak points. Then we're trial dogs, finally getting to show off those Perry Mason chops in scenes which almost never really happen. Throughout the process—if we're smart—we're always wearing the appeals hat, making sure that everything's by the book so that the conviction—if and when it comes—will stand up on appeal.

He nodded at the grand jurors as they filed in. It was hardly a formal proceeding in appearance. Those who had arrived for their first session in suits and ties or skirts had long since shed the business attire for comfortable slacks or jeans. They sat in chairs behind three tiers of raised and slightly circled tables. Trask thought it looked like a small college classroom.

To his right was a court reporter, transcribing the session so that it could be reviewed by a defense counsel and/or a judge at a later point. Across the room was a single table, at which the grand jury foreperson and secretary were sitting. In the center and to Trask's right was a single desk where the witness—one Special Agent John Foote of the Federal Bureau of Investigation—was waiting, facing the tiered rows of grand jurors. Trask smiled and nodded at Foote, who smiled and nodded back.

John's a pro at this. Jurors love him, grand jury or trial. He wrinkles up that big white moustache like an old Tom Selleck, flashes his eyes, and he might as well be Santa Claus. He has the deep voice to go with it, too.

The last of the grand jurors filed in from their lunch break, and the foreperson announced that a quorum was present.

"Our next case is United States v. WaShaun Stewart, Jr., also known as 'Gloomy.' Mr. Trask, you have the floor."

Trask nodded.

"Thank you. Our witness this afternoon is Special Agent John Foote of the FBI."

Trask read the oath to Foote as John raised his right hand.

"I do."

For the next two hours, Trask methodically led Foote through the events of Gloomy's young, but extensive, criminal career. The overall conspiracy charged was one to sell cocaine—both powder and 'crack'—and marijuana. In order to do so most successfully, Foote pointed out, Gloomy's 51st Street Crips had to win turf wars with their main rivals, the 33rd Street or "Trey Wall" Bloods. They did drive-by shootings to protect their market areas, stole dope supplies from their rivals, and killed when they thought they needed to do so. That was why they stole a minivan on one occasion, because the sliding side door let them roll up on their unsuspecting targets, slide the door open with one easy motion, and then focus the firepower of three or four AK-47s on a small area—a street corner, a home, or another car. The theft of the minivan thus became an "overt act" instead of a charge. It was an action taken in furtherance of a federal crime—the conspiracy—and even though the car theft was not itself a federal crime, it could be proved at trial because it was *part* of a federal offense.

The highlights—or lowlights, depending on one's perspective—of the lengthy presentation were the five murders committed by Gloomy. He shot a rival's cousin in a passing car when he missed and hit the cousin by mistake. He ambushed an errand boy for the Trey Wall who was delivering two kilos of cocaine to a gang leader, nearly cutting the kid in half and knocking him off his motorcycle with automatic weapon fire. There was another drive-by shooting which hit four members of the Crips with fire from the minivan, and one of the victims died. In the most sickening episode, Gloomy had shot a member of his own gang in the leg after suspecting that he had "gone soft," a conclusion that Gloomy reached after seeing the victim talking with a Trey Wall member on a high school campus during a lunch break. With the wounded kid lying in the street and begging for his life, Gloomy had taken his pistol and shot the victim between the eyes. The last homicide was the episode in which Gloomy had put two bullets into the back of a Trey Wall member's head while the victim was walking down the street listening to music.

After it was all done, only one grand juror had questions for Foote.

"The kid—Gloomy—he's barely an adult?"

"That's correct. He only recently turned eighteen."

"Why? Why kill so many at that young an age?"

Foote did his Selleck moustache smile and nodded. "That's a question that we all ask in this business. We never seem to find an answer that makes sense, at least not to us."

Trask, Foote, and the court reporter all left the room and waited outside the entrance door while the grand jury voted on the indictment. It didn't take long. A buzzer sounded fifteen minutes later.

Trask and the court reporter went back inside.

"You have a true bill," the foreperson announced.

"Thank you all for your time and attention," Trask said, before bending over to sign the indictment.

He was walking back toward the door when a woman in the front row waved her hand.

"Yes, ma'am?" Trask asked.

"Get that guy. He deserves to go away forever."

Trask nodded.

He left the room and handed the file to the attorney who was handling indictment returns—the formal presentation and filing of the indictments to a magistrate judge of the district court—that day.

"When are you returning them, Bob?"

"About fifteen minutes. Magistrate Judge Powers."

Trask checked his watch. The case would officially be filed about 4:15 p.m. Trask waited in the hallway to see if any of the grand jurors had more questions or comments about the presentation. It was always valuable feedback.

After a few minutes passed, he walked to the stairs and went up one floor. The magistrate judges—there were three of them—had their chambers on the inner wing of the fourth floor. Anyone wishing to visit those chambers had to have a pass card or had to be buzzed in after declaring themselves on an intercom. There were some rooms in the outer hallways, however. This was where the administrative staff—the courtroom deputy clerks assigned to the magistrate judges—had their offices.

Trask had always taken care to treat the members of the court staff with respect. Some of the other lawyers wanted to strut around and lord it over anyone they viewed to be a member of a different caste. It was a stupid play, to say the least. Having friends within the inner workings of the courts could always pay dividends.

One of the courtroom deputies, a woman named Sharon Dodge, had always been friendly to Trask and appeared to appreciate the courtesy he showed her. Sharon was the administrative clerk to Magistrate Judge Powers, and one of her duties was to draw judges—both the magistrate judges and the district judges—off their respective "wheels" whenever a new case was filed. She had told Trask that he was always welcome to check with her after an indictment return to see which judges had been drawn for a new matter. Accordingly, Trask was now in the habit of checking with Sharon a few minutes after indictment returns.

Sharon shared an office with another courtroom deputy clerk, Theresa Owens, who handled the caseload for Magistrate Judge Horney.

ReeSHARD HorNAY. Trask smiled as he thought of Cam's pronunciation.

Sharon's desk was right inside the doorway, while Theresa's cubicle was to the right and out of sight unless a visitor actually stepped inside.

Trask walked up to the open doorway and was about to say hello to Sharon when she saw him. In one, swift motion, she leaned back in her chair so that her head would not be visible to Theresa's side of the cubicle wall and shook her head from side to side. Her eyes doubled the warning with a hard glance.

She nodded toward the other cubicle and gave Trask a discreet wave. He nodded and walked back out of the hallway toward the front of the floor and the elevators.

I wonder what that was all about.

He headed back to his office on the fifth floor.

Cam Turner was waiting for him.

"You need to see these," Cam said, handing Trask two sheets of paper as he unlocked his office door. "I just got the email notices."

"Come on in," Trask said as he stepped into his office.

Cam closed the door behind him.

"The first page is our case assignment, I see," Trask said. "Judge Powers handled the returns. I tried to get my usual insider cue from Sharon, but she waved me off before I could speak to her. Something was going on in the next cubicle with Theresa."

"Read on, and you'll figure that out," Cam said.

Trask's eyes returned to the papers.

"Gloomy's case was assigned to your friend, Magistrate Judge *HorNAY*," Trask said, a small grimace running across his face. "The wheel runs over us again. At least we drew Judge Thomas for trial. Our real judge can overrule the junior varsity magistrate if he pulls anything too outlandish."

"Next page," Cam said.

Trask pulled the next sheet of paper from behind the judge assignment sheet. He read a few lines, the frown on his face turning to a full scowl as he finished.

"What the hell, Cam? This is an order directing us to appear before Horney to explain the form and substance of our indictment!"

"I know. It came out about ten minutes after the return, which means two things: First, it almost certainly had to be drafted before the indictments were drawn off the wheel, and that means that Horney didn't really *draw* this one; he *pulled* it and assigned it to himself. Second, if the indictment just got returned, he hasn't even had time to read the damned indictment. It was seventy-five pages long. So why does he have a reason to question anything about it?"

"I smell a rat, a swamp rat," Trask said angrily.

"You mean a *Marsh* rat," Cam corrected him. "Ray gets copies of all the indictments—even your SLC cases—for the whole crim division in his weekly read file. I think that little session we saw in the slop chute was more than Marsh and Horney swapping tales of their alma mater. Either at that or some other time, Ray has to have slipped an advance copy of the indictment to Horney, and Ray probably filled his head with some sort of crap about you and our case against Gloomy."

"Let's work through this," Trask said, taking a seat in the chair behind his desk as Cam sat down in a chair facing him. "Senator Drake retired last year, so that makes Burke the current senior Senator from Missouri. That means Burke can anoint the next federal judge in Missouri, especially since Burke is also on the Senate Judiciary Committee. The president has no idea who the best nominees are for the federal bench in every state, so he normally defers to the senior political power broker from that state, and for now, that's Burke."

"And *ReeSHARD HorNAY*, being a junior varsity jurist, a mere magistrate judge, would love to curry favor not only with Senator Burke, but with Burke's in-law, that being Ray the Marsh rat," Cam offered. "Horny Dick wants to be a district judge instead of a mere magistrate."

"We're on the same page," Trask said, nodding. "Our case—my case in Marsh's mind—getting scuttled can be played in the press as an unfortunate but necessary action taken by a courageous junior jurist. They can even play to the minority community's sensibilities since Gloomy is black and that's all the analysis that some require. They won't consider that all of his victims were black as well, or that the poison he was selling was going almost exclusively to black customers.

"I get demoted, or fired, Ray gets his revenge for all the perceived wrongs I committed against him in D.C. Horney gets to be a real judge, and J.P. Barrett probably gets shoved aside as well, making room for a new appointee as the district's United States Attorney."

"Possibly one Raymond Marsh," Cam said, shaking his head. "How do we play this?"

"Our wild card is Judge Thomas," Trask said. "From what I've seen, he's shrewd enough to see a play like this for what it is. Our indictment is completely proper. I drafted it to avoid any stretches. If Horney stretches at all in trying to dismiss any part of it, I think our appeal of the magistrate's report and recommendation to the district court will result in a dismissal of the R and R, *not* a dismissal of our indictment. We'll play nice and give Horney a chance not to embarrass himself, but if he wants to play hardball, so can we. I'll be ready. When's that hearing again?"

Trask reached for the copy of the order. "Two p.m. tomorrow. He didn't want us to have a lot of prep time, did he?"

"You won't need it."

Trask gave Cam his version of "the look." "Your confidence is inspiring. I hope it's not misplaced."

"Got a minute?" Trask stuck his head into Barrett's office before heading home. He gave Barrett a briefing on the events of the last hour.

"I want to kill him," Barrett said, referring to Marsh. "What do you recommend, other than that?"

"If we can embarrass Ray as badly in front of Horney as I think he was embarrassed in your staff meeting, it might prevent Horney from doing anything stupid. I think that can be arranged."

"Do you want me to be there for the hearing?"

"I wouldn't recommend it; just in case I'm wrong. It would give you some separation from the issues."

Barrett nodded. "Thanks for keeping me in the loop."

"Sure. One more thing."

Trask told Barrett about the chemical analysis on the cards found at the two crime scenes.

"The handing out of those cards laced with 'pink' qualifies as an illegal distribution of a controlled substance. Pink has been listed in Schedule I of the Code of Federal Regulations. I'd like to open an investigation of that as a Senior Litigation Counsel case."

Barrett did a double take. "Marsh will have a fit!"

"Not if he doesn't know about it. I won't list a defendant, because I don't have one at the moment. We haven't identified a subject of the investigation by name. My investigation opening sheet will just mention that we've noticed the introduction of a new and dangerous drug into the area. I'm picking it up because no one has any experience with it yet, and I'd like to handle the matter before handing similar cases out to the other attorneys."

"Isn't this an obvious back door into the county's serial killer case, Jeff?"

"Not *necessarily*. I thought about that quite a bit last night. We have two of the incidents involving the cards laced with DMSO and pink. We've *assumed* that those are related to the serial killer, and if I'm being honest, I still think that they are. The point is that's an *assumption* we've been making. None of the remains have been tested for pink, and we don't *know* that the guy passing out those cards is our butcher. He may just be grabbing women for sexual abuse, and he may be holding them as captives somewhere. They could still be alive. One way we'd know if the card guy is the butcher is if we find the Brown girl's body all cut up. She had a tattoo. And we have DNA for comparison. Since a card was left at the scene of her abduction, there's the connection.

"The second way we could confirm that the butcher *is* the one using the cards would be through a pathology tox screen on one of his victims. That's tough, because we have no idea how long he keeps his victims alive before he kills them, and whether the dope from the cards would still be present in their systems in sufficient quantities so that it would show up in any testing of the tissue. It would take a very fresh kill—if you'll pardon the insensitive way that sounds—for us to do a valid tox screen on whatever torso or limb he wants to discard, and we'd have to find it fairly fast. The chemists at the lab are telling us that the half-life of pink before the body processes and eliminates it is only about six hours."

"I see what you're saying." Barrett thought for a moment. "What if you do find that body part?"

"Then we test it, and if the tox comes back positive, then we tell the county we were working what was an apparently unrelated matter, and since we now have reason to believe that our targets are one and the same, we're more than willing to work the case with them. We may get farther along on a chargeable drug case before the county can file on any of their murders. We might find a pile of the dope at his house, for example, and we could charge him with possession with intent to distribute in a complaint the same day. At least that way we could get the bastard off the street before he tried to kill again. In the meantime, the county can put together their homicide cases."

Barrett nodded. "I like it. Approved." He raised a hand with a finger pointing skyward. "On one condition."

"What's that?"

"If you—God forbid, find Captain Brown's daughter dissected, or if you get that fresh body part and if it comes back positive for pink and DMSO, *I'll* be the one telling Marsh that those cases will be SLC matters."

Trask laughed. "Done. Thanks boss. Mind if I make a quick call?"

"Go right ahead."

Trask pulled out his cell phone and pressed a contact icon.

"Billy? Do me a favor and take two of the incidents off your wall in your conference room—the ones involving those cards." He paused. "That's right. Put them in a separate file. No, it's not going on our wheel." Another pause. "Who's assigned over here?" Trask repeated Graham's question as he looked at Barrett and smiled. "I am."

14

THE COURTROOM of Magistrate Judge Richard Horney was courtroom 4D, located on the eastern wing of the semi-circle which made up the fourth floor of the Charles Evans Whittaker federal courthouse. Whittaker, a Kansas Citian, had been the first American jurist to serve as both a United States district judge and a federal circuit court of appeals judge—serving on the 8th Circuit Court in St. Louis—before being nominated by President Eisenhower and confirmed to the Supreme Court.

The layout and furnishings of courtroom 4D were the same as for the courtrooms on the fifth floor where the district judges had their chambers and courtrooms. The ceilings were high, expensive chandeliers hung from those high ceilings, the paneling on the walls cost more than most American homes, and the judge's bench looked like a mahogany throne, flanked by smaller wooden thrones for the court reporter, the courtroom clerk, and the witness stand. The quality of American justice—whatever it was—bought by the taxpayers did not take place in shabby surroundings at the federal level.

The functional difference for the courtrooms on the fourth floor lay in the fact that their tenants were magistrate judges instead of district judges. District judges were appointed for life by the president, whereas magistrate judges were hired for terms of fifteen years by a panel of the district judges. The magistrates wore robes like the district judges, and the attorneys appearing before them called them "judge" and "Your Honor" just like they addressed the district judges. The authority of a magistrate judge was, however, nothing like that of a district judge.

District judges were empowered by the Constitution and underlying federal statutes to hold trials and to issue binding orders over those who appeared before them. Parties who disagreed with those orders had to appeal them to the 8th Circuit Court of Appeals. The district judges issued final rulings—subject to those appeals—on motions to suppress evidence in criminal trials, and they sentenced the defendants who were convicted in those trials. Magistrates, by contrast, were allowed to hold hearings only on such matters as the district judges delegated to them, and to issue—not binding orders—but reports and recommendations, called "R&Rs" by the attorneys, which were not binding on anyone. An R&R merely went upstairs to a district judge, who could issue an order adopting it in whole or in part, or the district judge could reverse the R&R entirely. In many ways, magistrate judges just performed the duties of robed law clerks for the district court.

The difference between the two types of judges had led Bob Lassiter, Trask's boss and mentor in Washington, D.C., to refer to the magistrate judges as "the junior varsity judiciary."

Trask and Cam Turner took their places at the counsel table for the government in Magistrate Judge Horney's courtroom. Across the room, Alvin Black, the appointed attorney for WaShaun Stewart, Jr., also known as "Gloomy," waited for his client to be brought up out of the lockup by deputies of the United States Marshals Service. Trask nodded pleasantly at Mr. Black, who was one of the local defense bar's "straight shooters." Alvin Black could be expected to vigorously defend his client, but to do so within the bounds of the law and the ethical canons which bound members of the bar. There would be no dirty tricks at Gloomy's trial unless they were pulled by Gloomy himself or by his disciples who remained on the streets.

The side door behind Mr. Black opened, and two, large deputy marshals escorted Gloomy into the courtroom. He was both handcuffed and shackled at the feet, and he wore the orange prison jumpsuit that was standard issue for federal prisoners. Trask always found himself shaking his head at the sight of WaShaun Stewart, Jr. Gloomy was hardly a threatening sight, barely five-eight and 160 pounds. The only danger one sensed in Gloomy's presence came when one looked into his eyes. They were cold and empty, and set deep in a face which was always wearing a sullen sneer.

If I knew he was coming, I could take him easily, one-on-one, Trask thought, *but on the street, I'd never see him; he'd be coming up from behind with an AK or a forty-five.*

The double doors to the rear of the courtroom opened, and two men entered the room and sat on opposite sides of the room in the wooden pews reserved for observers. One was a small man wearing thick glasses and a tweed sport coat. Trask recognized him as a reporter for *The Outlook,* an alternative lifestyle tabloid published weekly and distributed free locally through stands on the street corners of Kansas City. While *The Outlook* was hardly a mainstream publication like the area's main remaining newspaper, *The Kansas City Star*, Trask thought the tabloid's writers did a more thorough and objective job of journalism, once they took a story seriously. A feature on Gloomy's crime spree had been running in the tabloid for weeks, and Trask had found it hard to find fault with the reporting.

The other man who had entered the courtroom was Ray Marsh, who took a seat in the rear behind Trask and Turner.

"Jimmy Bishop is here from *The Outlook,"* Cam whispered to Trask.

"I know," Trask whispered back. "I called him about the hearing."

"You invited him?" Cam asked, still whispering.

"I did," Trask answered. "I did not, however, invite Marsh. Did you?"

Cam snorted and snickered at the same time.

Two women entered the courtroom through a door to the right of, and behind, the judge's bench. One was Theresa Owens, Magistrate Horney's courtroom clerk; the other was a court reporter, carrying her stenographer machine on a small tripod. They took about ten steps into the well of the courtroom before they stopped together.

"All rise! The court is now in session, the Honorable Richard HorNAY presiding!" Ms. Owens issued the proclamation with all the formality she could muster.

Behind the two women, the door opened again and Judge Horney, dressed in his black robe, strode purposefully to his throne while the two women proceeded to their stations. Trask saw a knowing glance pass between Horney and Marsh. He also noticed a quick frown when Horney noticed the reporter in the gallery.

"I think that next time, the ladies will be throwing rose petals in his path, don't you?" Cam whispered in Trask's ear.

Trask smiled. As Senior Litigation Counsel, the number of cases he handled was not that large; the size of the cases that he handled was. This was his first appearance before Magistrate Judge Horney. The other two magistrates—and even some of the district judges—usually entered their courtrooms *with* their clerks. Horney had definitely issued some staging instructions for his grand entrance.

"Be seated," Ms. Owens said from her clerk's station.

"Call the case, please," Horney ordered.

Wow, such formality, Trask thought. *This isn't a docket call with a dozen matters to take up. It's a special hearing and we're the only case for the afternoon. The other magistrates usually announce the case themselves.*

"The court calls the United States v. WaShaun Stewart," the clerk said. "Will counsel please enter their appearances?"

Trask stood at his table. "Jeffrey Trask and Cameron Turner for the United States."

I am NOT saying, "May it please the court" today. The court is not pleased with me, otherwise we wouldn't be here, and—so far—I am certainly not pleased with the court.

"May it please the court, Alvin Black for the defendant, WaShaun Stewart, Jr., who appears in person and in custody."

"Your client is a junior, Mr. Black?" Horney asked.

"He is, Your Honor."

"Madam clerk, please include that in announcing the title of this case in the future," Horney said, looking down at Theresa Owens.

"Yes, Your Honor," she said, her face turning crimson.

Trask glanced at Cam, who rolled his eyes.

Horney and Marsh must have been separated at birth; both love these public rebukes. That correction—if it was even necessary—should have been made privately and with a gentle, "Oh, by the way, Theresa," in front of it.

"Let's proceed," Horney said formally. "I called this hearing because—after being assigned this matter for preliminary review—"

Baloney, Trask thought. *This wasn't a draw off the wheel; you assigned it to yourself.*

"—I take my charge as a judge of this court seriously, and, therefore, read over the charges. I was concerned about the unusual form of this indictment, and whether it was properly drafted, and I was, therefore, properly concerned about how it was returned by the Grand Jury. I will, therefore—"

That's a lot of "therefores."

"—direct Mr. Trask or Mr. Cameron to come to the podium to respond to my concerns, and to state why they believe that this matter should go forward in its current form."

Trask nodded respectfully and walked around his table to the podium in the center of the well of the court.

Be nice, stay in control, he reminded himself. *The goal today is not to pick a fight with the fool in front of you. That's one you can't win. It's the fool behind you that gets the bullets, even if they're ricochets.*

"May it please the court," Trask began, in as calm and respectful a voice as he could muster, "I am afraid that I don't quite understand exactly what your concerns might be about the indictment. That said, I am, of course, prepared to address whatever questions you might have for us."

"Of course," Horney repeated. "I have several. First of all, Mr. Trask, I note that—despite the allegation that dozens are named as conspirators in this indictment—only this defendant is to be tried on this indictment. That's a bit unusual, isn't it?"

"It is," Trask agreed, "because we are in the unusual position of having agreed to dispositions in all of the co-conspirators' cases. That is due, in large part, because many of them did not want to face trial alongside Mr. Stewart, where they would have to be linked with him in a case involving several of his murders. Quite a few have, in fact, agreed to testify against him in exchange for their plea agreements."

"I see." Horney nodded matter-of-factly. "Furthermore, I have never seen an indictment this long before. The sheer length of this document—almost eighty pages if I recall—would seem to me to present a burden to the district court in merely reading it to the jury. How do you respond to that concern?"

I won't say that you've never seen one this long because you didn't practice much criminal law in your prior life, or that you haven't been on the magistrate's bench very long either. How do I say this?

"Respectfully, Judge, in practicing for years in the drug sections of both this district and in the office of the United States Attorney for the District of Columbia—"

"Oh? I was not aware that you had worked in Washington before coming here," Horney interrupted, shooting a slightly puzzled glance at Marsh in the rear of the courtroom.

"—Yes, I was also the Senior Litigation Counsel in that office before taking the same assignment here," Trask continued. "In my position here, my SLC cases are supervised directly by the United States Attorney, and not by any other member of the office."

"I see." Horney shot another puzzled look in Marsh's direction.

"At any rate, speaking indictments, such as this one, are not unusual in major drug conspiracy cases. The length of the indictment is in large part due to the inclusion of virtually every overt act that the evidence would show was committed by the conspirators in furtherance of the conspiracy. The district judge may, at his or her discretion, include those sections in reading the document to the jury, but that is not required. As the court can clearly see, a reading of only the formal counts of the indictment would not be an undue burden on the time of the district court and the jury.

"The other purpose of including the overt acts in the indictment is to inform the defense of the complete nature of the case against the defendant, and to obviate any need for filing a motion for a bill of particulars. In that manner, a speaking indictment offers some advantages to the defense in terms of case preparation and discovery. We could have had a much more abbreviated indictment, but then the defense counsel would have had to plod through hundreds of pages of reports without having much of a framework to work with. This way, Mr. Black won't have to guess which report or incident relates to which count of the indictment."

"Let's see what Mr. Black has to say about that, shall we?" Horney asked.

He expects Alvin to accept his invitation to attack us, Trask thought as he turned his head toward the defense table.

"I honestly can't disagree with anything Mr. Trask has offered," Black said, standing and shrugging his shoulders. "I've seen several speaking indictments like this myself. I find that they do make my job a lot easier, Judge. As I'm sure the court is aware, the drug conspiracy statute doesn't require that the government include *any* overt acts in support of the conspiracy count. I'd much rather see an indictment like this instead of the bare-bones alternative."

Horney said nothing for a moment, instead looking past Trask toward the rear of the courtroom again. "I'd still like to make sure that the overt acts included in this indictment actually relate to the counts charged," Horney finally said.

That's a bluff and a reach, and I'll call it. Hard. Trask paused. *Breathe. Don't attack. Leave him an out.*

"Respectfully, Your Honor, I'll first have to object to that request."

"You object, Mr. Trask? On what grounds?" Horney sat back on his throne, miffed that a challenge to his authority had been made.

"Judge, it is well-settled that the law presumes that a grand jury acts within the scope of its authority, and that an indictment returned by the grand jury is valid on its face. That alone is enough to call for a jury trial on the merits without any preliminary probe into the facts of the case. Both the government and the defense have now informed the court that we believe that the form of this indictment is proper, and the court has not informed the parties of any particular defect which *the court* sees in the form of the indictment. That being the case, it is improper for any court to try and look beyond the form of the indictment before trial. Otherwise, defendants could be demanding pre-trial hearings for all sorts of fishing expeditions."

"I suppose you have some authority for that proposition?" Horney asked.

Committed to memory about an hour ago, just in case. Trask turned and almost gave Cam Turner a wink.

"I do, Your Honor. *United States v. Costello*, 350 U.S. 359, decided in 1956, more recently cited by *United States v. R. Enterprises,* 498 U.S. 292, decided in 1991. Both those Supreme Court decisions were adhered to by the 8th Circuit's opinion in *United States v. Wadlington*, 233 F.3d 1067, decided in 2000."

"Mr. Black?" Horney asked. His voice remained steady, but he was almost begging for help.

"I'd love to be able to go on those fishing expeditions Mr. Trask mentioned, Your Honor, but I think that he has correctly stated the law."

"Well, gentlemen, *you* may be in agreement, but I seem to recall case law establishing some exceptions to that rule," Horney declared.

Like hell you do, Trask thought. *You just know I'd be out of line if I called you on that bluff, and you'll have your law clerks burning midnight oil after the hearing trying to find that exception while you take the matter "under advisement."*

"Therefore, Mr. Trask, I'm going to overrule your objection for purposes of this hearing, and we're going to make sure that your overt acts are actually connected to the criminal counts in the indictment as you claim. Why don't we start with overt act number one? Let's start at the beginning."

You really didn't read it, did you, Judge? You just took your friend Ray's word for everything, and now you've trapped yourself. The beginning is a really nice place to start.

"Very well, Your Honor," Trask replied. "As you know from your review of the indictment, Count One—the conspiracy count—charges the members of the conspiracy with conspiring to—among other things, distribute cocaine and marijuana, and to possess, with intent to distribute, cocaine and marijuana. In the Manner and Means section of Count One, the indictment also specifies that members of the conspiracy would illegally use and carry firearms while making these drug sales in order to guard their product and profits.

"Overt Act One alleges that the two ringleaders in the conspiracy, the defendant Stewart and his main lieutenant, Jimmy Norman, were the subjects of a high-speed car chase as they tried to elude the police, fleeing southward on Troost Avenue at speeds in excess of ninety miles-per-hour. In the course of that car chase, Stewart and Norman, the only occupants of the vehicle, were seen by officers throwing items out of the car windows. Police units assisting in the pursuit stopped and recovered the items shortly after they were thrown. These items included packages of cocaine, packages of marijuana, and two handguns. One of the handguns had latent fingerprints on it later identified as those of Jimmy Norman. Overt Act One was, *therefore,* clearly part and parcel of, and committed in furtherance of, Count One as alleged in the indictment."

Trask paused.

"Does the court require any further explanation regarding Overt Act One under Count One?"

Horney froze for a moment. Trask saw that Theresa Owens was trying not to giggle. Horney flipped through his copy of the indictment on the bench. After several minutes, he spoke again. "How about Overt Act Seventeen?"

Trask nodded. He paused just for a few seconds. He had no notes. He responded from memory.

"The court's concern on this overt act probably arises from two understandable points. First, the action alleged is that one Orion Dudley broke into a pawn shop and stole a handgun. Mr. Dudley is named as an *unindicted* co-conspirator in that count. The reason he is *not* now indicted in an active case is that he is now *deceased*. The reason he is deceased is that—as alleged in Count Five of the indictment, which is also incorporated into Count One as an overt act committed in furtherance of the conspiracy—Mr. Dudley was executed by the defendant, Mr. Stewart, who believed that Dudley had become a liability to his gang by fraternizing with members of a rival drug gang.

"The second obvious question might be why the local theft of a firearm could be included in a federal charge. The answer is that the firearm stolen by Mr. Dudley was then given by Mr. Dudley to the defendant WaShaun Stewart, who later used that same weapon to kill Dudley by shooting him between the eyes at point-blank range. The gun was, *therefore*, used in the course of the charged conspiracy, by an indicted co-conspirator, for the purpose of maintaining order within the criminal conspiracy, and to permanently silence a member of the conspiracy who the defendant thought was going rogue. We have informant testimony to offer as evidence on this point at trial."

Trask paused again.

"Does the court require further explanation with regard to this overt act?"

The bluff had been called. Horney folded. He glared angrily at Marsh, who stood and walked out the back of the courtroom. Horney regained his composure before speaking again.

"I'm sure, Mr. Trask, that you understand how seriously I take my role in preparing cases for trial in the district court." Horney smiled as if he was a father who had just been testing an offspring. "I am now quite satisfied that your indictment is proper in form, and that there is an adequate factual basis for the matters alleged therein. I will schedule this matter for the normal status hearings, including arraignment, which will take place tomorrow morning. Since I am the one who called this hearing and since I am now satisfied that the indictment is proper, and since I have heard no objections from the defense to the contrary—"

Horney looked at Alvin Black, who shook his head from side to side.

"—I will not be issuing a Report and Recommendation on these issues. Does either party have anything further?"

"No, sir," Trask said.

"No, Your Honor," Alvin Black replied.

"We are adjourned." Horney stood.

"All rise," Sharon Dodge said, smiling at Trask.

Trask stood by the podium until Horney had left the courtroom. He walked back over to the counsel table and Cam Turner.

"I know a good casino on the river where we can find a Texas hold 'em game," Cam said, smiling.

"Those involve luck; this didn't," Trask said, laughing. "We didn't just have good cards in this game, we had the whole deck. Let's get out of here."

"One question first, please, Mr. Trask?" Jimmy Bishop was standing just outside the swinging door to the well of the courtroom. He was holding his cell phone in his hand.

"Sure, if I can," Trask said. "I hope that phone isn't set to record. You know that anything official has to go through our public affairs guy upstairs."

"Understood. Off the record, what did I just see in here? Are hearings like that unusual?"

"Off the record," Trask repeated, looking at Bishop's phone. "They're not just unusual, they never happen."

"I figured. When can I get a copy of that indictment?"

"That's why these hearings never happen. Indictments like this one are usually sealed. This one, in fact, still is. They're unsealed at arraignment, which is now set in this case for tomorrow morning. It's a public document after that, Jim, and you can pick a copy up at the clerk's office, right after the hearing."

"Thanks, and thanks for the exclusive on whatever this was."

Trask laughed. "It was just a heads-up, not an exclusive. You're welcome, for what it was worth. And—off the record again?"

"Sure."

"If this hadn't gone the way it did, there would have been a much bigger story. We'd have appealed and probably gotten a quick reversal, if not upstairs, then on an expedited appeal at the 8th Circuit."

"Okay."

They headed for the doors at the back of the courtroom. Cam was the first to push the double doors open into the center hallway outside. Trask followed Cam and turned to hold the door for Bishop, who was following him. When Trask turned back around, he saw Foote, Billy Graham, and Becky Suzuki waiting a few feet away in the hallway. He didn't see Raymond Marsh until Marsh jumped in front of him.

Before Trask could even mentally process what was happening, Marsh shoved him. The bigger man's weight pushed Trask off balance, down and backward, and into a wall. Trask regained his balance. He stood up and glared at Marsh.

"Don't *ever* do that again, Ray. I mean it." Trask's tone was measured, but it was also angry and warning.

Marsh stepped in front of him again. Trask read Marsh's eyes, then his peripheral vision caught the muscle twitch as Marsh's right shoulder started forward.

Marsh's right was a roundhouse, thrown wildly. Trask's countering left both blocked the first punch and struck Marsh squarely in the face. The jab also set up Trask's combination right which followed a fraction of a second later, sending Marsh falling backward into the arms of John Foote, who had been rushing over to stop the fight. Foote looked at Marsh's face as he lowered Ray slowly to the floor. Marsh's eyes were closed, and his body was limp.

"He's out—like a light, Jeff," Foote said.

"Nice right," Billy observed.

"I'm calling an ambulance," Becky said.

"I'll go tell J.P.," Cam said.

"*Now*, I have something to write about," Jimmy Bishop said. "By the way, Mr. Trask, I caught the whole thing on my phone cam."

"Shit!" Trask said quietly to himself as he turned away from Bishop.

15

"Do me a favor, please, Jeff. Just sit for a few minutes and don't say anything." J. P. Barrett pointed to a chair in his conference room. Barrett picked up the remote for the television set mounted on the wall. "I want to see this for myself."

He has a right to be pissed, Trask thought. *Now he'll have to answer questions from D.C. on why the two top attorneys in his criminal division were duking it out, and how that ended up on local TV newscasts. I just reacted. I should have ducked and dodged. Marsh would have probably busted his own hand on the wall. Now* mine *feels like it needs X-rays.*

Trask took a couple of deep breaths.

This is the first time J.P. has treated me like anything other than a friend and a trusted colleague. He's usually asking for my advice; now I'm an employee in time-out.

Trask looked at the TV screen. It was just now five o'clock.

"Our lead story tonight comes from the federal courthouse," the local news anchor began. "It may not be the first time we've heard of a heated confrontation between lawyers there, but this time, the attorneys involved are both from the same side of the case, and this time, the dispute involved much more than words.

"The video you are about to see was recorded by a local journalist on his cell phone camera. The scene took place following a status hearing on an indictment recently returned against WaShaun 'Gloomy' Stewart, Jr. The lawyers you will see on the screen are Raymond Marsh, the chief of the United States Attorney's Office's criminal division, and Jeffrey Trask, the office's Senior Litigation Counsel."

The screen changed from the anchor desk to what Jimmy Bishop had captured on his phone. The recorded video had been clipped to begin with Marsh's shove that had sent Trask back into the wall. It ended with an unconscious Marsh being lowered to the floor by John Foote. There was no audio.

"Well, Marcia," the male anchor said turning to his co-anchor as the screen returned to their studio, " I guess the only thing we know for sure at this point is that Mr. Marsh was the loser in whatever that was."

"No doubt about that, Gary," Marcia said giggling, just before J.P. Barrett turned off the television.

"Hmph!" J.P. Barrett leaned back in his chair and shook his head. He looked at Trask and finally smiled. "The way I see it *now*, he didn't give you much of a choice, did he?"

"I could have probably gotten out of it some other way. Sorry. I'm not proud of it. I didn't know Bishop was recording anything. He agreed to make my answers to his questions off the record. I know it's not a good look for the office."

"I've already heard from both the Director at OEO and from OPR in Washington," Barrett said. "They expect this to make the national news tonight. They're waiting for a response from me."

Trask nodded. The Director of the Executive Office—known as "OEO"—at the Department of Justice was usually the smiling face who handed out awards for exceptional performance in an annual gathering in the Great Hall of Justice in the department's main building in D.C. Trask had been the recipient of two such awards, and the plaques hung on the wall of his office. The Office of Professional Responsibility—or "OPR"—was to DOJ what an internal affairs division was to a police department. They investigated and punished those who got out of line.

If both the carrot and the stick are pissed at me, this could hurt.

"After seeing what I saw—unless I'm missing something—my response will be that Ray initiated the attack without provocation, left you no way out, and that you acted in self-defense." Barrett shook his head in near disbelief. "When Ray gets out of the hospital tomorrow—they tell me it's a mild concussion—I'll ask for his resignation. If he doesn't give me one, I'll fire him. Washington wanted me to suspend you. I reserved judgment on that until I saw the video. I'm not going to suspend you, Jeff, unless you tell me that I need to know about something that may have happened off-screen."

"We never even spoke," Trask said. "I was too busy answering all the silly questions that Horney had for us. Of course, those probably came indirectly from Ray, and neither he nor Horney were happy with our responses. Horney grudgingly approved the indictment—as if he had a choice—and even said he wasn't going to bother writing an R&R. Ray just jumped me in the hallway outside the courtroom. I never saw him coming."

"Did you box a lot at the Academy? That was a nice, straight right." Barrett was smiling now.

"Not really." Trask answered, relieved that the tension was easing. "One season of intramurals and some PE classes. I think I *might* have won as many fights as I lost. Got knocked out myself once."

Barrett laughed. "The other guy must have been pretty good."

"A California Golden Gloves champ," Trask said, nodding. "My coach didn't tell me about that until right before the fight started. I thought I needed to do something radical to stay alive, so right after we touched gloves, I threw the biggest haymaker right I had. It caught him square on the chin, and I thought he was going down, so I closed in to throw another one. Then I saw him smiling up at me."

"Really? What happened then?"

"I have no idea."

Barrett laughed loud and long. "That was the knockout."

"Yeah. I woke up to smelling salts and a couple of medics asking if I needed to go to the hospital. I was no great shakes in the ring, boss. Ray Marsh is just—how did Cam put it the other day—a big puff ball, and—like you said—he didn't give me much choice."

Trask paused.

"What are you going to do about Senator Burke?"

"If and when he calls," Barrett answered, "I'll ask him first if he's seen the video. I'll have a recording made of the newscasts tonight in case I need to send him one. I probably won't have to, since I expect it'll make the national news. I don't think I'll have any problem justifying the termination, even with Burke. You were actually lucky that this Bishop character videoed it."

Trask nodded.

"I had some witnesses there if you need to talk to them. Cam Turner and our case agents were all standing close by when it went down. They had something for me on our other matter."

"If OPR is silly enough to want to make a mountain out of this mole hill, they can interview everybody." Barrett pointed to the television. "Like they say, a picture is worth a thousand words. I think a *moving* picture may be worth a million."

"Thanks for the support," Trask said. "There is one more thing. It has nothing to do with Ray."

"Good. What?"

"The reason that Foote, Billy Graham, and Becky Suzuki were waiting for us outside the courtroom is that another body's been found—at least part of one."

"Jesus."

"Yeah, another torso, sawed up like the others. A convenience store owner on Independence Avenue was closing up last night and found it in his dumpster."

Barrett frowned. "Was it Captain Brown's daughter?"

"No. She has a small, distinctive tattoo on one shoulder. This wasn't her."

"I guess we can be grateful for that."

"Yeah, for now."

"Go home, Jeff. Put some ice on those knuckles."

"Thanks. They need some."

The phone on the conference table rang. Barrett looked at the number on the call screen.

"Another D.C. area code. Not OEO or OPR this time. Probably Burke."

Trask waved on his way out.

Lynn met him at the door with the pups and an ice pack.

"Welcome home, Rocky."

"You're not the first to call me that today."

"I probably won't be the last, either. You've already had calls from five states. I chased the reporters away and wrote down the friends' numbers."

"Thanks." Trask shook his head. "We have any beer?"

"I picked some up."

"I love you."

"I know. You can just call me 'Adrian' tonight if you want. I laid your sweats out if you want a workout, but if you want to run to the top of something with stairs, you'll have to drive back downtown."

"Yo, Adrian!"

"Yes?"

"Stop it."

16

"So how was the mandatory day off?" Cam asked, his head sticking inside Trask's office doorway.

"Interesting," Trask said, chuckling. "If J.P. hadn't ordered me to stay home, I'd certainly have missed out on some new life experiences."

"Really?" Cam walked in and shut the door. He sat down in one of the chairs beside Trask's desk.

"Oh yeah. I made the mistake of going out in public yesterday, just a little run to the grocery store for Lynn."

"You got recognized."

"More than I ever wanted to be. That damned video must have played a hundred times over the past two days. Every local channel ran it on both the early and late news, and then every national broadcast and cable network ran it on their shows."

"What kind of reaction did you get?"

"Four high-fives and a lecture from some wannabe sociologist on the evils of toxic masculinity."

Cam laughed. "A pretty good ratio, at least."

"Ratios don't win jury trials, Cam. I worry about turning off our potential jurors. Verdicts have to be unanimous."

"Yeah, I read that someplace." Turner opened a sheet of paper he had held rolled in his hand. "I read *this* yesterday afternoon. Magistrate Judge ReeSHARD HorNAY has informed us that—pursuant to a request by the defendant WaShaun Stewart and don't forget the Junior—he is granting attorney Alvin Black's request to withdraw as Mr. Stewart, Junior's counsel. Apparently, Mr. Stewart, Junior thought Mr. Black was rolling over too easily in our hearing on Tuesday. Alvin filed a motion agreeing with his client's position that the attorney-client relationship has been irretrievably damaged, and HorNAY granted it."

"Dammit!" Trask stood up and headed for his Keurig. "Want some coffee?"

"No. Thanks."

Trask returned to his desk. "So now we have to wait and see who gets appointed to replace Alvin, then the new counsel requests a delay of three months or so on the trial date so he—or she—has time to read all the discovery and prepare for trial. We go from an ethical counsel who wouldn't ambush us with any garbage to a who-knows-what kind of mouthpiece, and all our witnesses worry and fidget in the meantime."

"Almost entirely correct."

"Almost?"

"No replacement attorney to be appointed by the court. HorNAY's order goes on to state that the defendant Stewart, Junior will be retaining his own counsel now. His family apparently found some cash."

"Gee, I wonder where that came from," Trask said sarcastically.

"Are we implying that Gloomy had some dope proceeds stashed somewhere that we had not previously identified?"

"We are."

"I thought so. At any rate, the judge gave Gloomy a week to name his new lawyer."

"I'll call our team in for a sit-down. They'll have to cajole our witnesses longer than they had planned. Anything else happen in my absence?"

"Barrett called Marsh in. Ray refused to resign, so J.P. fired him, with the blessings of both OEO and OPR. Your video apparently made Washington want to wash their hands of everything as quickly as possible. Marsh was escorted from the building. A couple of the secretaries boxed up his personal stuff and gave it to him at the door to the lobby downstairs. At least one TV truck was there to capture that little story."

"Ray probably called them."

"My guess as well," Cam said nodding. "Want to do lunch?"

"Give me a rain check. I need to take a drive. I missed breakfast this morning, and I need some thinking time as well as food."

"Understood. When are we meeting?"

"Please call John Foote and see if he can be here at two with Graham and Suzuki."

"Will do."

Trask pulled the Jeep out of the garage. He drove eastward, with no specific destination in mind. The Average White Band's "Pick up the Pieces" was playing in his head. He turned off the interstate after a short distance and headed north, soon finding himself on Independence Avenue.

Here's our local "track" where most of the victims got snatched. The dangerous world of a working girl—or of a college student with a flat tire—finding themselves in a real-life version of one of those gore flicks, with no hero coming to the rescue. What a way to go out.

He drove east again, his eyes tracing the sidewalks on either side of the roadway. A young woman in a skirt far too short for the weather met his gaze with her own. He glanced down at his watch as he passed her.

Eleven-fifteen—in the morning—and she's already on the job.

His mental jukebox shifted to "Naughty, Naughty," by John Parr.

He saw a burger joint with a drive-through and pulled in.

No, I will not be dining in today. I will be slumped behind the wheel of my car in your parking lot, eating my lunch and hoping that I will not be recognized.

He ordered and picked his food up at the window, then pulled into a space as far away from any other cars in the lot as he could find. When he finished eating, he called Lynn.

"Hey there, slugger!"

"Oh, please."

"Can't help it."

"Any more calls meriting a response?"

"None of that kind. Three more from pesky members of the press. I politely told them to pound sand. How do they have your number, anyway?"

"It's the digital age. We can run and try to hide, but it doesn't work. I'll change it soon enough. It's just a pain in the butt to notify everyone that we *want* to be able to call us."

"How's work today?"

Trask told her about his conversation with Cam.

"So that's why Channel Thirteen has Ray carrying boxes away from the courthouse."

"Yep."

"When you make an enemy, you make an enemy."

"Not my choice."

"I know, babe. I'm sorry to see you going through this. I hate that your trial will be delayed. I'd like to do a vacation at some point this year. We could both use one."

"I agree. We'll set something up when the calendar finally looks open."

"Just turn Ray down if he demands a rematch."

Trask snorted. "Later, babe."

He pulled out of the parking lot and turned south, back toward I-70.

17

TRASK ENTERED his unit conference room to find Foote, Graham, Suzuki, and Cam Turner sitting at the table.

"Sorry I'm late, guys. Mr. Barrett wanted a couple of minutes of my time."

"Anything important?" Cam asked.

"Actually, yes," Trask answered. "I'll tell you about it later. Right now, I just want to fill our team in on the developments with Gloomy's trial."

Trask shrugged as he looked at the investigators.

"I'm afraid we're looking at a lengthy delay. Probably three or four months. Gloomy wants a new attorney, and Horney is letting him find one."

"Maybe Judge Horney would like to help us babysit half a dozen nervous snitches," Foote said, snorting. "I'll have to call headquarters for some more case funds. We have four witnesses in motels outside of town so they can't be located and snuffed out."

"I understand. Out of my control, guys," Trask said. "The last thing I wanted to see was Alvin Black getting kicked off the case. He would have made all our jobs easier. Not that he would have rolled over; it's just that he doesn't play fast and loose with the rules."

"Alvin's good people," Graham said, nodding in agreement. "Who do you think will step in?"

"I have no idea," Trask said. "Horney's notice indicated that Gloomy's family had come up with some cash to hire the mouthpiece of his choice."

"That can't be good for us," Foote observed. "We'll anticipate the worst."

"Good idea," Trask said.

He changed the subject.

"Anything more on the newest torso?"

"We only know that it's not Captain Brown's daughter because of the tats," Billy said. "This gal had a small tramp stamp, but no butterfly on the shoulder."

Trask saw Becky give Graham a nudge.

"We have a potential lead," Billy said. "There's a guy who wants to talk to us. Want to ride on the interview?"

Trask thought for a moment. The serial killer still wasn't a federal case. Still, if the lead could possibly point to the tainted business cards, he wanted to be there. Besides, Ray Marsh wasn't around anymore to bitch about it. He decided not to ask any questions.

"Sure. Why not? Where are we going?"

"Ever been to Dogpatch?" Graham asked him.

"Not on purpose," Trask said, chuckling. "I took a wrong turn once."

"Am I going?" Cam asked.

"Actually, no," Trask said. "You're going up the hall to talk to J.P."

"About?"

"He'll fill you in on what I was going to talk to you about."

"I have to see another attorney about another case," Foote said. "Besides, I've already been to Dogpatch."

"You can ride with us, Jeff," Billy said.

Blue Summit, Missouri, otherwise known as "Dogpatch," was an unincorporated area located between the incorporated cities of Kansas City and Independence, Missouri. Normally, those competing municipalities would have jumped at any chance of expanding both their boundaries and their tax bases by trying to annex a bordering, unincorporated section of occupied land. Neither city had moved to annex Dogpatch, however. Neither city wanted it.

Billy turned off the interstate and began meandering northeastward through the narrow streets pockmarked by what seemed to be an endless sequence of potholes. There were simply too many to avoid, and Trask, sitting in the back seat, felt his teeth chattering from the series of impacts.

"Wish I had stock in the nearest shock and alignment shop," he said.

"I'll tell our mechanic to look the ride over if we make it out alive," Billy said.

"I may need a bathroom when we stop," Becky said. "I think I'm about to lose a kidney."

They turned north. Trask saw a row of 1940s vintage houses, the largest no more than 1,200 square feet, lining the east side of the street.

Single family, detached, slums, Trask thought.

The opposite, west side of the road was unimproved and wooded.

"That side leads to some old graveyards," Billy said, nodding to his left. "We've found buried bodies, illegal dumping grounds, homeless camps—all kinds of grunge in those woods. Good old Dogpatch."

"I think I'd rather camp in those woods than in some of these shacks on the other side," Trask observed.

"That's why it's still the county's problem instead of KC's or Independence's," Becky said. "No tax revenue, just a welfare dump. It's a monetary sinkhole. High crime and low rent."

"And who are we visiting?" Trask inquired.

"Whoever lives here." Billy pulled into a driveway at the north end of the block where the road took a right turn.

Trask looked up the driveway toward the house. As Dogpatch residences went, this one was well-maintained. The paint on the exterior siding wasn't peeling, and the yard was mowed. A picture window in the front room looked out on the rest of the block below it. Trask saw that a ramp, as well as stairs, led to the front door.

Someone here has to roll in and out.

"Give me a second before we go in," Suzuki said, opening a laptop. She accessed one of her databases. "There's been a double-homicide at this address. 2017. Ruled justifiable, self-defense. The resident's name was Devin Miller."

"That's the guy who called us," Billy said. "We'll go in alert."

When they reached the front door, Graham pushed the doorbell. Trask saw that it was one with a camera and microphone built in.

"Badges?" a voice requested through the doorbell system.

Graham and Suzuki flashed their shields. Trask pulled his credential wallet out, opened it, and held it up in front of the camera eye. An electronic buzzing sounded at the door, and Trask heard a metallic click.

Electronic lock.

"Come on in," the doorbell said.

Trask followed Graham and Suzuki through the doorway. They entered a small living room that was well-lit by the sunlight coming through the picture window. A man in a wheelchair held out his hand, and each of the visitors shook it as they introduced themselves.

"You can call me Red, or even Redbird," Miller said.

Trask saw plenty of reasons for the nickname. Miller had red hair on his head and in his beard, streaked with ample amounts of gray. He looked to be about seventy. There were also dozens of souvenirs relating to the St. Louis Cardinals on shelves lining the walls.

"Not a Royals fan yet, huh?" Graham asked.

"The Cards were here first," Miller said, "and they've always been good. I grew up in this house listening to their games on an old brick of a transistor radio. Harry Caray and Jack Buck. Bob Gibson on the mound throwing complete games. Musial, Brock, Bill White, Ken Boyer. I never latched on to Finley's Athletics when they were here for a cup of coffee. By the time the Royals came to town I was already committed."

Miller looked at Billy Graham as if he were reading Graham's mind.

"Don't even think of bringing up the '85 series."

"Okay, I won't," Graham said, chuckling and holding his hands up in front of him.

"Can we talk about the shooting that happened here before we move on to anything else?" Suzuki asked.

"Sure," Miller said. "As you may have noticed, this ain't the best subdivision in the area. I used to live in a good one, by the way, out east in Blue Springs. Lost that house in a divorce after this happened—"

He pointed to his legs. Trask saw that one of the legs had been amputated just above the knee. The other stump was below the knee. Miller followed his glance.

"Drove over an IED just outside Baghdad," Miller explained. "I had already retired from the Army, but when the bastards hit New York on nine-eleven, I went back in and went over for the war. My ex disagreed with my decision, and I got the divorce papers in a field hospital before they med-evac'd me home. She'd have probably left me anyway. The thing between these stumps got pretty torn up in the blast, too. Now it just helps empty my bladder.

"Anyway, I lost the Blue Springs house about the same time as my mom died, so I just moved back in here. I live rent-free 'cause the mortgage was paid before I inherited it. I just have to deal with the neighborhood. Two of my neighbors decided they could rob the crippled dude, and they came through the front door ready to put me down. My granddad was in the first World War. Infantry. He came home with this old trench gun—"

"Hey careful there!" Graham warned as Miller lifted the butt of a shotgun from where it had been concealed in a sling behind the backrest of the wheelchair.

I never even saw that thing, Trask thought. *I bet the burglars didn't see it either.*

"Oh, sorry," Miller apologized. "Didn't mean to startle anybody. Anyway, they came through the door and I blew 'em back outside with this thing. Almost a hundred years to the day from Armistice Day. It still works good. I never got charged with nothing. Self-defense."

Miller took another look at Trask. "Hey, you should be familiar with that, huh? Ain't you the lawyer that's been on the news?"

"I'm afraid so," Trask admitted. "Why don't you tell us why you called, Mr. Miller?"

"Red or Redbird," Miller said. "Sure. Like I was saying, this thing between my stumps don't completely function anymore, but I still like to talk to somebody now and then, and there's a gal down the block there—"

He nodded toward the picture window.

"—who—well, she's a hooker—but I just pay her to help clean up a little and then sit down and talk with me some. I guess you could say we're friends by now."

"What's her name, Red?" Billy asked.

"I just know her by her first name, Sally."

Becky Suzuki glanced at Trask, who raised an eyebrow.

"That means something to you?" Red asked Trask.

He doesn't miss anything. We'll have to avoid anything that might cue him.

"It could," Trask said. "What about Sally?"

"She comes here every Tuesday," Miller said, "or at least she's supposed to. She cleans up for me, we play some cards, and I have somebody to talk to for a while. I pay her, and she doesn't have to earn the money lyin' on her back.

"When she came in last week, she cleaned the place, then we got to talkin' about stuff. I had the TV on, and they were doin' a story on some of the body parts that have been showin' up around town. Sally got real quiet, then she said that she might know who was killin' all these girls. She said she had been out walkin' Independence Avenue, and this guy in a pickup gave her some kind of card that made her faint. I asked her if she could recognize the guy, and she said she probably could. I asked her what he looked like, but she wouldn't tell me. She said she didn't want to get me involved, and she made me promise not to tell anybody what she said."

"Why are you telling us now?" Becky asked him.

"I was tellin' her that she should go to the cops, that it might save somebody's life, you know? She just doesn't trust the police. She said they've harassed her for years, and that she'd rather just keep quiet. I asked her to think it over, and she said she would, but then she didn't show up this past Tuesday. That's the first time she ever missed a day with me. I called her a bunch of times, but she never answered her phone. I got to worryin' about her, and then I thought every day that went by, some other girl might be gettin' cut up, so I called you guys. I figured maybe you could talk to her, check on her … maybe convince her to help, you know?"

"Which house is hers?" Graham asked, looking out the window.

"The green one, third one down the block there."

"We'll go see if she's home," Billy said.

"Do us a favor, Red," Trask requested. "If you see us get inside, call her number. It might help us find her—or at least her phone—if she left it there."

"Sure."

They walked down the block to the little green house. Once on the porch, Graham tried the knob on the front door. The door swung open.

"Hello? Sally? Anyone home? Police officers!" Graham had his hand on his pistol, still in its holster on his belt. "Hello?"

There was no answer. They swept the little house, but it was unoccupied.

Trask looked around. *No sign of any struggle. No indication she was surprised in here. Nothing ransacked, even with the door unlocked. In this neighborhood.* He heard a cell phone ringing in the bedroom.

Becky Suzuki beat him to it. She was pointing to the phone in an open bedstand drawer.

"Good call, Jeff."

"Old trick. Sometimes they work more than once."

The ringing stopped. Becky pulled a plastic bag out of one of her pants pockets and dropped the phone into it. "We can dump this back at the office. Do we need a warrant?"

"I wouldn't worry about that at this point."

"Works for me." She put the bag containing the phone into her pocket.

Trask nodded toward the open door of a small bathroom that connected to the bedroom.

"See if you can find a hairbrush in there. If we find some hairs with root balls still attached, we might be able to get some DNA."

"Another good idea."

Seconds later, she appeared in the doorway of the bathroom, holding a brush that she had dropped into another plastic bag.

"Voila!"

"Good deal," Trask said.

They met Billy back in the living room.

"Let's walk back up the street," Trask said. "We'll lock up on the way out."

"Nothing that made the house look like a crime scene," Billy said. "Good thing, too, or we'd have had to call the Sheriff's office. They have jurisdiction here."

"Who leaves their phone at home these days?" Becky asked.

"Only when I forget it," Trask said. "If she turns up, we'll be happy to give it back to her. I doubt she'll complain."

Becky stopped to drop the evidence in the trunk of the car. They reached Miller's door and he buzzed them in again.

"You said this is the first time she's missed an appointment with you, Red?" Becky asked.

"Yep."

"And how long have you been meeting with her?" Graham had his notepad out.

"Every Tuesday for the last six months or so. She did miss one day—said she had a date she couldn't break—but she called me in advance to let me know. She came by the next morning … on a Wednesday."

"You've got a real good view of this block through that big window," Trask observed. "See anything unusual around her house on Monday or Monday night, maybe Tuesday morning?"

"Nah," Miller shook his head. "She never brought her business home with her. I never see cars parked out front or anything like that. She doesn't even have a car of her own. Sometimes one of her girlfriends picks her up and brings her home. Other times she calls a cab. I can't remember any cars down there over the past week."

"And she usually picks up the phone when you call her?" Trask asked.

"Yep. First or second ring. I called her—like you said to—when I saw you guys go in. Nobody picked up."

"Thanks for trying," Suzuki said, "and thanks for calling us. We'll let you know if we hear anything, and please call us again if you hear from her."

She handed Red her business card.

"Quite the lead," Trask observed as they hit I-70 and turned west. "Now we have a witness who might be able to identify our guy, but the witness disappears before we can even try to persuade her to talk to us. Even then, it's more than we had before."

"We'll see what surprises we can find on the phone," Becky said. "It shouldn't be hard to unlock."

Graham's radio squawked in the front seat.

"What's up, Sarge?"

"Who's with you, Billy?"

Trask recognized the voice of Tommy Land.

"Becky and Jeff Trask."

"They can hear this, too. Bonita Baylor has just hired a new guy in the Jackson County prosecutor's office. It's Ray Marsh."

"You're *shittin'* me!" Graham protested.

"No, and that's not all. She's assigned him to your serial killer case, Billy."

"I think I'm going to throw up," Becky said.

Trask stared out the window and shook his head.

18

The Allman Brothers' "Whipping Post" was playing on the stereo. Trask sat on the "bad couch"—the one that had been relegated to downstairs dog duty—with his feet on the matching "bad coffee table." To his right, a fire blazed in the wood stove insert that he'd had installed in the fireplace. Koko the Husky lay on the couch to his left, her head resting on a bad pillow. Kodi the Border Jack lay to his right, her head resting on his leg. Kodi lifted her head when she heard Lynn coming down the stairs to the left.

"I figured you'd need this," she said.

She handed him a glass containing a clear liquid and ice.

"Two fingers of Crown Royal, and two fingers of water, right?" she asked.

"Perfect. Thanks."

"I always know you need more than a beer when I hear this dark stuff playing." She nodded toward the stereo.

He smiled. "The Allman Brothers. Whiskey-drinkin' music."

"So, tell me how you plan to deal with this mess now."

"We had a good session back at CCU after Tommy's radio call," Trask said. "Since John Foote is FBI, he's keeping *my* case—anything having to do with the drug-laced cards. Like I said before, we might *suspect* that those incidents are related to the butchered bodies, but we don't know that yet, so we walled it off into a separate case. Foote will just take all the police reports on those two incidents—Sally the hooker and Captain Brown's daughter—and staple them to the back of some 302s—the FBI case report forms—and they'll leave the CCU building with John. I had already told Billy to take those off his wall.

"There aren't any autopsies—yet—to tie those two victims to our butcher. We have no bodies. For now, it's an official FBI federal dope case assigned to yours truly. Unless we get some proof of the linkage between the two investigations, it'll stay that way."

"What if that proof shows up?"

"Then J.P. Barrett and his new crim chief will have to sit down with Bonita Baylor and come to some sort of understanding."

"Who's the new crim chief? I thought J.P. had offered that to you before Marsh got dumped in his lap."

"He did, but we both agreed that after the little to-do in the courthouse, it would look bad if I got the job after knocking my predecessor out of it. No need to rub salt in Senator Burke's wounds right now. Besides, giving another supervisory position to someone else in the office means a chance to reward a deserving party with a raise and one of those coveted downstairs parking slots. No more two-block walks in the cold and no more $100-a-month parking bills."

"So, who's the lucky party?"

"I recommended Cam Turner, and J.P. agreed. He's a fine prosecutor, and he has lots of managerial and supervisory experience from his blue-suit JAG days. The younger folks in the office are always asking him for advice anyway."

"I bet Cam's happy."

"Grinning from ear to ear. He finally feels appreciated. He'd never admit it, but I think he always wondered why Barrett brought me in as SLC from outside the office. Cam had put in for it, and he was as deserving of that job as I was."

"Now you're both in the staff meetings."

"Yeah, and now I have two bosses I can deal with. It's all good on that end. I'll just have to handle the Gloomy thing without Cam now. He'll have too much on his plate with his new assignment."

"Is *your* plate clear enough to handle that alone?"

"Sure. There's only one defendant left, one defense counsel, and the case is prepped for trial. We'll just have to see who shows up to represent the little thug."

"Are you completely out of the case on—what did you call him—the butcher?"

"I am, *officially*. Billy and Becky Suzuki know to keep me in the loop, but to do it all off-paper. John Foote will still be working with them at CCU, too. They all know the ground rules: no reports, no emails, no cell phone calls. No memos for record. Nothing traceable. Local phone calls on land lines are okay. They don't generate any records."

"What about Marsh? Won't he be asking questions? He knows the cops would rather work with you, and that they'll probably be filling you in."

"All true, but like we say, there's what we know and what we can prove. Ray's not enough of an investigator himself to find what the real investigators aren't feeding him. He'll probably work at the county the same way he worked in our building—just stay in his ivory tower and demand that his minions bring him whatever he wants."

She paused.

Here come the real questions, Trask thought. *These will be the parts of the case she'd be working if she was still carrying a badge. She's already been working them in her head.*

"When you were at Sally's house, you found the door unlocked?"

"Yep."

"And no sign of anything being stolen?"

"Not that we noticed. Of course, we'd never been in the place before. There were no signs of any struggle or disturbance. The bed was made. There was a little TV still in the living room. If any of the other denizens of Dogpatch had known they could have run off with that, they would have. Most of the furniture was Walmart grade art-deco, but it would have probably been an upgrade for most of the joints in the neighborhood. It didn't look like anything had been taken."

"And she had no car?"

"Nope, and no place to park one. There was no garage, not even a carport, and if she left a vehicle on the curb out there at night, odds are that only the frame would have been left by morning."

"She left with someone. Either someone she knew, or at gun point."

"My conclusion, too."

"What kind of locks were on the door?"

"A deadbolt and a pushbutton on the doorknob. You couldn't lock the deadbolt from outside without a key, but you could push the button and pull the door closed behind you. That's what we did when we left."

"When she left, she didn't even do that."

"Nope."

"Gunpoint."

The creaking hinges on the old garage door woke her. She slowly raised her head from the soiled mattress that made up the floor of her cage. Even that slight effort was a challenge. She hadn't eaten for days, surviving only on the water in the doggie bowl in the corner of the cage.

Her eyes began to focus as the sunlight filtered through the opening door. He stood there with the gun in his hand, looking at her, saying nothing. She felt herself shaking, partially from fear, partially from weakness. The horrible screams from somewhere nearby had finally stopped during the night. She had actually slept for a couple of hours after that, but she felt in her soul that whatever had caused those screams awaited her.

It's my turn now. God help me.

The pitiful whimpers that came involuntarily from her throat almost surprised her. She thought of trying to beg, but she never began the sentences her mind was trying to form. She watched as he unlocked the padlock on the cage door and pulled the heavy wire frame open. He waved the pistol, motioning her to crawl out. She shook her head, her cries louder now, more desperate.

He motioned with the gun one more time, and when she again refused to comply, he grabbed her by the hair and dragged her out. She felt something cut her ankle while he pulled her out of the garage and across a short distance of gravel to another door. He opened it and dragged her inside where he forced her into another cage—a smaller one, with white ceramic walls on either side. She heard him walk out the other end of the room, and she smelled a strong odor as he left.

She reached down to her right ankle, feeling the burning. Her fingers came back to her face covered with blood from the gash. She pulled up the corner of the pad on the floor of the cage and began to write in blood with her quivering finger.

"My name was Sally."

19

THEY SAT around the table in Trask's drug unit conference room. They had agreed that all meetings concerning what they now called the "federal" case would be held in the courthouse, away from any eyes and ears that might want to report their discussions to the county prosecutors.

"It could be Red Miller," Becky Suzuki offered. "Think about it. He hates women after his divorce, he can't do anything to them sexually, if he was telling the truth about his war injuries—and no man I know would ever want to even fake impotence—he knew where Sally lived, there's at least enough to consider."

"We'll never stop considering all possibilities," Trask said.

"I don't buy it," Foote said. "I didn't get those vibes from him. He struck me as just a very lonely old guy who'd lost his only friend, and I don't think he's lying about his injuries, especially after seeing how high that one leg was amputated. If he's our butcher, why would he call us at all?"

"He might be fishing to see where we are on the case," Billy said, raising an eyebrow in Becky's direction.

He's trying to support her a little, even if he doesn't buy the theory himself, Trask thought.

"Why would he direct us to Sally's house, then?" Foote asked. "Pretty risky if he's the perp."

"He knows he didn't leave anything for us to find there," Becky said.

"Anything's possible," Trask said, "and we'll keep considering, but we don't have enough to move in that direction yet."

"What about surveillance on him?" Becky asked. "A pole camera on his house, or maybe a GPS on his van. I ran him in the system, and he has one of those specialized handicap vans that he can drive. It's probably locked up tight in that garage to the right of his house."

"I'm sure it is," Trask said, "which would mean we'd need a warrant to slap the GPS on the van. It's on private property. We don't have enough to articulate probable cause for that. Our judges up here would laugh me out of the room, and I'm sure that we don't want to ask one of the Jackson County judges for a warrant right now. Bonita Baylor and Ray Marsh would hear about it in minutes."

"I see what you're saying," Becky said, nodding in resignation.

"The pole cam might be a good idea somewhere else," Foote added, "but not in Dogpatch. There are five convicted felons out there for every block. They've been through enough trials and discovery processes to know about pole cams. They'd see the phone company or power company truck for the ruse that it would be, and they'd be ripping the thing down and selling it the second our truck got out of the neighborhood."

"Just a thought," she said.

"And not a bad one. Please keep 'em coming," Trask said. "What else?"

"We've added a couple of things to our perp's possible profile, based on what you told us about DMSO," Billy said. "Our guy may have some high school or college or even pro athletic experience, or he may have a chemistry background, or he may have worked at some point in the pulpwood processing industry."

"Good ideas," Trask agreed. "Anything else?"

Nobody said anything.

"Then we're still where we were when we started. Keep thinking. Keep working. Same time Monday, please. Have a good weekend."

WaShaun Stewart, Jr., "Gloomy" to both his friends and his enemies, and to the Kansas City, Missouri Police, the FBI, the DEA, and the ATF, did not like what he was hearing.

"Normally," the attorney continued, speaking through the screen that separated them, "I'd say we would at least have a shot at an acquittal, even if it was a long shot, but yours is not a normal case. First of all, there's not just one murder charged, Mr. Stewart, there are several. Second, there's normally a chance that the prosecutor will make some error at trial that we could appeal. We'll see what happens at trial. If there's a conviction, there's an appeal. Win the appeal, and there is always a chance some critical witness would recant or just disappear by the time we had the re-trial.

"The problem here is that you don't have a normal prosecutor. Jeff Trask is the AUSA handling your case, and he doesn't make mistakes. I've tried a couple of major cases against him, and I had a hell of a time finding any errors at all to assert on appeal. The errors I did assert were losers from the start. We had to file *something*—it was a life sentence case after all—so that's what I did, but I knew the conviction would be affirmed.

"We have computers for legal research. You can plug an attorney's name in the system to do a search for any appellate opinions. If the attorney tried the case or just argued the case on appeal, the opinion will come up. Plug Jeff Trask in, and all you get is 'affirmed,' 'affirmed,' 'affirmed,' 'affirmed.' He doesn't lose trials, and when he wins those, he doesn't lose on appeal.

"The bottom line is, yes, I'll handle your case, but my best advice is to take the inexpensive way out. My fee will be much cheaper if it's a guilty plea. Express some remorse, and maybe the court will go lighter on your sentence. A victory here would be anything less than a life sentence, and even that is still a long shot. Think it over. Give me a call next week if that's the way you want to proceed."

Gloomy nodded, but he said nothing.

That's the same bullshit the last guy said. I ain't payin' that kind of money just to get sent away forever.

A deputy United States Marshal unlocked the door to the conference side of the holding cell, and the attorney left. Moments later, the same deputy opened the door behind Gloomy, and motioned him out. Stewart slid his shackled feet out of the cell.

"Just head to the elevator," the deputy told him. "Time to go back to CCA."

Gloomy snorted. CoreCivic, the private jail facility in Lansing, Kansas, had formerly been known as the Corrections Corporation of America, or CCA, before changing its corporate name. Some of the deputies and attorneys found the habit of calling it "CCA" hard to break.

The courts had—in their collective wisdom or lack thereof—decided at some time in the distant past that it was unfair to house "detainees"—prisoners who were still facing trial and who therefore were not yet *officially* convicts—with actual convicts. The result was that detainees like Gloomy—even those charged with murder or with multiple murders—could not be housed with those horrible convicts, even though the convicts in question may have been convicted of something far less egregious, like fraud. The convicts went to the federal pen at Leavenworth down the road, or to some other federal prison to be designated by the Bureau of Prisons.

It was on the trip back to CoreCivic and his holding cell that Gloomy Stewart decided he was not going to go to trial against Jeff Trask. Yes, he would keep his one more attorney appointment at the courthouse on Monday. That attorney would doubtless hand him the same advice that he'd already heard twice. It didn't matter. He would not be making the trip to hear the advice. If his plan worked, he would also not be making the trip to the courthouse from CoreCivic.

As usual, a Saturday morning meant a morning walk with the pups. March had roared in a couple of days earlier, but the winds were lighter and warmer for the day, so Trask allowed his dog team to tow him for a mile or so longer. Lynn was waiting for them when they returned.

"I have their breakfast waiting," she said. "Yours is waiting somewhere up the road."

"I love you, too. What's up?"

"Nothing. I just need to shop for some clothes, and I know you hate waiting and hovering. Your range bag is in your car, and you need some practice, anyway."

Trask shrugged and turned back toward the Jeep.

I do need the practice. Don't want to forget Billy's lessons.

There was a newer firing range on 291 North in the northeast part of town. It was a nice facility. In addition to the firing range, there was an attached retail store selling weapons, magazines, ammo, and some tactical clothing. There was also a small snack bar.

After stopping at a fast-food drive-thru, Trask ate his breakfast on the way to the range.

He worked his way through 100 rounds. The second target he used was better than the first. The grouping was starting to tighten up—down in diameter to about four inches now—and there was no "left and low" to worry him anymore. He packed up and headed out of the range area into the retail lobby when he saw Billy Graham.

"You have to pay to shoot now?" Trask asked.

"The academy range is busy all day with a couple of new rookie classes," Graham said. "This has always been my backup place. Besides, I called your house, and Lynn told me you'd be here. How'd you shoot?"

Trask showed him the second target.

"Better. Much better." Graham nodded as he looked at the holes in the paper. "I have something for you."

Billy reached into his own range bag and pulled out a holster rigged into a series of black nylon straps.

"It's a tactical rig—you carry the gun on your thigh—and the holster's a custom fit for your 239. I told you I wore mine out. I used to carry it as a backup to my long gun when I was assigned to one of the tactical squads. Since Sig doesn't make the gun anymore, I don't really have any use for it."

"So, I can wear this the next time I'm following one of your TAC teams on a raid?" Trask asked.

Graham laughed. "Sure, as long as it's empty. The TAC sergeant might not want an armed lawyer on his six during an operation. It's something nice to put the gun in when you're here or at another range. Missouri's an open carry state, so you can actually sport it anywhere if you want, although I wouldn't recommend it. You'd be the first one the bad guys targeted if they saw you were armed. I always carry concealed."

"Same here. What's really going on, Billy? You could have dropped this off at the office next week."

"Let's sit down for a few," Graham said, pointing to the snack bar corner of the store. Trask followed and joined him at a table.

"Becky and I went back to CCU after we left your office yesterday," Graham said. "Bonita Baylor and Ray Marsh were both in Tommy's office when we got there. He waved us in and introduced us. We tried to be friendly and professional, but Ms. Baylor went all control freak on us. She read us the riot act, and she made damn sure we understood that anything having to do with her serial killer investigation is supposed to go to Marsh and nobody else."

"At least she got Ray out of his office," Trask noted.

"I'm not sure that was a good thing. He saw my wall display in the conference room. He told us he might be down 'a few times a week' for updates, since he was the attorney assigned to manage the investigation."

Trask nodded and let out a long sigh.

"It's nuts that it has to be this way, Billy. We're all *supposed* to be on the same team, and if I didn't know from prior experience with Marsh that he screws up everything he touches, we would be. That said, the goal still has to be identifying our butcher and taking him off the street to save lives. If something indicates that sharing what we find in our investigation will get us there a second quicker, I'm there, Marsh or no Marsh."

"I'm with you."

"We'll keep our eyes out for that development along with everything else we're looking for, okay?"

"Sure."

"Do we have anything else to consider for now?"

"No. No more leads."

"We need some luck."

"I'd rather be lucky than good."

Trask smiled. "I'd rather be both."

"Your target—" Billy said, "—is looking a lot better. Practice with some dry fire at home and that grouping will get even smaller."

"Thanks. See you Monday, and thanks for filling me in."

20

Gloomy hid his smile until the jailer slammed the door behind him. Stewart turned and held his handcuffed wrists through the slot in the door until the cuffs were unlocked and removed. Then he grinned.

The solitary confinement cell in the Livingstone County Jail was exactly what Gloomy had expected. The fight he had started at CoreCivic had resulted in his transfer to the oldest jail in the United States Marshals' contract network. There were plenty of times when CoreCivic couldn't handle all the detainees waiting for trial, and some of the overflow prisoners had to be locked up at county jails in the area. The Marshals Service paid the counties for their hospitality.

Stewart had heard from some of the others at CoreCivic about how the system handled troublemakers. They'd be shipped out to the counties, and—if they had been *real* problems—the detainees could expect to be sent to the worst dumps the marshals could find. This one certainly qualified. It was cold, antiquated, and from what Gloomy had heard, the food sucked. It was due to be closed at the end of the year.

None of that mattered. Gloomy had what he needed: a private isolation cell, a bar of soap, time, and an almost certain portion of instant mashed potatoes with brown gravy as part of his evening meal.

He sat down and got to work immediately. The soap was about four inches long, and big enough for his purposes if he was careful. He had the advantage of years of experience—even at his young age—with guns. His father, an "OG" or original gangster with the 51st Street Crips, had taught him how to shoot and handle a pistol at age five. Gloomy could usually tell the make and model of a pistol just by holding it, even with his eyes closed.

It has to be a micro-compact, like one of those little nines, or maybe a .38.

He decided to model his creation after a little Taurus he had carried as a pocket gun. He whittled the soap in his lap using his fingernails, sitting with his back to the door in case any passing guards stopped to look in on him through the window. He was halfway through the project when he heard the slot slide open.

"Dinner, Stewart," the jailer barked as he slid a plastic tray in through the slot.

Gloomy tucked the soap in his waistband and walked the two steps to the tray. It was just what he expected: some sort of mystery meat, a spoonful of English peas—not the tasty baby kind, but the big rubbery ones he had played table basketball with in elementary school—and lumpy mashed potatoes with brown gravy. The dinner beverage was a cardboard container of milk. The utensils were a plastic knife and a plastic spork.

He gulped down a few mouthfuls of the meat and even some of the potatoes, being careful not to waste the gravy. The precious brown fluid was pushed to a corner of the tray using some of the potatoes as a dam to contain it there. After swigging down the meat, he used the paper napkin from the dinner tray to plug the drain in the sink on the wall and poured the gravy into the sink. He finished the potatoes in the tray and returned to his sculpting.

The plastic dinnerware made the job easier. An hour later, the remnants of the bar of soap bore a striking resemblance to a small Taurus 9mm pistol. A white one.

Shoe polish would have been easier, but they won't be giving me that. Brown will have to do instead of black.

Gloomy put the soap gun in the sink just before the slot opened again. He returned the tray and his plastic tools to the jailer. After another hour, he checked on his creation. Enough of the brown gravy coloring had stuck to the soap to turn it into a facsimile of the popular "desert tan" color. He nodded with approval.

Trask smiled across the conference table at his new crim chief. It was Cam's first Monday morning staff meeting in the front office.

"In case anyone hasn't heard yet," J.P. Barrett began, "we have a new chief of our criminal division. Welcome, Cam," he said, nodding at Turner. "I won't put you on the spot just yet by asking for a division update. I think you're probably just getting your feet wet."

"I appreciate that," Cam said, smiling, "and I really appreciate the parking spot."

Barrett turned to his left and looked at Trask. "Why don't we start with Jeff, then? Any news on the Gloomy front?"

"The marshals are telling me that he has a final meeting with a possible defense counsel this afternoon," Trask said. "He talked to two last week, but nobody signed up. I don't know if the fees are too high for a long trial, or if our defendant just isn't liking the advice he's getting. At any rate, his week to find counsel runs out tomorrow. If we don't see someone entering their appearance on his case, I imagine we'll be back in front of Judge Horney, and our man Gloomy will have some explaining to do.

"They also told me that he started a real ruckus at CoreCivic last week, and the staff there is fed up with him. That got him transferred to an isolation cell at Livingstone County."

"I thought they were closing that jail down," Barrett said.

"That's supposed to happen later this year," Trask agreed. "For now, it's still open, and they just got a new resident detainee."

"That's a long bus ride down here from Chillicothe," Cam observed. "Not much on the scenery front, either."

"Gloomy will get to see it twice today," Trask said. "Down and back. He might get out of isolation if he stops stirring up trouble, but he's stuck there 'til the trial's over, whenever that might be."

"How about our drug-soaked business card case?" Barrett asked. "Anything new there?"

Trask shook his head. "Nothing at all."

"Let's go, Stewart," the deputy said.

Gloomy stuck his hands through the slot to be cuffed. The cell door opened, and one of the three black-shirted deputy sheriffs put the shackles on his ankles. They flanked him and escorted him through the white-walled hallways until they reached the dock where the transport bus was waiting.

"Just one for the feds in KC," one of the deputies said to the driver. "Attorney consult. You might as well wait on him. Shouldn't take too long, Jim."

"It's already 2:30, and it'll be after dark before we get back," the driver complained. "I'll radio when I'm about fifteen minutes out."

"That'll work. We'll be here."

They cuffed Gloomy to the front seat in the prisoner cage behind the bus driver. Stewart saw that the driver—a portly, balding man about fifty—wore the same black uniform of the Livingstone County Sheriff's Office.

This old cracker's just waiting to retire. If I get away from him, he sure ain't catching me in a chase.

Gloomy also saw the gun and keys hanging from the man's wide, black leather belt. He turned his attention to the bus. There was a metal cage with a door separating the prisoner section from the driver.

If I play this right, he'll be opening that for me.

Gloomy weighed his options.

Do I try it on the way down, or wait for the trip back up? It might be better in the dark. I can make for the trees, and I'll stand a better chance of getting someplace where I can hide. This damn orange suit will stand out like a pumpkin in daylight. I'll talk up this old fool on the way down. Butter him up, maybe make him let his guard down.

The bus pulled away from the jail and headed southwest toward Kansas City.

I can pick my spot on the trip down there, too.

Gloomy squirmed a little, repositioning the soap gun that he'd hidden in his underwear. Small as it was, it still didn't feel comfortable wedged next to his privates.

"So, there's just the two of us. What's going on in KC today?" the driver asked him.

"Just trying to find a lawyer to take my case," Gloomy answered.

"What's the problem with that? They want too much money?"

"Yeah. They always want too much money. You got that right."

"I know you can't talk about the facts of your case, but what are you charged with?"

They never told him what I was charged with?

"Dope case."

The driver nodded. "Seems like that's all the feds do these days."

"I just don't feel like taking the fall for what somebody else done," Gloomy said, putting on his best innocent face. "I'll be doin' a lot of time if I get convicted."

"Maybe this lawyer can help you out, then," Jim said.

"Yeah, I sure hope so."

Gloomy studied the opposite side of the highway as they drove toward Kansas City. He looked for the perfect spot, an isolated turnoff where the bus could stop outside the glare of the lights of passing cars. A wooded area would be best. He memorized the mile markers whenever he saw a location that might fit the bill.

"Spring's almost here. It's starting to warm up a little," the deputy observed. "Things are turning green again."

"Yeah," was all Gloomy could muster. He went back to studying exits and mile markers.

The trip back. After dark.

His eyes shifted to the dark colored jacket the deputy had hung behind his seat.

It may be getting warmer, but it's still cold outside. He won't be needing that as much as I will.

"How long you think your attorney visit will take?"

"About an hour. It'll be shorter if he gives me the same line I heard from the other two."

"Okay. I'll just grab some coffee in the snack bar and wait for the marshals to tell me when you're done."

"Okay."

I just have to make sure it'll be dark by the time we get back to my spot.

The attorney did, in fact, give him the same advice, but Gloomy appeared to be interested, asking what appeared to be genuine questions whenever he could think of them. The interview dragged on for ninety minutes before the lawyer ran out of gas in his pitch.

"So, what do you think?" he asked.

"I need to talk to my family. I'll call them tonight and let you know tomorrow," Gloomy promised.

"Sounds like a plan."

The lawyer pushed a button to let the marshals know he was finished. The lock on the door clicked behind him.

"I'll wait for your call tomorrow," he said on his way out the door.

And you'll just keep waiting.

Fifteen minutes passed. Gloomy wondered why he was waiting, then figured it out.

They had to call Deputy Jim and wait for him to get back up from the snack bar.

The door behind him opened, and Gloomy shuffled his shackled feet back down a hallway to the elevator and the bus. The driver was waiting with the engine running,

"I figured I'd warm it up a little for you."

"Thanks," Gloomy said. "Appreciate it."

They drove slowly through the rush hour traffic as they made their way out of Kansas City.

"That took a little longer than you said. Did ya get some good news?"

"Maybe. Gotta call and talk to the family tonight."

"Sure. Mind if I turn on the radio?"

"No."

A country station started playing. Gloomy almost snorted, but then thought better of it.

Let him get as comfortable as possible.

The bus reached the farms and ranchlands outside the metro area. Gloomy started watching the mile markers. When they were eight miles south of his chosen spot, Gloomy slowly lowered the fly on the jumpsuit, and pulled out the soap carving.

"You can turn that shit off now."

The change in his passenger's tone caused the driver to look back over his shoulder. He looked straight into what he thought was the barrel of a pistol pointing at him through the metal screen.

"How the hell did you get that?!" the deputy asked, panicked.

"They don't search attorneys as careful as they search prisoners," Gloomy said. "Don't be stupid and you'll live through this, understand?"

"Yeah, okay. What do you want me to do?"

"Start slowing down. We'll be pulling off to the right in a couple of miles. Hand me the key to these cuffs and shackles."

The deputy passed it backward through the screen. Gloomy transferred his soap carving to his left hand, keeping it behind the driver's back where it was less visible. He freed himself from the restraints and pulled himself upright on the screen behind the deputy.

"That right coming up. Take it. Slow."

The bus pulled off the highway onto a rural road.

"Go about a hundred yards and pull over and stop."

"Please, young man, I got a family to take care of."

"Then do what I tell you."

The bus stopped.

"Take off your gun belt and drop it on the floor."

The driver complied.

"Keep your seat and don't turn around. Where's the key to this cage door?"

The deputy held it up in his right hand.

"Unlock it, but stay in your seat."

The deputy reached for the lock and turned it. Gloomy heard the metallic click. He pulled the door open and grabbed the gun belt from the floor. He pulled the gun out of the holster.

A Glock .40. That'll work.

Gloomy grabbed the keys from the ignition and tossed them to the back of the bus. He handed the cuffs to the deputy.

"Cuff yourself to the steering wheel."

The driver locked the cuffs around his right wrist, slid the chain and the other cuff through the spokes of the wheel, then clicked the left cuff closed.

"*Please—*"

"Shut the fuck up."

Gloomy threw the handcuff key to the back of the bus. He looked at the deputy's left shoulder.

No shoulder mic. The only radio is the one on the dash.

He reached for the mic on the dashboard and jerked it hard. The wires ripped loose. Gloomy tossed it toward the back where he'd thrown the key. He grabbed the jacket from the hook behind the driver's seat and pointed the pistol at the driver's head.

"*Oh God, no! Please—*"

21

"HELLO?" Trask automatically checked his watch as he answered the phone.

Almost nine. Kinda late.

"Jeff, it's Cam."

"Mr. big cheese division chief. What's up?"

"Well, the first thing on my agenda tomorrow is to revise the calling tree protocol put in place by my predecessor. That control freak Marsh apparently told every secretary and every law enforcement agency in the state that every call on every criminal matter involving the office had to first be routed through him, so instead of calling you on your case, the marshals called me first."

"On which case?"

"Gloomy. He's apparently managed to escape."

"What?!!"

"The transport bus he was in left the courthouse around closing time, but never made it back to Chillicothe."

Trask shook his head and tried to think. "What do we know so far?"

"Nothing. Just that he's missing, along with the bus and the driver."

"Could some of his old crew have ambushed the bus?"

"Anything's possible, but they'd have to be clairvoyant. The marshals said that Gloomy didn't make any calls to the outside all weekend, either from the county lockup or while he was talking to his potential lawyer at the courthouse."

"Who was that?"

"Tom Benson. No way Tom would have relayed any messages to the gang for Gloomy."

"I agree. He's straight."

"What's the marshals' plan for now?"

"They have no idea where the bus may be, or even if it started out for Chillicothe. They said they'd get a chopper up in the morning and start up I-35, since that's the way the bus was *supposed* to go. The state police are ready to send dog teams out once the bus is located. The FBI said they could put their plane up, too."

"Okay. Did you call Foote?"

"Yeah, and he said he'd call Billy and Mrs. Billy."

"They're *married?*"

"Not yet. Just a matter of time, though, in my opinion."

Trask chuckled. "You're probably right."

"Anyway, I thought you'd appreciate a heads-up instead of getting blindsided in the morning."

"I do. Thanks. See you at the office."

Trask clicked the call off and headed for the front closet that was just inside the front door of the great room. He took the twelve-gauge from the back corner in the closet and checked it. It was loaded.

Lynn was watching TV from the couch across the room.

"What's that about?"

"Gloomy's loose."

He started into the woods to the east of the road before doubling back behind the bus in the darkness. He waited for a single car to pass before crossing the road and heading northwest. Although he'd spent his entire life in the city and had virtually no idea of what to do in the great outdoors, Gloomy had seen his share of TV movies and crime shows.

The cops will have dogs on my scent as soon as they find the bus. Gotta find a way to shake them.

He considered jacking another passing car—he had the deputy's Glock after all—but decided not to risk it.

If they don't stop, and if I can't stop them, they'll report me to the cops immediately. If I just keep moving, they probably won't find the bus 'til morning. I need the extra time.

He kept to the woods, avoiding any open fields when he came to them. He kept circling toward the north and west.

I got an uncle in St. Jo. It's a long way, but maybe I can make it that far in a day or so. Can't head home. That's the first place they'll look for me.

He was glad that he'd taken the deputy's jacket. The sun was down now, and the cold was setting in. He was also glad the snow had melted. He wouldn't leave tracks in the white stuff. It would make him harder to track. He stepped out of a grove of trees and almost fell into a ditch. He saw there was a creek at the bottom of it.

I can lose the dogs by wading in the creek.

He took off the laceless sneakers they'd given him to wear at the county jail, and also removed his socks. He rolled up the cuffs on the orange jumpsuit. His first steps into the water were a shock.

Damn! That's cold as hell! Now I know where all the snow went.

He sloshed northward in the shallow water, figuring he'd have to walk a good distance in the creek before climbing out again.

They'll have the dogs walking the banks in both directions of where they lost me. Got to stay in this cold shit for a while.

He pushed on northward, his teeth chattering from the cold. He had no idea how far he'd gone when he finally climbed out of the creek bed.

If that ain't far enough, it'll have to do anyway. I can't feel my feet anymore.

He used the jacket lining to dry his feet and lower legs before putting the socks and sneakers back on. He was starting to shake violently from the cold.

Gotta find someplace to warm up for a while. Maybe rest for an hour or so. If I warm up, I can travel some more before the sun comes up.

He was back in the woods, moving north, when he saw two, dark buildings in a small clearing to his right. The one to the left was taller and square, the other building on the right was longer, a low, concrete-block rectangle.

No lights. That's good. Maybe nobody's around. Looks like a garage on the left. Maybe I can grab some wheels.

He headed for the building to the left. There was a padlock hanging through a metal loop where the doors met, but it was unlocked. Gloomy slowly pulled one of the doors open and peeked inside. He saw an older pickup truck.

Damn. That's an old piece of shit. Hope it's not a standard. I never learned how to drive a clutch.

He moved slowly through the darkness toward the driver's door. He opened it, and then winced when the hinges protested with a loud, metallic creak. He froze and waited for several minutes, the Glock at the ready in his right hand.

Nobody's coming. Good.

He climbed into the driver's seat.

No clutch pedal. That's a start.

He bent to his right and looked at the steering column.

If I can find a screwdriver, I think I can punch the ignition. Hope it runs. Hope it has gas.

He climbed back down out of the truck and started peering through the darkness at the walls of the old garage.

There's gotta be a damn screwdriver around here somewhere.

A faint noise behind him caused him to turn. The butt of the rifle slamming into his face caused him to black out.

22

"Our airplane spotted the bus about here." Foote pointed to a spot on the map. "As you can see, it had turned off I-35 and gone east about half a mile on this farm road. This is all a little northeast of the town of Holt."

Trask looked around the CCU bullpen. It had been set up almost like a small auditorium, with metal folding chairs filling the floor between the desks that lined the walls. Those chairs were now filled with law enforcement officers of several varieties. He recognized officers and agents from the Kansas City, Missouri Police Department, the FBI, DEA, ATF, the United States Marshals Service, and Missouri State Police. He stood to the left of Foote with Billy Graham and Becky Suzuki and watched as Foote continued the briefing.

"The bus driver is one lucky man. As most of you know, Gloomy Stewart doesn't hesitate to kill when he feels like pulling a trigger. He just pistol whipped the Livingstone County deputy who was driving the bus, and we expect that deputy to make a full recovery. Slight concussion. The driver faked being unconscious, and he was able to see Gloomy heading east into the woods to the right of the truck. He told us that Gloomy had gotten a gun somewhere when he got back on the bus at the courthouse.

"Gloomy said something about getting it from a lawyer he met with. We've interviewed the lawyer, and we think that statement was misinformation. The attorney went through the metal detectors at the courthouse, and he's not the kind of guy to make a stupid play like that. I'll turn it over to Sgt. Robbins of the State Police for a moment. He can tell you what the dog teams found."

Sgt Robbins, dressed in the uniform of the Missouri State Police K-9 units, took the laser pointer offered him by Foote and stepped up to the map.

"As John said, the driver saw Gloomy enter the woods about here—" he pointed to a spot up the road in front of the bus, "—and we were able to pick up a scent and trail him into the woods. He went into the trees for about sixty yards, then circled back around to the rear of the bus, before crossing the county road about here—" he pointed to another spot on the map, "—and going west-northwest through the trees on the other side of the road, heading in a direction that would have taken him north of Holt.

"We were able to trail him for about a half-mile until he hit New Hope Creek, about here." The laser indicated another location. "He apparently knew enough to stay in the water, despite the temperature, because we went up and down both banks of the creek for a mile in either direction. We were never able to pick up the scent again. The spot where he entered the creek is the last location we have for him.

"We got a good bit of rain out that way this morning, so any further scent is probably washed out by now. We've retrieved some bedding from his cell at the jail, so we can freshen the scent for our units and start working again if anyone finds a promising starting point, so we'll see you out there."

Robbins handed the laser pointer back to Foote.

"Description is a black male, late teens, about five-nine and 165 pounds," Foote continued. "Here's a photo." He pointed at a mug shot displayed to the right of the map. "Last known clothing is an orange, Livingstone County Jail jumpsuit. He took the deputy's black service uniform jacket when he left the bus. He also took the deputy's service weapon, a Glock .40 caliber. He's charged with five homicides, and may be good for more, so 'armed and dangerous' is an understatement. Nobody works this without a partner on his or her hip. Understood?"

A silent chorus of nods answered him.

"Good luck and be very careful."

"Want to ride with us?" Graham asked Trask.

"Sure."

"We'll be doing knock and talks north of that last location," Billy explained. "It'll probably be farmhouses, maybe a store or two."

"Should I get my nine out of my car trunk?" Trask asked.

"Tommy Land would have my ass if I said yes." Billy shook his head. Then he leaned his head closer and whispered, "Next time, don't ask or tell. We have a spare body armor vest for you in our trunk in case anything gets weird. You'll have to wear that."

Trask nodded. "At least it isn't a hundred degrees outside."

He followed them out and hopped into the unmarked car's back seat. They followed the caravan of other unmarked units and marked police cruisers up the interstate.

"Quite the convoy we have today," Billy said as he drove. "The last time I saw this many in a line was for a state trooper's funeral."

"Let's try to avoid having another one," Trask said. "Every one of these units has an assignment?"

"Yeah. John and the other federal agents met with the State Police last night. Some are going out on search patrols, and a lot of us will be doing the door-to-door area canvass. We all have grid assignments to work. Maybe we'll get lucky and find him."

"Easier said than done," Becky said.

"The Essex, 1963," Trask said.

"What?!"

"A crossover pop hit for a bunch of Marines on active duty, as I recall."

"And you know this because?" Becky asked.

"Because he read it or heard it somewhere," Billy answered for Trask. "At least there's relevant info in that head in addition to all the other stuff."

"You can't just erase things like that?" Becky asked.

"That's easier said than done," Trask quipped.

Becky moaned.

They turned off I-35 and headed toward the little town of Holt before veering off on a two-lane, rural road and heading northeast. Graham pulled the car into the driveway of a farmhouse on the left side of the road. Becky checked the address on the car's computer.

"This should be a William Kirby," she said.

"First stop," Billy said as they got out of the car and headed for the front door.

A man in overalls met them on the porch before they reached it.

"Help ya?"

"Maybe," Billy said. "Mr. Kirby? Been listening to the radio or TV?"

"Sure. Figured that was why you were here. Seen his face on every channel last night. The guy who escaped?"

"That's right. Seen or heard anything?" Billy asked.

"Nope. Keepin' my gun close, though."

"That would be a good idea," Graham said. "Another good idea is to dial 911 if you see him. Call us if you hear something or have a question." Billy handed the man a business card. "Don't try to be a hero yourself. He's a bad dude."

"Understood. Hope you find him."

"Thanks. So do we."

They returned to their car and continued up the road.

"No nerves evident there," Becky observed.

"I agree," Billy said. "He wasn't hiding anything." Graham glanced at Trask through the rearview mirror. "Anybody looks nervous or strange, there's always a possibility Gloomy's hiding behind the door watching."

Trask just nodded.

They drove another quarter mile up the road.

"At least it's not a subdivision," Trask noted. "Spread-out farms, and only on one side of the road. What do we do when we run out of places in your grid section?"

"Call for instructions," Billy said. "They'll give us another one."

He turned into another driveway.

"Morris and Evelyn Hemeter," Becky said.

The previous interview essentially repeated itself, with Becky taking the lead in a contact with Mrs. Hemeter, a housewife. They backed out of the driveway and continued to the next farm.

Becky checked the computer again. "Thomas Leggett."

They interrupted a man taking groceries out of the back of a minivan.

"Mr. Leggett? How's it going?" Billy asked.

"Fair enough. What can I help you with?"

"We're just checking to make sure that everybody's staying safe. We have an escapee in the area."

"Escapee?"

"You haven't heard about it on the news?"

"Nope. Just got home from visiting some relatives in Iowa. Had the radio on a satellite music station."

"Okay. We have a murder suspect who escaped from a transport bus in the area. There are lots of officers out looking for him. We just wanted to make sure that everyone's staying safe and keeping alert."

The man patted his belt just behind his right side. "I hear ya."

"He's carrying, too. Call 911 first, okay?"

"Like I said: I hear ya."

"Okay. Wife and kids with you?"

"Inside."

"Make sure they know, too. Might be a good idea to keep the kids inside for a while."

The man shrugged and nodded.

"Have a good one," Billy said.

"You, too."

They drove another mile northward before Billy stopped across from the entrance to a dirt road. The road led into a heavily wooded area on the left of the paved route. There was a chain strung across the entrance between two metal poles sunk into concrete bases. To the right of the entrance was a wooden sign mounted on a wooden post reading, "Venison and Taxidermy."

"There's some sort of button under the sign," Billy said. "Looks like a little speaker, too. Maybe an intercom."

Trask studied the system as Billy pulled the car across the road, onto the dirt and up to the chain. There was a power wire running up the pole above the button, and Trask thought he saw a security camera behind some tree branches at the top of the pole.

Billy got out and walked around to the button.

"Yeah?" a voice squawked over the speaker. "Who are you and what do you want?"

"Police," Billy answered. "We're looking for a fugitive, an escapee. Can you come talk with us for a minute or two, please?"

There was a short pause. “Sure. Be right there. It’s going to take a minute. I’m a couple hundred yards back from the road.”

“We’ll wait for you.”

It took almost five minutes before a man appeared, coming up the dirt road on a golf cart that was towing a lightweight metal trailer. The driver of the golf cart stopped on his side of the chain and hopped out. Trask looked him over.

Five-nine, 190 pounds. Mid-fifties. Gray, thinning hair, dark brown eyes. Jeans and a brown Carhartt jacket.

Trask joined Becky and Graham at the chain.

“Willard Dewey,” the man said, offering them his hand.

They introduced themselves and showed their badges.

“We’re looking for this guy,” Billy said. He held up his cell phone, showing Dewey a photo of Gloomy Stewart. “He escaped from custody near here last night. He’s a very dangerous gang member, wanted for more than one murder. We’re out looking for him and warning everyone in the area not to make contact with him. Just wondering if you’ve seen or heard anything unusual around your place.”

Dewey cackled a hoarse laugh. “Naw—not that anything *usual* happens around here—anyway, I ain’t seen him. I just got here this morning. I don’t have a house back there, just my processing shop.”

Trask pointed to the sign.

“That’s right,” Dewey answered before Trask could ask. “I clean and butcher deer for hunters, do some mounting, too. Pretty busy when the season hits in November. The road back there’s a mess, so I just roll up here on my cart, throw the carcasses on that little trailer—I shoulda said ‘carcass;’ no way I could haul more than one on that rig—and haul ’em back to my little shop. We’re way outta season now, of course. I was just in doin’ some cleanin’ up and repair work.”

“But you haven’t seen anything of our fugitive?” Becky asked.

“Nope.”

“He’s armed,” she informed him.

“Well, hell, so am I!” Dewey cackled again. I gotta couple deer rifles back there, too. That’s another reason I’m out here today. Doin’ some work on my guns.”

Billy handed him a business card.

"911 if you see him. Call us second," Billy said.

"Got it."

"Anybody else have a place near here?" Becky asked, looking northward. All she could see was the road, and they were nearing the end of their grid assignment.

"Just my competition."

"Who would that be?" Trask asked.

"Another deer processor—Butch somethin' or other, Butch the deer butcher—I never can remember last names—'bout three-quarters of a mile up the road there. I doubt he's around, with it being out of season now. His place isn't marked. You'll just see a chain across a dirt entrance, like mine here."

"Does he have a buzzer like you?" Billy asked.

"Naw. If he's there, the chain's down and you can drive back. If he ain't around, the chain's up and locked. I call him my competition, but there's plenty of work for both of us come the season. No hard feelin's or nothin' like that. If one of us is too busy, we send the business next door."

"Got it," Billy said. "Thanks, Mr. Dewey."

"Anytime. You folks have a good rest of the day."

"You, too," Becky said.

They returned to the car. They drove to the next entrance and saw the chain across the road up and locked.

Billy shrugged. "Private property. Can't enter without consent. We'll have someone look him up and meet him out here to do a sweep of his property. I'll let the air units know, too. They can do a flyover today." He grabbed the radio mic and called Sgt. Land.

"As far as we can tell, this section's clean, boss. Got another one for us?"

23

"GOOD FLICK," Billy said, as he opened Becky's apartment door for her. "Some decent action, no politics, and fairly realistic. Nobody outrunning machinegun fire, no hero snap-shooting a bad guy off a roof half a mile away without aiming his pistol."

Becky kissed him. "Want to come in for a bit?"

"Always." He smiled. "But then I always leave sad." He poked out his bottom lip in his best pout.

She giggled. "I've told you I was raised in a traditional values home. That's one reason you love me, and you know it."

"I suppose so," he said. "Anyway, it was good to get away from work for a while—and just be together."

"Want something to drink?" she asked. "A coke maybe?"

"Sounds good."

She stepped to the fridge to get it. When she closed the door and turned back towards him, he was holding a jewelry box in his hand.

"I … don't really know how to do this," he said haltingly. "I hope it fits, that is if you say yes."

"Say yes to what?" she giggled again.

"Alright, alright." He dropped to a knee. "Ms. Suzuki, I love you. Always have since the moment I met you, and it's just gotten worse—I mean stronger—since then. Would you do me the great honor of becoming Mrs. Graham?"

She smiled. "Stand up, silly Billy."

He did.

She kissed him as long and hard as she ever had before.

"Of course, I will. I love you."

She looked at his hand holding the box and giggled again.

"I think you're supposed to open that and show me the ring."

"Oh, yeah."

He pulled the top back on the jewelry box and held it up to her.

"Oh my God, Billy! It's gorgeous, and you paid too much!"

"Do you *really* like it?"

"I love it, and I love you."

She put the ring on her finger, smiling as the light hit the diamond.

"It's perfect. Come here," she said.

She kissed him again and started unbuttoning his shirt.

"Really?" he asked. "I thought you said I had to put a ring on it first."

"I think you just did."

"I thought you meant the other one."

"I did, but I'm human, too, and I think we've waited long enough, unless you disagree."

He started unbuttoning her blouse, and she laughed again. He pulled his cell phone out of his pants pocket to put it on the counter beside them, but it went off in his hand.

"Not now," he complained.

"Duty calls," she said. "It won't be the last time, but we'll make plenty of our own time."

"Graham," he said into the phone. His face fell. "We'll be right there."

They pulled up outside the yellow crime scene tape.

A uniformed patrol officer recognized them and waved them forward. They stepped through a small crowd that had started to gather near the front of the convenience store. The patrol officer held the tape up so they could duck under it.

"The manager called us. Dumpster on the side," the officer said.

Billy nodded. He walked over to the trash bin and looked over the edge. The torso of a young woman lay on top of the usual pile of plastic bags and loose garbage. There were no arms or legs attached to the torso, which was naked.

He threw her away like she was litter, Billy thought.

A crime scene tech with a camera was standing nearby.

"I've taken the first round of shots," the tech said.

Billy nodded.

"No cameras on this side of the building," Becky said, her eyes sweeping the area.

Billy snorted. "Of course not. That might make it easy."

He saw John Foote's large frame ducking under the crime scene tape. Foote nodded to them as he passed them. He glanced over the edge of the dumpster and shook his head.

"Have you checked yet?" he asked Billy.

"No. Didn't really want to."

Foote nodded again. He pulled on a pair of plastic gloves and reached down, gently turning the torso on its side. He waved the crime scene tech over.

"Better get this one."

The tech took another couple of photographs.

Foote gently lowered the torso back into place.

"Butterfly tattoo on the back of the left shoulder," he half-whispered.

Billy nodded. "I'll call Tommy. He'll call Captain Brown."

Becky stepped close to Billy and squeezed his hand.

"If I didn't personally hate this bastard before, I do now," she said. "He just turned the happiest day of my life into the saddest night of Sam Brown's."

She squeezed Billy's hand again.

"Want me to call Jeff?"

24

Trask and Cam Turner sat around a coffee table with J. P. Barrett in Barrett's office.

"We're sure that it's Captain Brown's daughter?" Barrett asked.

"I'm afraid there's no doubt at all now," Trask answered. "The tattoo was there, and Sam and his wife had submitted DNA samples just in case … well, just in case something like this happened. The ME called me this morning. The DNA was a match, too."

"An indescribable tragedy," Barrett said. "I can't imagine what they must be going through." He shook his head. "Any word on a funeral service for their daughter?"

"Not yet," Cam said. "I worked with Sam on a few cases over the past couple of years. I called him to say how sorry I was to hear about the confirmation. He said that—rather than having other body parts turning up here and there—they had arranged to have Beverly's body frozen until they could have a single ceremony."

"God, what a horrible situation!" Barrett stood up and paced a little. "And her death also brings us to the unpleasant reason for this meeting."

He returned to the table and sat down again.

"I talked at some length with Bonita Baylor this morning, after I got off the phone with the attorney general. First of all, we've been given very explicit orders by the AG that the county will run the homicide prosecutions, unless and until the evidence raises some sort of federal connection to the murders themselves. I did receive permission to continue to investigate the drug angle as a federal matter, but Baylor—and, of course, our friend Ray Marsh—gets to call the shots on the murders."

Barrett looked at Trask. "Sorry, Jeff. We gave it a shot."

Trask nodded. "It's the right call. They have jurisdiction; we don't."

"So," Barrett continued, "the bottom line is, absent some extreme exigent circumstances, they make the calls on the murders. That means investigation, charging decisions, arrest. But—"

He paused.

"—we continue to work the dope angle. We are not surrendering our discretion on those matters, and I informed Ms. Baylor that I was detailing you, Jeff, to the Career Criminal Unit as a designated legal and investigative advisor on the drug case. I want you down there until one of two things happens first: (1) we identify this butcher and take him off the street, or (2) you find Gloomy. If that happens, you'll be busy back here getting ready for his trial again."

"Understood," Trask said. "How did Baylor take that news?"

"She didn't like it one bit. She said that if we were going to work it that way, she was going to assign Marsh to CCU as well."

"Wonderful," Trask said sarcastically.

"It gets worse," Cam added. "She's hired a retired police detective as an investigator for her office—"

"I read that in the paper," Trask said. "I thought that he was designated only to work police misconduct cases—kind of a one-man internal affairs bureau to placate the folks always alleging police brutality and excessive force."

"Not anymore," Barrett said. "He'll be going to CCU with Marsh."

"To counter any advice I might give, and to report back to Baylor," Trask noted.

"That's about the size of it," Cam agreed.

"Once I committed you, I didn't feel like I could back out," Barrett said. "She called my bet and raised it."

"At least I'm still in the hunt," Trask said. "As long as we get this guy, I don't care who gets the credit for it."

"We're all on that page," Barrett agreed. "What's the latest on the search for Gloomy?"

"Still in the wind," Trask answered. "We had a loose end in the sector northeast of Holt that Billy Graham and Becky Suzuki worked—I was riding with them—a venison processor who wasn't around. The marshals ran the property info and were able to get the guy's wife on the phone. She gave consent, so they checked it out. The building was locked down tight—padlocks on the outside, windows all secure—so it's a checked box now. Gloomy wasn't hiding there. There's a multi-state alert out for him, and the TV stations are running public service announcements. We're just waiting for some promising leads."

Barrett nodded. "That's the other reason I want you at CCU for now. The minute those leads come in, I want you to know about them."

"Understood," Trask said. He changed the subject. "Just FYI, Graham and Suzuki are now officially engaged. Lynn and I are treating them to a celebration dinner tonight at the freight yard bar-be-que. You're invited, Cam. Seven?"

"Count me in," Turner said.

"Boss?" Trask asked.

"Sorry," Barrett said. "I better maintain some separation from the other players for now."

WaShaun Stewart, Jr. cowered against the back of the cage in the old garage, shaking in fear.

He had come to with a terrible headache. The throbbing in his brain had been aggravated by the fact that he had been forced to spend the entire night listening to screams and some sort of machinery. The noises seemed to be coming from the inside of another building a short distance away. He was sure that the screams were from two separate women, since they often came simultaneously. He had no idea what was happening to the women; he did know he had never heard anything like those screams before. He was certain of one thing: he wanted no part of whatever was going on inside the other structure.

There had been no contact with whoever had knocked him out and put him in the cage. Gloomy had worn his fingers into bloody pulps in a futile attempt at prying an opening in the heavy-gauge wire pen. He had even tried digging through the floor, only to find that the dirt at the bottom of the cage just covered more of the metal mesh that formed the walls.

Sometime before dawn, the screams stopped for a while. The quiet put him into a daze. Stewart didn't know if he had slept or not. He didn't want to accept what seemed to be the reality of his situation, so what may have been a nightmare blended with what was actually occurring, creating a fog that was more than his mind could process.

He heard the screaming start again.

Just one woman this time? Yeah. Just one.

An interval of quiet. A short interval. Then a faint, pitiful sobbing.

She's not screaming, just crying now.

The doors to the old garage creaked open, the sunlight blinding him for a moment. The silhouette of a man stood in the doorway. Gloomy tried to shield his eyes from the glare.

What's that in his hand? A gun? A spear of some kind?

The figure came toward him, still a silent shadow framed by the bright sunlight surrounding it. He pressed harder against the back of the cage. The end of a pole suddenly shot through the mesh toward him, and he felt a sharp pain in his left thigh. He screamed, as much from fear and surprise as from pain. Then he blacked out again.

"Here's to our favorite new couple. Congratulations!" Trask held up his glass in a toast. "And a chance to pay Becky back for the last feast we had here."

Diners at several tables around them joined in a brief round of applause.

"I have an announcement to make as well," John Foote said from his seat next to Becky. He raised his wine glass. "I am announcing the opening of a formal, federal, financial investigation into Detective Billy Graham." Foote took Becky's left hand and held it up, displaying the engagement ring. "No way in hell do you buy a rock like that on a cop's salary. I know. I used to be one."

"Not that you'd know how much an engagement ring costs," Billy responded.

When the chuckles died down, Becky leaned across the table toward Lynn.

"We need some advice from someone who's done this the right way," she said. "How do you two stay happy together?"

"How do you know we're *both* happy?" Trask asked.

Lynn gave him a playful elbow in the ribs. "That's one way," she said. "Try to make each other laugh a little every day."

"I'll remember that," Becky said, smiling at Billy. "What else?"

"No cheap shots," Lynn said. "There's a little truth in that old saying that familiarity breeds contempt. The more you know about someone, the more there is to criticize *if you look for things to criticize.* There's always a cheap shot around if you're looking to take one. When you see those opportunities, remember all the good things, the things that made you fall in love in the first place. Look the devil in the face and smile, pass on by the criticism, and stay positive. Too much criticism can fracture the fragile male ego."

"I'll write that down for you," Billy said to Becky as he took out his pocket notepad. "Just in case you forget that one."

She tried to ignore him. She turned to Trask. "You agree? Any additions?"

"On a more serious note, I think that you two are starting with one of the same big advantages that we had," Trask said, putting his arm around Lynn. "You've seen each other *work.* Whether we want to admit it or not, a lot of what makes us who we are lies in our chosen professions. Lynn and I had common occupational interests; so do you and Billy. The fact that both of you do it well means there's something for each of you to respect in the other. I've seen each one of you learn from the other. The willingness to do that in other avenues of life will take you a long way."

"Amen," said Cam.

"You just said 'Amen' to Billy Graham," Foote remarked. He held up his glass again, then saw it was empty. "Damn. Oops. Sorry, Reverend."

Graham dipped his fingers in his water glass and flicked them toward Foote. "You are forgiven yet again."

"Blessed be the Colt Peacemakers," Foote responded. He turned to Trask. "I hear you're moving in with us tomorrow."

"Bright and early, to be followed in short order by one Raymond Marsh."

"Who will be towing a retired detective Dan Fuel," Cam added.

"The new county police inquisitor?" Foote asked. "I hadn't heard that one."

"I'm afraid so," Trask said. "Bonita Baylor decided to double up on my boss when he told her I wasn't taking my toys and going home." He looked at Billy. "What do I need to know about Mr. Fuel?"

"It takes a certain personality to have IAD as your career goal," Billy said. "You make your own career out of trying to ruin other cops' careers. I know the job needs to be done, but most of us rotate through Internal Affairs when we're *forced* to go there—it's an ugly and involuntary assignment. Bad cops need to go, but most of the cases I saw in IAD were just failures of human nature: bad judgment, not real corruption. You're never happy about taking people who used to be good officers off the beat. Fuel loved doing it. He's a sanctimonious prick. I guess Baylor couldn't find enough cops around to prosecute, so she's playing to her election base by turning Marsh and Fuel loose on us. 'Standing up to the feds.' That'll be her next campaign slogan."

"Why, Reverend!" Foote said in mock surprise.

"Looks like you're going to be having even more fun," Lynn said to Trask.

"Like a root canal without anesthetic."

25

HE WOKE up in another cage. He was groggy again, this time from the drugs that had been injected into his leg by the syringe on the end of the pole. As his eyes cleared, he saw the man watching him from across the room. When he finally managed to sit up in the cage, the man disappeared to Gloomy's left.

He bent over toward the front of his new cage, his eyes trying to follow his captor, but the white ceramic wall jutting out past the side of the cage prevented him from seeing around the corner. It did not, however, prevent him from hearing what was coming from that direction.

The woman's frantic pleas were pitiful at first, but they soon turned into the same nerve-scorching screams he had heard the night before. The realization hit him.

He waited for me to wake up before he started. He wanted me to hear this.

The screams came in waves. Horrifying, futile cries for relief that would never come mixed with protests against a searing pain that would never stop. In between, there were intervals of the metallic whirring of a bench grinder. Gloomy tried covering his ears, but the shrieking—first from the woman and then from the grinding wheel—tore through his hands and into his brain through his eardrums.

One of the women I heard last night was in this cage, waiting her turn! That's why there were two voices screaming. Now there's just one!

There was another interval of relative quiet, with the screams subsiding into guttural moans, pleas, and whimpering. Then the screaming resumed, only there were now *two* voices screaming again. This time, one of those voices belonged to WaShaun Stewart, Jr.

Trask watched as Billy added the columns to his event wall in the conference room. Graham was re-posting the kidnapping of Beverly Brown and the attempted abduction of Red Miller's friend, Sally. Both Graham and Trask turned when they heard voices in the hallway. They saw Raymond Marsh and Dan Fuel standing in the doorway.

"Is that what you were hiding from me, Detective?" Marsh asked, a nasty, accusatory tone in his voice.

Fuel stood behind Marsh, smiling. He was a slender, beak-nosed, balding man in his mid-fifties.

"It's what we had opened as a federal drug case, Ray," Trask said, trying to protect Billy. "Before the Brown girl's torso was found and identified, we had nothing connecting those dope-soaked cards and this serial killer. Once that connection was made, I told J.P. Barrett that this murder and the attempted kidnapping of the hooker belonged down here with the task force."

"You know you had a hunch all along that they were connected, Trask. Don't try to deny that." Marsh was almost snarling.

Same old Ray. Same anger management issues.

"I've never operated on hunches, Ray," Trask said calmly, knowing his control would irritate Marsh even more. "That's not my job. I follow evidence. You should try that some time."

"And you should remember your place while you're down here, Mr. Trask," Fuel said. "This is a Jackson County matter now."

"As it should be," Trask said, staring hard at Fuel. "And I—as a *federal* prosecutor—am here to give whatever assistance I can lend to your efforts."

Trask smiled confidently at Fuel as if he were warning off a street mugger.

I don't work for your county, your prosecutor, or you, backstabber. Don't try me.

Trask and Billy left the room as Marsh and Fuel began to scan the pages pinned to the wall. Billy followed Trask into Tommy Land's office. They shut the door behind them.

Land looked up from his desk.

"Jeff, do I have you to thank for this little clusterfuck?"

"That would be the Honorable J.P. Barrett, United States Attorney for the Western District of Missouri. I am doing his bidding by reporting to you for a while."

"And Tweedledee and Tweedledum in the conference room?"

"Bonita Baylor's idea, in response to Barrett's idea."

"That's what I thought. I'm going to give those two morons their own office space down the hall, out of the bullpen. It'll make them feel important, it'll keep them *somewhat* out of our hair, *and* it'll keep me—or someone else—from shooting them when they aren't looking. Hell, Marsh is bad enough, but putting Fuel in here is like sticking a cat in a dog pound. He's screwed several good cops since the county hired him back."

"A resumption of his IAD career," Billy Graham noted.

Land took a breath and shook his head. "Unbelievable. Where do *you* want to park yourself?" he asked Trask.

Trask shrugged. "Anywhere but in the office with those two."

Land laughed a little and took another breath. "That felt good. Of course, after the video I saw on the news, I might like to see a cage rematch of you and Marsh."

"No comment."

"There's an empty desk along the back wall next to Foote. Knock yourself out. Or someone else if you feel like it."

"I'm here to help. Just let me know how."

"Do what you do best, Jeff. Think."

Trask nodded and headed for his new desk.

Gloomy felt himself shaking uncontrollably. The last screams had stopped several minutes before, but there had been long periods of what sounded like sawing. Then the sawing finally stopped, and he heard footsteps approaching his pen from the left. He pressed instinctively against the back of the cage.

He's coming for me now! It's my turn!

Instead, the footsteps—rubber boots tromping and squeaking on the concrete slab floor—passed close by the front of his cage. The man was holding a severed head—holding it low as he passed so that Gloomy could get a good look at it. A hand in a rubber glove held the woman's lifeless skull by her hair—her mouth pulled open by a slack lower jaw, her eyes frozen, staring at Gloomy—as blood dripped from her neatly-sawed neck.

26

TRASK LEFT the federal courthouse about 10:00 a.m. and headed for the CCU building. Even though J.P. Barrett had detailed him to Sgt. Land's task force for the foreseeable future, Trask still had his drug section to supervise, and an hour of file reviews in the morning, combined with another hour in the afternoon, let him keep his finger on the pulse of the unit.

I haven't seen that one before, he thought, as he pulled into one of the parking spaces in front of CCU. A new Dodge Charger, dark blue, and painted with the words, "Jackson County Prosecutor's Office," was parked in the slot next to him. *I guess Marsh and Fuel got a new ride to go with their new assignments.*

Trask went inside and sat down at his new desk next to John Foote.

"I know you just got here, but we need to take a ride," Foote said.

"Okay." Trask shrugged and followed Foote back out to the parking area. They walked past Trask's Jeep and the new Charger.

"I see you've noticed Fuel's new wheels," Foote said as they got to his Expedition.

"Just the outside."

"They gave him a police radio so he could monitor any division's calls," Foote said. "A real big brother to look over everybody's shoulders."

Trask climbed into the front passenger seat of the Expedition. "Where are we going?"

"You tell me. I just needed to get out of there for a bit. It's been a helluva morning."

Trask thought for a moment. "The ME's office. I have a few questions for our friend, Dr. Carter."

"Works for me."

"What's been going on?"

"Marsh and Fuel have been concentrating on the Brown girl and Sally the hooker," Foote began. "They're obsessed with those two events rather than the other victims because they think there must be a reason you were hiding those files from them. They've been in the bullpen grilling Billy and Becky since the doors opened this morning. They were talking about getting a warrant to search Red Miller's house."

Trask grunted. "With what for probable cause?"

Foote nodded. "Exactly, and that's what Billy asked them as well. He told Marsh, 'All you have for an affidavit is that Miller knew Sally, who has disappeared, and that his pecker doesn't work.'"

"An accurate summary. I was there with them for the interview."

"Right. But then Fuel piped in with, 'We could always ask him for consent.'"

"Which Red Miller, not knowing any better, would probably give them."

"Yeah, and he doesn't know that he'll be consenting to a police search, not a Bureau search."

Trask knew the difference, having seen both. The FBI was thorough, but they usually tried to put everything back in its place, to leave a house like they found it. The cops literally tossed a house, leaving everything in the middle of a room's floor. For a double amputee like Miller, it would take him a week to put his home back together.

"That would suck."

"Maybe somebody should tell him not to consent."

Trask paused. "Bad idea, John. Baylor and her hounds are just looking for interference like that right now. Let me think about this."

Foote did exactly that, keeping quiet until they reached the Medical Examiner's building.

"I'll meet you inside," Trask told Foote.

He waited until John had gone through the front door, then Trask pulled out his cell phone. He punched in a search phrase, found the phone number for *The Outlook*, and called the number. He asked for Jimmy Bishop.

"Mr. Trask?" Bishop answered.

"Would you be interested in a confidential tip this morning, Jimmy?"

"Always. I won't give you up."

"Like my statements weren't being recorded at the courthouse?"

"That was an accident. I swear it."

"It's okay; I'm glad you got the video. It saved me some grief."

"That's good. What do you have?"

"You ever been to Dogpatch?"

Gloomy finally collapsed, the product of exhaustion and weakness. He'd only had a few sips of water in the last three days, and being forced to hunch over in the cages had contributed to the strain on his body. He listened again for any sign that his captor might be in the building. He hadn't heard any signs of life in the room for hours, so he finally curled up in a fetal ball and let himself sleep.

He was awakened by another stabbing pain in his leg. His eyes flew open just in time to see the pole with the drug dart on the end of it being pulled back out of the cage. He was unconscious again in seconds.

When he awoke an hour later, he found that he couldn't move his arms or legs. He looked up at the ceiling and saw his reflection in a mirror.

"Any estimate on how long she'd been dead?" Trask asked. "The Brown girl? The torso?"

"Hard to be precise," Dr. Carter said, "At least in terms of hours. Too many variables. Even with the variables, though, I'd say she'd been killed within the twenty-four-hour period prior to the torso being found in the dumpster. It was a fresh homicide."

Trask looked at Foote. “He’s keeping his victims alive before he kills them. She’d been missing for days.”

“I’d agree with that for another reason,” Carter said. “We always check the contents of the stomach as part of the autopsy. Her stomach was empty, shrunken. She hadn’t eaten in quite a while.”

“Anything on the toxicology screen?” Foote asked.

“No. Not that I expected to see anything,” Carter answered. “If your theory about the pink is accurate, it’s half-life in the body is so short it would have all been dissipated—excreted or dissolved—in much less time than that period of captivity.”

“He wanted them fully aware when he started to work on them,” Trask thought out loud.

Foote’s phone buzzed.

“Yeah, Billy? Shit. I’ll tell Jeff. Thanks.” He clicked off the call. “Marsh and Fuel are on the way out to Miller’s place.”

Trask nodded. “Figured as much.”

Trask sipped a Dos Equis as the local evening newscast began on the TV. Lynn stood behind him as the anchor introduced the first story.

“Our lead story tonight is one of what is alleged to be police abuse, and in an ironic twist, the officer involved is the same officer recently hired by the Jackson County Prosecutor’s Office to monitor allegations of excessive force by the police. A local journalist captured the aftermath of a search at the home of a veteran of both Gulf Wars, a veteran who lost both his legs in defense of his country.”

The television screen shifted to scenes of the inside of Red Miller’s house. Each room was a disaster area, with drawers emptied and furniture overturned into the middle of the floor.

Jimmy came prepared; took his good videocam.

“I interviewed Mr. Miller,” Jimmy Bishop said, speaking into his camera, “the owner of this home and a veteran who lost both his legs in the second Gulf War. He told this reporter that he had consented to what he thought would be a courteous and careful search of his home. You can see just how courteous and careful that search turned out to be. Mr. Miller said that some priceless articles in his baseball memorabilia collections were damaged in this search, and that those items are irreplaceable.

“Mr. Miller indicated that—because of his disability—it will take him several days to return his home to a useable condition. Many of the areas of the home cannot now be accessed by Mr. Miller, who cannot navigate those rooms in his wheelchair because the searchers left such a mess in his house.

“Mr. Miller identified the officers conducting this search as Dan Fuel and Raymond Marsh of the Jackson County Prosecutor’s Office. He said they refused to tell him what they were looking for and left without taking a single item for evidence. If that is true—”

Bishop paused for effect, sweeping the wrecked living room with his camera.

“—then all of this was for nothing.”

The scene returned to the news anchor desk.

“We reached out to Bonita Baylor, the Jackson County Prosecuting Attorney for a response,” the anchor said. “She has not yet provided us with that response.”

“What a couple of shitheads!” Lynn exclaimed. “I wonder how Jimmy what’s-his-name got there so fast.”

“Good reporters have their sources,” Trask said. “It’s Jimmy Bishop, the kid from *The Outlook*.” He took a long pull on his beer.

27

"ONE OF MY friends at the county courthouse called," Tommy Land said. "He was in the hallway outside Bonita Baylor's office when Marsh and Fuel got there this morning. She apparently threatened to fire both of them, then she ordered them to go back out to Red Miller's place and help him clean up. I don't think the newscasts last night fit her re-election theme. The problem was —when the dummies got back to Dogpatch—a whole bunch of VFW old-timers got in their faces. They had seen the news last night and were already helping Red put his house back together. I guess Marsh and Fuel ended up looking down the barrels of several shotguns. They were threatened with eating large quantities of buckshot if they trespassed on Miller's property."

"Too bad we didn't get video of *that* on the news," Trask said. "The kid from *The Outlook* must be slipping."

"Something like that," Land said, looking at Trask for any signs of an admission.

"What?"

"Nothing. Anyway, Marsh and Fuel are back at the county in their old offices where Ms. Baylor can keep a closer eye on them. They are at least *physically* out of our hair for now. We still have to report any developments on the serial killer to Marsh, and Fuel is supposedly still monitoring the investigation

—meaning any officer involved in the investigation—but they won't be working in our building here."

"I guess we have Jimmy Bishop to thank for that."

Land looked at Trask again. "Yeah, I guess."

They were interrupted by Becky Suzuki standing in the door of Land's office.

"We have another severed leg in the river."

"Where this time?" Land asked.

"Just downstream from the Chouteau Bridge."

"Of course," Land responded.

Trask nodded. *That bridge is a convenient spot: not as heavily trafficked as the downtown bridges, and a great place to throw evidence into the biggest dumpster in the metro—the muddy Missouri River.*

"You and Billy," Land made the assignment.

"And me." Trask assigned himself.

Land nodded.

They pulled up behind a couple of marked units already parked on a road close to the river. A uniformed officer waved them down toward the water. Trask followed Billy and Becky as they walked through trees and brush until they reached the bank. Two more uniformed officers and a crime scene technician were waiting. Yellow crime scene tape had been stretched to form a three-sided barrier. The fourth side of the cordon was the river.

"A fisherman walking the bank found it and called it in," one of the patrol officers said. "We're waiting on the ME's guy to get here to transport it to the morgue."

Billy nodded. "Got all your pics?" he asked the crime scene tech.

"Yeah. I'm getting good at these. You have to make sure the sun's not reflecting back at you off the water."

He pointed to the leg. It was still under an inch or two of water. The leg was bare, severed at the top of the thigh, and hung up under a piece of driftwood that was partially stuck in the riverbank.

"Maybe it'll match to Captain Brown's daughter," Becky said. "The sooner we collect everything, the sooner they can bury her."

I'd like all *of my daughter's body parts please,* Trask thought. *What a horrible position to be in. I can't imagine what the Browns are going through with this. Maybe some numbness will set in for them.*

"The DNA process is a lot faster than it used to be," Billy said. "We should know in a couple of days."

He took his own camera out and took a couple of photos.

Those will be on the conference room wall soon.

Trask's cell phone buzzed in his pocket. The screen indicated that the contact was Sgt. Tommy Land, KCMOPD.

"What's up, boss?"

"Yeah, like you *really* work for me," Land said, chuckling.

"Until otherwise assigned."

"Be that as it may, a couple of things. One, when we finish this call, you need to call Cam Turner."

"Okay."

"Two, I've had the commanders of Central and East Patrol divisions brief their people to be on the lookout for more body parts showing up on Independence Avenue. Central Patrol has the west end; East Patrol has the eastern side. We're checking dumpsters at convenience stores and gas stations fairly regularly, and we're trying to make sure all the owners keep their surveillance cams operational."

"Okay."

"One of Central Patrol's units checked a dumpster at a convenience store about an hour ago. He found a pair of sneakers with no laces lying in the garbage. We're pulling the video from the surveillance camera to see what we can see. The shoes had the letters 'LCJ' stenciled on them, top and back."

"Would that mean Livingstone County Jail?"

"It would. I called up there to see what size they had issued Gloomy, and the sneaks we found are the same size. They were pretty muddy, but I was told there might be a small streak of blood on one, so I had 'em take the shoe to the lab for a DNA confirmation."

"Nice work, boss."

"Thanks. In the meantime, I've put everybody on notice to assume that Gloomy's back in town."

"Fair enough."

"Call Cam."

"Will do."

Trask called Turner.

"Glad you called in," Cam said. "You have a status hearing on Gloomy's case in front of Magistrate Judge ReeSHARD HorNAY in thirty minutes. Can you cover it?"

"Doesn't he know that Gloomy's in escape status? How the hell are we supposed to have a status hearing without a defendant or defense counsel? Stewart never even hired anybody to replace Alvin Black!"

"I'm just the messenger. Can you get back in time?"

Trask checked his watch. "Yeah, I'll be there."

Trask had Billy and Becky drop him at the front of the courthouse. He took the elevator to the fourth floor and made it to Horney's courtroom with two minutes and fourteen seconds to spare. Theresa Owens smiled at him from the clerk's desk.

"You're usually here about five minutes early. We were about to call your office."

"We were at the riverbank near the Chouteau Bridge," Trask said.

"Oh no! More body parts?"

"I'm afraid so."

"That's horrible. That case won't be coming up here, will it?"

"Probably not."

A light on her desk let Ms. Owens know that the Hon. Richard Horney was about to make his entrance.

"All rise!" she announced.

Since he had no audience—only his staff and Trask, no defendant or opposing counsel in the courtroom—Horney walked in briskly, waving them to be seated as he climbed into his throne.

"We originally had this date and time set for a pre-trial conference in this matter, Mr. Trask, but the Marshals' Service informs me that they still have not returned the defendant to custody. Is that correct?"

"Yes, Your Honor. Mr. Stewart remains in escape status."

"Exactly how did he manage that, if you don't mind me asking?"

"Our contact with the transport deputy indicated that Mr. Stewart pulled a gun—or at least what the deputy *thought* was a gun—on the deputy during the return transport from the courthouse here to Livingstone County. When the jail personnel searched Stewart's cell back in the county jail, they found a good deal of soap shavings and the remnants of a bar of soap concealed in his bunk. It was their best guess that Stewart had carved a gun out of the soap and used that to bluff the bus driver. He took the driver's *real* handgun, hit him with it, cuffed the driver to the steering wheel, and got away on foot. Dogs were used in a search of the area, but they were unable to locate Stewart."

"Mr. Stewart has not shown much respect for this court, has he?"

Trask did his best to maintain a poker face. *For the Court?!! Is THAT what this hearing is about? Gloomy has no respect for anybody or anything. He kills five people and slings poison all over town, but you're concerned with his failure to appear for a hearing after escaping from custody?*

"No, Your Honor, he has not."

"I'm issuing a bench warrant for his arrest." Horney stood proudly and slammed his gavel down to emphasize the imperial edict he had just issued.

Well, I'm sure THAT will solve EVERYTHING then. A hundred cops out looking for his hide can't turn him up, but I'm sure your bench warrant will have him here in short order, prostrating himself and seeking your majesty's forgiveness.

"Yes, Your Honor."

"We are adjourned," Horney declared.

Trask thanked Cam for the lift back to CCU. He checked in with Tommy Land in his office.

"Any more developments?" he asked Land.

"Shoes are at the lab. Leg is at the morgue. We should have the surveillance video from the convenience store tomorrow. How about on your end?"

"If and when we ever catch Gloomy, we can add failure to appear to the list of counts against him. Judge Horney seemed convinced the additional beef would bring him in forthwith."

"This is where I reach into my desk drawer and pull out a bottle of whiskey," Land quipped. "In the movies."

"I wonder who's writing *this* script," Trask said.

"We've asked patrol to double their drive-throughs around 51st Street," Land said. "If Gloomy's back, we're sure to see some action pick up. He'll be going after witnesses, people he thinks were witnesses or who might become witnesses. He'll be shooting up the Trey Wall again, too."

"Foote?"

"I've asked John and his Bureau contacts to double the watch teams on our cooperating witnesses at the out-of-town hotels. This is getting expensive."

"Glad I don't have to do budgets."

"You got that right."

Trask walked into the conference room. He found Graham and Suzuki there, staring at the event summaries on the wall.

"I have one question," Billy said. "It's not his turf; it's too far north. Why would Gloomy ditch his prison sneaks on Independence Avenue?"

28

TRASK LOOKED over Billy's shoulder at the computer monitor. Becky Suzuki and John Foote stood on either side of him, doing the same.

"Here's where it starts," Billy said. He pressed a key, and the surveillance video began at the cued spot.

A figure entered the frame from the top, from behind the convenience store. He was wearing a blue, Kansas City Royals hooded sweatshirt, a blue, Kansas City Royals baseball cap, sunglasses, and gloves. The bill of the baseball cap totally concealed the man's face. In less than five seconds, the man approached the dumpster, threw the sneakers inside, and disappeared the way he came.

"That gives us the square root of nothing," Foote said.

"Maybe a little more than nothing," Becky protested. "Gloomy's a Crip, and Crips wear blue. All that Royals gear was blue. The guy looked to be about the same height as Gloomy, and—if it *is* Gloomy—he certainly knows that every cop in town is looking for him, so he'd be pretty likely to hide his face as much as possible."

"Granted," Billy said. "But opening day is around the corner, so there are only about a hundred-thousand guys in town wearing Royals gear at the moment."

"And who else would have a reason to be carrying those sneakers around and tossing 'em?" she asked.

"Good point," Trask said. "And one for which I have no answer. Half the hoodies *wearing* hoodies in that neighborhood might find those sneaks, lace them up, and wear them like a badge of honor. The jail stencils would qualify as a style statement. Gloomy is one of the few who would certainly *not* want to be wearing them right now."

"Thank you." Becky gave Billy's shoulder a playful poke.

"We have to assume that it's him, for now," Foote said. "We could start interviewing all the relatives on 51st Street again, but we'd just get the same lies we always got before. I say we wait and let him make the first play."

"That makes the most sense," Trask agreed. "I just hope nobody else dies in the process."

"Maybe Judge Horney's bench warrant will do the trick and he'll turn himself in," Billy said.

Becky poked him again.

Tommy Land came walking out of his office and into the bullpen.

"The lab called. The DNA came back. The leg was Beverly Brown's."

"Now they're just missing three limbs and a head," Foote said. "Maybe our butcher will be real nice and leave 'em all in one spot. Of course, the next head we find will be the first one."

"Why do you think he stopped dropping the body parts around the track?" Billy asked.

Trask looked at Land, giving him a cue.

"I had asked Central and East Patrol to start watching all the stores and gas stations," Land said. "The increased visibility probably made him go back to the river for his dumps."

"Do we want to pull back on that?" Foote asked, looking at Trask, and then Land.

"Your call," Trask said to Land. "We've got a better chance of recovering and identifying limbs and torsos if we find them on dry land. There's a lot less tissue damage than what we get from the river and the things swimming in it. Maybe your emphasis on cameras will turn up something better than this one." He pointed at Billy's monitor.

"I'll make the calls," Land said, nodding. "Same emphasis, less visibility. Maybe we can at least speed up Beverly Brown's funeral. I've also got to forward the DNA lab report to Ray Marsh."

"That'll get things moving," Foote said.

"Something else is moving," Trask said. "I'll be in the head for a minute."

He walked to the far end of the bullpen and the men's room. As soon as he closed the stall and sat down, his cell phone buzzed.

It never fails. Always in the bathroom. I'll call them back in a bit.

He checked the number as he left the bathroom.

I wonder what HE wants.

Trask stepped out into the parking lot. He hit the dial icon for the number. The call was answered at *The Outlook.*

"Jimmy Bishop, please." Trask didn't wait long.

"Mr. Trask?"

"What's up, Jimmy?"

"You saw the news. How'd I do?"

"You're asking me for a grade?"

"Yeah, I guess I am."

"You didn't lie. It didn't look like it was tailored to a political agenda. I'll take that from a journalist these days."

"I'll take *that* as at least a passing grade, then."

"Okay. What can I *really* do for you, Jimmy?"

"I hear you guys found another body part."

"That's not officially on my plate, Jimmy. The serial killer investigation is a Jackson County matter, assigned to your friend and mine, Ray Marsh."

"I don't think he'll be taking my calls."

"I think you're right, but I wouldn't call Ray if I were you. He's not the one running for re-election and who would jump at the chance for any good, free publicity."

"Bonita Baylor?"

"That's the one. I have a hunch she might welcome a chance to clear the air with your publication. I will give you one suggestion, though."

"What's that?"

"The location where the leg was found is pretty important, from what I understand."

"Thanks. That's good to know."

"Will this be on TV again, or in print?"

"Print. *The Outlook* comes out again in two days. If Ms. Baylor takes my call today, I should be able to make the deadline."

"I look forward to reading it. Jimmy?"

"Yes?"

"All this is off the record again, okay?"

"You got it."

Trask ended the call, then opened the call memory on his phone and erased it. He started back inside, but met Billy and Becky coming out the door as he was going in.

"It's an arm this time. In the river at Sugar Creek," Billy said.

29

TRASK SAT at his desk in the CCU, next to John Foote, who was reading the new edition of *The Outlook* out loud. Graham, Suzuki, and Land stood beside Foote's desk eating doughnuts while John read.

The Bishop kid followed the lead, alright, Trask thought. *Good. Maybe I mean "leak," instead of "lead." Whatever. He followed it. As long as he protects his source, it's all good.*

"In a statement made today to this reporter, Jackson County Prosecuting Attorney Bonita Baylor indicated that she had directed the police to focus their recovery efforts on the banks of the Missouri River, where two severed limbs have been recently recovered."

I wonder how the Chief of Police feels about Ms. Baylor directing his investigation. Even on the fed side, we know to suggest, *rather than order. The Chief has to pay attention to Bonita to get his cases in court, but he doesn't work* for *her.*

"Ms. Baylor also said that the recent search in Blue Summit of the residence of Devin Miller had been what she called a 'terribly unfortunate mistake,' although members of her office who had conducted that search had been following what they believed to be valid leads at the time.

"'We offered our most sincere apologies to Mr. Miller after the incident,' Baylor said. 'We wish him the best. This series of gruesome murders has us all on edge.' Baylor told *The Outlook* that her office and the Kansas City Police Department would follow every lead offered to them in an effort to bring the killer to justice. She said that a dedicated call-in line had been set up *in her office* for anyone wishing to report any leads, and she said that all tips would receive appropriate investigative attention."

"That should give Marsh and Fuel something to do with their time," Foote said. "I remember having to man the FBI complaint center phone after the twin towers got hit in 2001. We got calls from every ghost chaser in a three-state area."

Foote changed his voice into a rural drawl.

"*I'd like to report a bunch of Arabs driving south on 71 Highway.*

How do you know they were Arabs, sir?

I seen 'em. They was in a blue pickup truck.

How were they dressed, sir? Turbans?

Normal. They didn't have turbans on or nuthin.' Prob'ly didn't want anybody to know they was Arabs, ya know?

Did you happen to get the tag number?

Naw, they was goin' fast and headin' the other direction.

Thank you for the call, sir."

"What if something valid comes in on that line?" Trask asked. "It's not like Ray and Fuel are going to jump in their new car and drive down here to share it with us."

"We'll just have to get there first," Land said. "Citizen tips can make a case, but even *we* don't know exactly what we're looking for yet. I trust our professional eyes and ears to find something before the public does. I hope that'll be the case."

He paused and shook his head.

"At least Bonita and her two ace sleuths haven't leaked the deaf-mute thing to the press yet."

"Should *we* leak that?" Billy asked. "Might generate some *valid* citizen tips."

"I don't think so," Land said. "It's too singular. We could get bogus confessions, copycats, and it might chase our guy to ground for quite a while. I'd rather have him out there making mistakes."

"And killing more girls?" Becky asked. She realized what she'd just said. "Sorry. "

"It's okay," Land said. "I just think that if we can get him back to his old hunting ground—the track, Independence Avenue—we've got a better chance of grabbing him *before* he kills again, maybe while he's dropping off another piece of a victim, maybe while he's looking for another one."

"*The Outlook* article might help with that," Billy said. "It made it sound like we're pitching tents on the riverbanks now."

Graham's cell phone rang. He took the call, frowning as he turned the phone off.

"That was the lab. We thought the arm might be another part of the Brown girl. It wasn't. They *did* get another DNA match, though."

He looked at Becky.

"Good job on collecting samples at her house. It was Miller's friend, Sally."

"You call Miller," Land told Billy. "Tell him about Sally. Thank him for his cooperation with us and apologize to him again for Marsh and Fuel tossing his house. Let him know we tried to stop that before it happened."

"Okay, boss." Billy nodded.

"I get to call Marsh again," Land said.

30

TRASK AND LYNN watched the evening news after feeding the pups.

"Bonita Baylor had a news conference earlier this afternoon on the serial killer," Lynn said. "That'll be the lead story on an otherwise slow news day. It'll be a replay. It was on live about 1:00. You'll love Marsh."

"Sorry I missed it earlier. We were out hunting Gloomy in his old neighborhood. No luck, of course."

Trask watched as Baylor tried to reassure the city that everything was under control.

Sure, you have all the best resources out looking for this butcher. But—so far—he's made an ass out of all of us, just more so you and your team than anyone else.

"We are now manning our task force line twenty-four hours a day. All it will take to bring this killer to justice is for an alert citizen or citizens to call. We are ready to act on your tips. I would now like to introduce my assistant, Raymond Marsh, who will be leading the prosecution of this matter."

"She's trying to rehabilitate him by putting him on TV," Trask told Lynn.

"You got that right. Just watch."

"We *have* made mistakes so far in this investigation," Marsh began, "but those mistakes were motivated by a desire to save lives, to get this killer off our streets as soon as possible. We felt at the time that the stakes justified a gamble. We guessed wrong, and we would like to again extend our sincere apologies to the gentleman whose house was searched. We have been able to officially clear him in this case."

"How the hell did they do that?" Trask asked. "I don't think Red Miller is good for any of these murders, but we certainly haven't been able to clear him."

"Shhh!" Lynn pointed back to the TV screen.

Marsh was still at the microphone. "That erroneous lead was in large part developed as part of a federal investigation which—at the time—had been improperly concealed from this office. Because the gentleman in Blue Summit had been a suspect in that federal case, and because we had not been provided with *all* of the relevant information prior to our search, we drew conclusions which we would not have drawn, had we been presented with all the facts."

Trask's normally controlled demeanor left him in a heartbeat.

"What a lying, two-faced, sack of horse shit!" he yelled.

Lynn stepped in front of the TV.

"It's an expensive set, Jeff. Don't throw anything at it."

Trask slumped back in his chair in disbelief.

"Of all the nerve—"

Marsh continued. "Ms. Baylor has provided Investigator Fuel and me with all the resources this city and county can assemble. Rest assured that we are on this case and we *will solve it!"*

Trask turned the TV off.

"I can't take any more of that."

"You got the gist of it."

Trask's cell phone went off.

"I'll put your dinner in the fridge," Lynn said.

"Jeff?" Cam Turner asked.

"He's not here," Trask said.

"Well then, I hope he's on the phone with CCU," Turner said, laughing. "Did you catch the news?"

"Just turned it off. Didn't want to hurl."

"Call your new office as soon as you can. They have a surprise for you."

"Okay."

Trask phoned Tommy Land.

"I just got off the phone with Cam Turner," Land said.

"That's not possible. I just got off the phone with him," Trask replied.

"Okay, Mr. Literal. I talked to him a few minutes ago, right before he called you. After that presser with Marsh today, I figured Cam and Barrett might want to hold one of their own based on what just went down."

"So tell me what just went down, already."

"Right. We had to go pick up another amputated limb. Guess where."

"The river."

"No."

"The track?"

"Nope."

"I give up."

"Just off Ward parkway in the high-rent district, south of the Plaza. On Ray Marsh's front porch."

"WHAT?!"

"Yep. Our killer apparently saw the news conference, too, and wanted to give Marsh the finger, only he couldn't do that in public, so he gave him a leg, so to speak."

"Surveillance cams?"

"Same old Jeff, back to working the case. Nope. No camera, not even one on the doorbell. Marsh said he hadn't had the time to get a system installed yet. He just moved in. He walked out on his porch after his dog barked, and the leg was lying there. One of those deaf-mute cards was under the leg, too. Lucky for Marsh he didn't pick it up. He nearly broke his neck, anyway. Tripped over the leg and fell off the porch."

"Think it's the Brown girl's? Or Sally's?"

"Not a chance. This one's black. It's at the morgue now. There's another twist. Doc Carter at the morgue said that it's not a female leg. He's gonna run the DNA tests to make sure, but he said that after looking at the feet—I mean the foot; there's only one foot on one leg, you know—he's pretty sure this one belonged to a guy. He said it still looks like the same killer, though, from the method of amputation."

Trask sat in silence for a moment.

"Jeff?"

"I'm here."

"What do you think?"

"I do think Cam and Barrett need to hold their own presser tomorrow, and I think I need a drink."

31

"J.P. JUST ISSUED A WRITTEN PRESS STATEMENT," Cam said. "He didn't want to do a full-blown conference and get into any more of a back-and-forth with Bonita Baylor than he had to. He told the press that Devin Miller was never a suspect in any federal investigation, and that this office never improperly withheld information from Marsh or Baylor concerning the serial killer."

"Sounds good," Trask said, continuing to type. He was behind his desk in his regularly assigned office in the federal courthouse.

"What are you working on?" Cam asked him.

"Motion to Suspend Trial Based Upon Anticipated Notice of Death," Trask said. "We got the DNA results back on Marsh's leg just before you walked in. I mean on the leg from Marsh's porch. I think if we ran Marsh's DNA it might come back as an alien life form. Anyway, it *was* a guy's leg, not a woman's. And it matched a sample we'd taken on a buccal swab downstairs when we arrested the guy."

"And that guy was?"

"WaShaun Stewart, Jr.," Trask said. "Gloomy. We don't know as an absolute certainty that he's dead—he may just be missing a leg—but odds are we won't be taking him to trial. At any rate, if he isn't dead, he's very likely to need a continuance to recuperate from his amputation."

"Wow!" Cam said. "You're on a roll, aren't you?"

"Oh, yeah. Lost one serial killer to another one. That's a first, even for me. Not a good day to hit the casinos. I'd lose holding a royal flush."

"I think I know one thing you'll win," Cam said.

"Really? What's that?"

"I think the court will probably grant that motion you're working on."

"You may leave now," Trask said. "I'm going back to CCU to see if Jimmy Hoffa's body turns up."

"I thought it would be a good idea to just sit in here and brainstorm for a bit," Sgt. Land said. Trask, Foote, Graham, and Suzuki had joined him in the CCU conference room. Trask saw that Billy had already added an incident summary for WaShaun Stewart, Jr., to the event wall.

"Billy, do you want me to transfer my Gloomy wall hangings over here now?" he asked Graham.

"No, I think you can close everything but his murder at this point," Billy replied. "Besides, the room isn't big enough. Not enough wall space."

"Let's get serious," Land said. "I've got every suit and brass collar in town looking over my shoulder now, and that's just the PD. The prosecutor's office is even worse. Baylor and Marsh are hopping mad now because of that leg and because J.P. Barrett essentially called them liars this morning."

"And whose fault was that?" Trask asked. "You tell a lie and try to blame someone else, and you get called on it."

"I know, I know," Land said, nodding. "Like you said, though, we're all *supposed* to be on the same team, and trying to stop this guy. Thoughts?"

He looked at John Foote.

"Well, to start with," Foote said, "Billy's instincts were spot on. That obviously was *not* Gloomy throwing the prison sneaks in the dumpster. So, we can add a couple of items of Royals gear to the perp's profile."

Some snickers followed.

"Anything besides that, John?" Land asked. "Maybe something helpful?"

"Sure. Gloomy disappeared up by Holt. That's not too far from where Beverly Brown had her flat tire. A few miles away, maybe, but—as has been suggested before—our guy may live or work up that way, northeast of town."

"He hunts the track—Independence Avenue—but takes targets of opportunity if they appear in front of him, and that's two targets of opportunity who disappeared up that way," Billy said.

"And if that's accurate, our guy may live or work along New Hope Creek, or at least somewhere in Holt," Trask observed. "We don't know how long or far Gloomy was in the water, or which direction he headed after the dogs lost him, but I agree that we should be thinking about that area. Something else has been bugging me though."

"What's that?" Land asked.

"Well, we now have a pattern. Bev Brown gets taken at the site of her flat tire, but her torso doesn't show up until several days later. The ME says it was a fresh kill, and her stomach was empty. The bottom line is she was held captive for that interval of time. Sally the hooker gets taken out of her home in Dogpatch, and—like the Brown girl—probably gets dissected days later. Now we see the same thing with Gloomy. He disappears, we look for him for days, and only after a few days does his leg show up on Marsh's doorstep, and it's another fresh dissection. Time of death in each case was within a day of the body part showing up."

"The captivities may have even overlapped," Becky noted.

Trask nodded. "I was thinking the same thing. Our perp is showing a common trait of serial killers, and that's escalation. He gets off on the terror he inflicts, and he needs a steady stream of victims to keep his adrenaline going. He may even have one victim waiting while he butchers another one. Like Becky said, the captivities are probably overlapping."

"And if he's keeping at least two victims locked up at any particular time, he has to keep hunting," Billy said. "We don't have any new missing persons reports in the area. Who does he slaughter after Gloomy?"

"I don't think he'll be reluctant to go hunting again," Foote said. "He picked up Marsh's challenge from the press conference and threw it right back in his face. The move with Gloomy's leg was as brazen as anything I've ever seen."

"He knows the track like the back of his hand," Trask said. "Predators generally stick to their favorite, most productive hunting grounds."

"And he was able to ditch Gloomy's sneakers on the track right under our noses," Becky added.

"That was another brazen move," Foote said. "He obviously knew where the surveillance cam was on the side of the store, and how to avoid getting identified while he was throwing another clue at us."

"He also knew how to switch his dumps to the river when we put too many units on the track." Graham shrugged. "So, what do we do?"

"As far as the track goes, pull back but keep watching," Land said. "I already put that word out to the patrol divisions."

"Is Gloomy's identity out yet?" Trask asked. "I mean, that it was his leg on Marsh's porch?"

"No," Land said. "I asked the ME to sit on it as long as he could."

"Good," Trask said. "I almost put it out on front street today myself, but I haven't filed the motion yet. We're supposed to notify the court if a defendant dies so that they can clear their docket. It can wait a couple of days."

"What do you have in mind?" Land asked.

"We aren't going to get anywhere asking folks if they know anything about people being dissected in their neighborhood," Trask said. "If they knew something that specific, we'd have heard it by now. But as long as Gloomy's death isn't public knowledge, we have an excuse to go back up around Holt and pretend that we're still tracking him. We ask neighbors about neighbors with that as an excuse. We hope we get lucky."

"If that's the best idea you have, it's also the worst I've heard today," Land replied. "But it's also the *only* idea I've heard today, and it *is* a reason and a way to poke around our new target zone. Let's get up there before Marsh or Baylor talks to the ME and puts the word out on Gloomy. Jeff, you ride with Billy and Becky. Work north from the last point the dogs smelled Gloomy."

"That's the sector we had last time," Billy said.

"Good. Maybe someone will open up a little more to some familiar faces," Land said. "I'll ride with John. We'll go south."

32

"WE'LL TRY to see inside the homes this time," Billy said. "We do front door approaches if we can. Maybe they'll invite us in."

"Here we are again," Becky said as they pulled into the first driveway. "William Kirby."

They got out, walked to the door, and rang the doorbell.

Trask looked at his watch.

Just after four. Some of them may not be home yet.

Kirby was. The front door opened.

"Oh, it's you folks again. Still looking for that guy?"

"Yes, sir, we are," Billy said. "We still haven't found him. Anything unusual in the area since we were here last?"

"Nope. Same old Holt, Missouri. Quiet as a mouse."

Billy looked past Kirby into the front room.

"Hey, that's a real nice duck there on your mantle. Did you bag that one?" Graham asked.

"Yeah. Two seasons ago. Pretty Mallard, huh? Come on in and have a look."

He waved them inside. They entered the living room, and Billy concentrated on the duck.

Smooth. Becky and I can look at other things while they're occupied, Trask thought.

"It sure is. Did you do the mounting?" Billy asked.

"Naw. Guy up the road a bit, fellow named Dewey. He does some taxidermy work in addition to deer processing. Most of his mounts are deer heads, but he's pretty good with birds, too. I had to freeze that one for a bit before he could get to it. The cold did a little damage, but he was able to repair the damaged feathers and fix it up."

"Very pretty work," Graham said. "If I get one this year I know where to take it. Thanks."

"Do you live alone, Mr. Kirby?" Becky asked.

"Yeah. Wife died about four years back. Kids are grown and gone now."

"Just wondered if there was someone else in the home who might have seen or heard something," Becky explained.

"Afraid not. Got a couple of dogs in the backyard, but they haven't been raising a ruckus or anything like that."

Billy took a final look at the duck.

"Thanks for giving us a little more of your time," Graham said. "Please stay alert and be careful."

"Mr. Kirby, who are your neighbors to the north?" Trask asked. "They're our next stop."

"Mo Hemeter and his wife. They got a teenage boy still at home. Billy. Think he's in middle school. Doesn't drive yet."

"You've seen them out and about like normal?" Billy asked. "We're always worried that a fugitive like this one might be holding someone hostage, hiding in their home."

"Nothing out of the ordinary," Kirby said. "Billy catches the school bus out front. I saw him this morning, and I've seen Mo and his wife drive by a couple of times. They wave and I wave back."

Billy nodded. "Thanks again. We'll still check on them."

They walked back to the car.

"Do you really hunt duck?" Trask asked Billy as they drove down the road.

"No, I don't kill things other than fish," Billy replied. "It's quieter, and my future wife here wouldn't approve."

"I don't hate hunters," Becky said. "As long as it's for conservation or food, I understand it. I just couldn't do it myself."

"Gotcha," Trask said.

They pulled into the driveway of the Hemeter property.

When they rang the doorbell, a young boy—about fourteen— answered the door.

"Billy?" Graham asked him.

"Yes, sir."

"My name's Billy, too. We're police officers." Graham showed his badge. "We were here a few days ago and spoke to your mom. Are your folks home?"

"No, sir. Dad's still at work and Mom's out shopping. She told me you were looking for that escaped guy."

"Yes, and we still are," Becky said. "Have you or your parents seen or heard anything unusual in the neighborhood?"

"No ma'am."

Becky handed him a business card. "Please keep your doors locked and call us if you do, okay?"

"Sure will."

They returned to the car.

"Don't want to go inside without the parents' permission," Billy said.

Trask nodded. "Who's next?"

"Thomas Leggett," Becky answered. "He was getting home from a road trip when we came through the last time."

"He's married, has kids, and carries," Trask remembered.

"That's the one."

Leggett wasn't home, and neither were his wife or his children.

"Dewey?" Trask asked.

"Dewey," Billy said.

They pulled into the entrance to the dirt road. Trask saw that the camera was still on the pole in the trees. Billy pushed the button on the intercom and waited.

"Yeah? Who is it?"

"Police officers, Mr. Dewey. We were here looking for a fugitive."

"Oh yeah. You find that guy yet?"

"No, that's why we're here again."

"Well, I still ain't seen him, and I'm not home today. I got that intercom system rigged to where I can answer it on my cell phone, so that's how you're talkin' to me now."

"Oh, okay," Billy said. "Still haven't heard or seen anything unusual?"

"Nope, nuthin' at all."

"Well, thanks for your time. Has your neighbor up the road been around?"

"Who? Leggett?"

"No, sir; the other direction—the other deer processor."

"Oh, I haven't seen him since the season ended."

"Have you talked to him by phone or anything?"

Dewey laughed, his cackling lasting a few seconds.

"Naw, I ain't talked to Butch, but then nobody has. Butch is a deaf-mute."

Trask and the others exchanged surprised looks.

"You didn't mention that the last time, Mr. Dewey," Becky said.

"That's because—what was your name, young lady?"

"Detective Suzuki."

"Suzuki like the motorcycles?"

"Same spelling."

"Well, Detective Suzuki, I don't remember you asking me about that, or I'd have sure told you."

"How do you share business with him?" Trask asked.

"He writes notes and reads lips some," Dewey said through the intercom. "His wife does that sign language stuff and can interpret for him. She's usually there with him. I think I did tell you last time that if the chain's down, he's there. If it's not, he's not."

"What does Butch do when he's not cutting up venison?" Trask asked.

"They're over-the-road truckers," Dewey said. "That's another reason they're not at that shop too often. It stays locked up most of the time."

"You've been very helpful, Mr. Dewey," Billy said. "Thanks for the time."

"Happy to help," Dewey said. "Good luck."

Trask joined Billy and Becky back in the car. Becky radioed Land. Trask said he would call Barrett. Land said he'd have to call Marsh. Trask said something profane under his breath.

33

GIVEN THE CHOICE, Trask had opted to participate in the search of Butch the deer butcher's property with Billy Graham and Becky Suzuki.

It would be more interesting to watch Foote interrogate Butch and his wife, but Marsh and Fuel will be sitting in on that. We did promise the county prosecutor that her people could handle the homicide interrogations and arrests, and this way I won't get arrested for strangling Ray Marsh when he screws up the questioning.

"Seems like we've made this trip before," Billy said as he drove toward Holt. "Did you expect the Gannons to consent to this search like they did?"

"I don't know what to expect about this case anymore," Trask said. "Nothing has been in line with the few expectations I *did* have to this point. I sure never expected Gloomy's case to merge with this one."

"Think John will have any luck with the interrogation?" Becky asked.

"If Marsh will actually let him do it, he just might," Trask replied. "He has a lot to work with. Both Gloomy and Beverly Brown disappeared near Gannon's place, and those cards point to him as well. I spoke with John last night, and he agreed that we should have Gannon bring in his truck logs. They'll either provide an alibi for him, or they won't.

"The trick to the whole session will be working through the sign language interpreters. John found one in the Bureau's district office. Her job will be to monitor Mrs. Gannon as she translates for her husband. That'll take some time and patience. Marsh will be the wild card. He's both impatient and—in my opinion—incompetent. Add those traits to the pressure he's under to make an arrest and you've got all the makings of a catastrophe."

"You don't think Gannon's good for the murders?" Billy asked.

"I actually hope that he *is* good for them." Trask said. "If he is, the killings stop, and we get to move on."

They turned off the highway, made some turns, and were back on the road to Gannon's shed, a short distance past Willard Dewey's taxidermy sign. Billy pulled into the dirt entrance. He pulled out a set of keys.

"Mrs. Gannon said that one of these unlocks the lock on the chain, and the other keys should work on the padlocks on the shed," Graham said.

He tried the first key on the padlock securing the chain across the road. The lock popped open, and Billy pulled the chain to the side. He climbed back into the car, and they drove about fifty yards back into the trees.

Billy got out and tried one of the other keys on the padlock hanging on the main door to the shed. The lock popped open, and Billy swung the door outward.

Trask followed the detectives inside. Billy flipped a wall switch, and a single, naked bulb hanging from the center of the ceiling illuminated the room. Trask noticed a large table in the center of the shed. There were two freezers lined up against one wall, and a work bench was set up on the opposite wall. A pair of old kitchen-style wall cabinets hung on the wall above the work bench.

"First impressions?" Graham asked as they looked around.

"Dusty as hell," Becky said. "Except for the floor. That's been swept. Otherwise, it doesn't look like anyone's been in here in months." She ran a latex-gloved finger along the table, leaving a track in the dust. She ran another finger along the work bench, with the same result.

"That would seem to work in Gannon's favor," Trask said. "We need to get some pics of everything."

"And this," Billy said, pointing to the inside of one of the cabinets he'd just opened. "But it doesn't look good for Gannon."

Trask stepped closer to the cabinet and looked inside. A half-full bottle was standing a few inches to the rear of the open door on the bottom shelf. The main label on the bottle read "DMSO." A paper plate lay beside the bottle. There was a residue of a pink-colored powder on the plate.

"Be really careful bagging that after we get some photos," Billy told Becky. "You might want to double-glove before touching that stuff."

"I need to call Sgt. Land," Billy said. "He can relay this to John by text, and John can use it in the interrogation."

"I'm going to walk around outside for a bit," Trask said.

"Okay," Graham said. "We'll be busy in here for a while."

Billy took a plastic glove from the box that Becky had open on the table, pulled one on, and flipped the door up on one of the freezers on his way to the door. He wished he hadn't. A severed human arm was lying at the bottom, frozen. Graham lurched backward.

Trask glanced inside the freezer.

"Yeah, you'll be busy," he said. "Better call a crime scene team. Land will want to hear about this, too."

Billy popped the door open on the other freezer and was relieved to see nothing inside. "This one's empty. It's not working; warm inside. No ice on the walls."

Billy made a call, then clicked his phone off. "Crime Scene's on the way."

"Now, I'm really going to walk around outside," Trask said.

He left the shed through the open door and walked around the exterior of the structure. The building stood in a clearing, with the brush and trees cleared for about ten feet in a circle surrounding the structure. He did not notice any identifiable footprints in the dirt around the front—the east side—or the north side, or the rear of the building to the west. When he reached the south side of the building, however, he did see an area where it appeared that the dirt had been disturbed, possibly swept with something crude.

Maybe a branch? It certainly wasn't a rake or a broom. There's another door here. Padlocked again.

He walked around to the front and went back into the shed.

"I think we should get photos of the ground on all sides outside," he told Becky. He turned to Billy. "Can I borrow those keys?"

Graham tossed them to him.

Trask walked back to the door on the south side. He tried all three keys. None worked on the padlock. He walked back inside.

"Billy, did Mrs. Gannon tell you that these keys unlocked both doors to this thing?"

"That's what she said. She said we should have one key for each lock."

"We don't have the key for the south door," Trask said.

"Maybe her husband changed the lock and didn't tell her," Billy said. "She didn't impress me as the kind of person who would be involved in something like this."

An hour later, a team of crime scene investigators arrived to process the shed.

"Medical Examiner's investigator is on the way to collect the arm and take it back to the morgue," the team chief told them.

"Good luck on finding any prints in all that dust," Becky said. "You might have to blow that crap off first."

"Thanks," the team chief said. "We'll take it from here. I think Sgt. Land wanted to see you all back at CCU ASAP."

"How'd it go?" Trask asked John Foote when they assembled in the conference room.

"I honestly don't know," Foote said. "We did the interview at my building. I told Marsh that if Gannon consented to a polygraph, we could go ahead and do it there, since we had a sign language interpreter already lined up.

"Butch and his wife came in willingly. She interpreted for him, and our sign language expert said that she wasn't manipulating either our questions or Butch's answers. They live on the south side of Holt, but they have that deer meat place on the north side. They claim that they haven't been in that shed for months, ever since the hunting season ended.

"Both of them seemed genuinely shocked by the whole thing. They said they'd been out on the road for the last month, and they had the truck logs to back up their story, and weight and motel receipts from all over the country. It would have taken a private jet and no flight records for them to get back here, do the dirty work, and then get back to their truck and continue building an alibi.

"I showed Gannon a photo of the card found at the scene where Beverly

Brown had her flat. He just kept shaking his head and signing to his wife. When we asked her what he meant, she kept saying, 'That's wrong, that's wrong.'

"If Tommy here hadn't called and told me what you found in the shed, I would've had no reservations at all about just cutting them loose. I had to ask them about the pink and the arm, of course. That's when everything went to hell. Marsh started screaming at both of them, accusing them of lying and being serial killers. He was so over the top that both the Gannons just clammed up and refused to answer any more questions.

"I stepped out of the room with Marsh and tried to calm him down. He was adamant that they were good for it, and said he was going to go to a judge immediately with an application to get arrest warrants for both of them. I asked him how he was going to explain the trucking logs to the judge. He said the logs were probably manufactured, and he didn't *have* to mention the logs to the judge. He and Fuel left to go type up their warrant."

"Did you mention the DMSO in front of Marsh, or just the pink?" Trask asked.

"Just the pink. Figured we'd hold back on something singular just for a double-check. Did the CSI team find any prints on the DMSO bottle?"

"No," Becky answered. "That's the last thing we waited to check on before we left."

"Anyway," Foote continued, "I told Marsh that he damn well *better* mention the trucking logs to the judge, 'cause I'd heard somewhere that he'd withheld exculpatory evidence before, and I'd hate to have to report him for doing it again."

"Thanks for reminding him," Trask said sarcastically. "I'm sure he'll thank you for it later."

"One more thing," Foote said. "When they were leaving, I heard Marsh tell Fuel to call Sam Brown and tell him they'd found his daughter's killer."

"Oh, no," Becky moaned.

"You don't think they did it either?" Foote asked her.

Becky looked at Trask. He took the cue.

"Several things," Trask began. "The shed floor had been swept, but the dust in the rest of the shed made it look like nobody had been there in months, just like the Gannons said. I also did a walk around the outside. No prints anywhere, but it *did* look like someone had swept the dirt in the rear of the place—on the west side and on the south near the other door—maybe to rub out some footprints as they left."

"Which could be why the shed floor was swept, too," Foote offered.

"Exactly. One other thing. The padlock on the south door of the shed didn't match the third key the Gannons gave us. The other two keys matched the main shed door and the road chain across the entrance."

"Why give us two keys that work and one that doesn't?" Billy asked.

"Hell, if you know there's dope in the cabinet and a severed arm in the freezer, why give us consent at all?" Foote asked.

"Where are the Gannons now?" Trask asked Foote.

"Marsh got his arrest warrants," Foote said. "We had just enough to justify holding them, and it's not like we could let them go as long as there was a chance in hell that they were good for these killings. I have no idea what Marsh did or didn't tell the judge, but I know he got the warrants 'cause he threw copies at me when he showed up with some uniforms to haul the Gannons off to the county lockup. Their initial appearance is tomorrow morning.

"They also consented to a search of their home in Holt. We're waiting for that team to get back, but one of the guys texted me a photo."

Foote showed Trask his phone. A photograph of a business card reading, "I am a deaf-mute," was displayed on the screen.

"They found this in what appeared to be Butch's desk. He had a whole stack of them. From what the team told me, it looks to be the same paper stock and font as the cards found at the crime scenes for Bev Brown and the attempted abduction of Sally on Independence Avenue. I'll forward the pic to all of your phones."

34

TRASK TOOK his seat in the back of the courtroom among the other spectators. Foote, Graham, and Suzuki shared the pew with him to his left. He looked into the well of the courtroom. Butch Gannon, a big, balding man, and his attorney sat at one of the tables reserved for defendants and their lawyers. A third person —a woman—sat at the table with them.

Alvin Black has Butch. Does he have a conflict of interest if Butch killed Gloomy? I don't guess so. Gloomy fired Black, and Gloomy's gone now, anyway. He won't be complaining about any conflict. That must be a sign language translator at the table with them.

Mrs. Gannon, a mousy, small woman attired in an orange Jackson County Jail jumpsuit like her husband, sat at a table behind Butch and Black. Another woman sat beside her.

I don't recognize her lawyer.

Trask saw that the prosecutor's table was occupied by both Ray Marsh and Bonita Baylor.

The conquering heroes appear in triumph.

Trask turned his attention back to the Gannons, studying their moves and faces.

He keeps turning and looking back at her. He's more concerned about her than he is about this hearing. They don't have to speak to communicate. They transfer more information in a glance than most couples do in words.

Trask looked around the spectator section of the courtroom.

Sam Brown is here, representing his little girl. Jimmy Bishop is here, too, ready to write the story.

The familiar call brought them all to their feet. "All rise!"

Trask recognized the judge as he entered.

Bob Bartle. Used to be one of the defense attorneys we saw on the federal side. Competent enough. He must have known the governor and gotten appointed on the last opening.

The court clerk called the case. Judge Bartle asked what the state's position was on the question of bail.

"Your Honor," Bonita Baylor began, "the state requests that the defendants be held without bail, or, in the alternative, that the court set a very high bail. As the court can see from the complaint filed against the defendants, the state has evidence which strongly suggests that these defendants are responsible for the brutal murders and mutilations of several victims. A search of the defendants' property resulted in the recovery of a drug linked to the kidnapping of at least one of the victims, and the severed arm of another victim was found in a freezer on the defendants' property. This evidence also established that these defendants pose a severe risk of danger to the community."

"What have you to say on the issue, Mr. Black?" the judge asked.

Black and Bartle are good friends. They go way back.

"I have been authorized by counsel for Mr. Gannon's co-defendant to speak on behalf of both defendants, Your Honor."

Black spoke at length about the trucking logs and characterized them as establishing an "airtight alibi, which the prosecution has chosen to ignore to this point."

"Given this evidence, which I would argue clearly establishes *not* just a reasonable doubt, but the *actual innocence* of both these defendants, I would request that a reasonable bond be set which would not punish these defendants, but which would—in accordance with the statutes governing bond in this state—only assure their presence at trial, a trial in which the defendants will prove their actual innocence beyond any doubt whatsoever."

That's quite a claim, Alvin—quite the burden of proof for you to shoulder.

Judge Bartle looked much more concerned than he had been when he entered the courtroom.

He came in expecting headlines about his quick and decisive action in denying bail. Now he's having to actually be a judge.

Much to Trask's surprise, the judge actually left the courtroom to take the ruling under advisement. When he came back, Judge Bartle appeared resolute, but not happy.

"I'm denying the state's suggestion that the court deny bail, but I am setting a substantial bail, given the severity of the charges in the complaint. Bail is set at one-million dollars each, with a requirement that a minimum of ten percent be posted before the defendants may be released."

"I have that here, Your Honor," Alvin Black said, standing as he spoke.

"You do?" the judge asked, startled.

Baylor stood up and objected. "But these are very dangerous criminals, Your Honor—"

"Sit down, Ms. Baylor. I've made my ruling," Bartle said. "While I'm at it, I suggest you begin working immediately on either rebutting or confirming the evidence which Mr. Black has argued is a dispositive alibi. By the way, your failure to address that evidence at all in the application for the arrest warrants in this case does not speak highly of your office."

The judge turned back to Alvin Black. "Mr. Black, you were saying?"

"Yes, Your Honor. The Gannons have a substantial amount of equity in their real estate and in their truck. I was able to secure a cash line of credit for them at their bank in anticipation of the court's ruling today. I am presenting a check for the bond amount to the court in satisfaction of the court's ruling."

Bartle shrugged. "Very well. Defendants will be transported back to the confinement facility for processing. You will be informed of the conditions of your release. You are not to leave this state without permission of the court. You will be informed of the next date and court appearance. We are adjourned."

Trask looked down the row to his right. He saw Jimmy Bishop rushing out to file a report with *The Outlook.* He also saw a very distraught Captain Sam Brown walking out of the courtroom with his head hanging down. At their table, Bonita Baylor was casting a very disapproving look at Raymond Marsh.

Trask turned to his left and the detectives.

He just shrugged.

The TV volume was up in his living room, as Trask didn't want to miss a word of the evening newscast.

"In a surprising and horrifying series of events late this afternoon, the saga of the area's serial killer—or killers—took yet another unexpected twist, and with that twist, four more lives," The news anchor began.

"Shortly after a hearing at which Butch Gannon and his wife Gail were released on bond, the father of one of the victims of these alleged killers, Captain Sam Brown of the Kansas City Police Department, was waiting when the Gannons were released from the Jackson County detention facility. Eyewitnesses on the scene report that Captain Brown shot and killed both Mr. and Mrs. Gannon. He then turned the gun on himself, committing suicide.

"When other officers went to Captain Brown's residence to notify his wife of his death, they found that she was also deceased. Mrs. Brown appeared to have overdosed on a quantity of pills, and she had left a note explaining that life was too difficult for her after the brutal murder of her daughter, Beverly. Mrs. Brown had apparently been dead for more than a day or two, according to medical examiner personnel on the scene.

"County prosecutor Bonita Baylor expressed regret at the deaths of the Gannons, saying that she would have much preferred to have secured their convictions at trial, after which she said she would have sought and obtained the death penalty for their crimes. She also expressed her sorrow at the deaths of Captain and Mrs. Brown, saying that their deaths had also been indirect results of the crimes committed by the Gannons."

The screen shifted to Bonita Baylor at the podium of a news conference, in which she said everything that the news anchor said she had said.

What original writing, Trask thought. *Journalism really is dead.*

"Alvin Black, the attorney for Butch Gannon, had a much different take on the events of the day," the anchor continued. "Mr. Black said that—had the case against the Gannons gone to trial—he would have easily proved that the charges against them were fabricated, since he was in possession of documents proving conclusively that the Gannons were away from the area at the time that the murders in question were committed."

The screen shifted to Alvin Black at the steps of the county courthouse, in which he said everything that the news anchor said he had said.

Trask felt Lynn rubbing his shoulders.

"What do you think?" she asked.

"I think that God forgives, and he might understand why Sam Brown and his wife did what they did. We always thought Sam was dealing with this horror as well as anyone could. We were apparently wrong. I've always wondered what I would do if anyone harmed you—or even the pups."

"What did you decide?"

"I'm not sure. Those of us in the system swear allegiance to it, but we're also the ones with the most contempt for it when it goes wrong, since we've seen it go so very wrong so very often. I'm sure that's what Sam Brown was thinking about today. God knows how long his wife had been lying in their bedroom, and he couldn't bring himself to see her taken to the morgue. He had to do something, and he did it."

"What do you think about the Gannons?"

"I don't think we've seen the end of this yet, and I hope I'm very mistaken about that."

35

"You've been practicing," Billy said as Trask reeled in the target on his lane. "There's no red left in that bull's-eye."

"I had a good coach," Trask said, smiling.

They walked out of the range area and took off their eyes and ears.

"I've been out here about twice a week for the last three weeks or so," Trask told Graham.

"Since the Gannons were killed," Billy noted. "We haven't had any more severed body parts turning up since we found Sally's other arm in that freezer. Maybe they *were* good for the murders, after all."

"Hmmph." Trask shook his head. "I still don't buy it. Call it a hunch, instincts, whatever. I think our perp is out there somewhere laughing at us all."

"He'll have a good laugh in a couple of days, then," Billy said. "The Chief is holding an award ceremony at the Academy in a couple of days. Tuesday, I think. He's giving Marsh a baton."

"Makes me want to sell mine," Trask remarked. "Not really. I think we earned those, and I'm proud of them."

"You should be proud of that target," Billy said, pointing at the perforated square. "You could qualify as expert, now. I'd take that one home and show it to Lynn."

"Think I will," Trask said. "Thanks again for all the help."

He walked out to the Jeep and stashed his range bag in the back. He started the car but stayed parked while his cell connection to the Jeep's Bluetooth activated.

"*The Outlook.*"

"Jimmy Bishop, please."

"Bishop."

"Jeff Trask, Jimmy."

"Hi! What are you up to now that the butchers are out of business?"

"Just routine stuff. Thought you might want a heads-up since you've been writing the story all along."

"Sure. What do you have?"

"The Chief of Police is awarding Ray Marsh a ceremonial baton at the Police Academy next week. I think it's Tuesday, but you might want to verify that with the department's PR folks. They can get you into the ceremony, too. Chief Walker is never one to turn down positive publicity."

"That'll be a feather in Marsh's cap, won't it?"

"Yeah. They don't give those out to everybody."

"No hard feelings for Marsh and his success?"

"Of course not. The goal is always getting the bad guys off the street and saving lives. If Ray's been able to do that, more power to him."

"Pretty magnanimous of you."

"Not really."

Bishop laughed. "That's as far as it goes, huh? Anyway, thanks for the tip. I'll be there."

"See ya."

Trask pulled the Jeep out of the parking lot and pushed the radio button. The oldies station was playing the Blues Magoos' "We Ain't Got Nuthin' Yet."

Exactly, Trask thought to himself. *1966, I think. The start of the real rock decade. I've always thought that popular music decades started on the fives. 1955 to 1965 was rockabilly and Elvis. 1965 to 1975 started real rock and roll. Disco from '75 to almost 1985. The end of the rock era from '85 to 1995. Then Hip-Hop and whatever all this whiny stuff is after that. Never thought I'd be part of a generation gap where music was concerned, but here I am.*

Time for a long trek with the pups when I get home. Love those dogs. No games; just trust and love. I just wish they could talk, sometimes.

The Outlook was always published on Wednesdays. Trask had grabbed a copy on his way to the office. He poured a cup of coffee and sat down behind his desk to read Bishop's article before turning on his computer.

"Police Chief Awards Ceremonial Baton to Jackson County Prosecutor"

Good headline, Jimmy. I was a high school All-American in journalism, once upon a time when the earth was cooling. Good fit in the column margins, too.

"In a ceremony held Tuesday afternoon at the Kansas City Police Academy, Chief of Police James Walker honored Assistant Jackson County Prosecuting Attorney Raymond Marsh for his work in bringing the notorious 'Kansas City Butchers' to justice.

"Chief Walker presented Marsh with a ceremonial baton, an award only presented for what the Chief called 'exceptional service' to the department and the community. Marsh was the lead prosecutor in the investigation which led to the arrests of Butch Gannon and his wife, after a severed arm of one of the victims was found in a venison processing shed owned by Gannon near Holt, Missouri.

"The Gannons were later shot and killed by police Captain Sam Brown as they left the Jackson County Detention Center. Brown's daughter Beverly was one of the victims who was kidnapped and mutilated by the serial killers after she had a flat tire on her way home from college in Liberty, Missouri. Captain Brown then shot and killed himself with his service weapon. His wife, distraught after her daughter's murder, also committed suicide."

Nice job, Jimmy. No fudging. Just the facts as they're currently known. No stupid "How do you feel about your relative's death and dismemberment?" interviews just to fill some column inches. Don't worry; some TV reporter will do those.

"The Gannons are also believed to have been responsible for the murder of WaShaun "Gloomy" Stewart, Jr., who was alleged to have been a gang leader and another serial killer in the area. Stewart had escaped from custody while pending trial in federal court. He then disappeared. In an ironic twist, characterized by authorities as the Gannons' thumbing their noses at law enforcement, Stewart's severed leg—identified through DNA comparison—was left on

Marsh's front porch. It now appears that Mr. Marsh—and not the Gannons—has had the last word in this macabre saga."

Okay. I know you had to close with something, but that's a little cheesy for my taste. At any rate, we'll see if this works. It did last time.

A rapping sound on Trask's doorframe made him look up. Cam Turner was standing in the doorway.

"I see you've already read it," Cam said. "I just wanted to make sure you weren't going to be next on the suicide list, with Ray getting an award for your work."

"Nah, I'm good. Thanks for checking."

"Lunch later?"

"Sure. My calendar's easy today. The wheel has just been spitting out minor cases for us lately."

"Good. I'll swing by."

Trask looked up from the TV and checked his watch for what was probably the twentieth time after dinner.

"Are you expecting a call or something?" Lynn asked.

"Something."

"Care to explain?"

"I think we're about to hear from the real butcher again."

"After almost a month? Maybe it *was* the Gannons after all. Are you sure you're not obsessing about this a little?"

"I don't know. I think he's still out there, and the Gannons were the victims of a good frame job. I just think that after Bishop's piece in *The Outlook* today, our guy may have a hard time holding back any longer. At the end of his last string, the killings weren't enough for him. He was in a new game with the police, making fun of Ray Marsh, all that. Stereotypical serial killer crap: Look at me! Look at me! I'm surprised we haven't heard something already. I get these feelings from time to time. You know that."

She walked over and sat on his lap.

"I *do* know that, and I also know that you're usually right. You won't be sleeping much tonight, will you?"

"Probably not."

He took a long breath.

"Do you know which species of shark is responsible for the majority of attacks on humans around the world?"

"Great whites?"

"Nope. They're good for TV, books, and movies because they're so huge. It's bull sharks. Ugly, mean, nasty bastards. They'll hit food—including people—in shallow waters. Only inches sometimes. They'll even swim up rivers and attack in fresh water.

"You know that my folks used to take us to the same vacation spot every year when we were growing up: Gulf Shores, Alabama. About two hours' drive from home, an extension of the Florida panhandle. Snow white sandy beaches, open gulf water, not like that brackish backwater along the Mississippi coast inside the barrier islands."

"I remember. You told me."

"When I was ten or twelve, I really got into surf fishing. I'd wade out a few yards—waist deep—and cast and wait. I was still always on the lookout for bull sharks. I'd watch up and down the beach for fins or shadows in the water. One day, Mom was sunbathing on the beach a few yards from where I was fishing. All of a sudden, she let out a scream. I looked to my left and saw a huge, black shadow in the water about four feet away, coming at me fast.

"I thought it was over. I was going to go down swinging, so I started to hit it with the butt of my surf rod, but when the shadow got to me it turned out to be a school of Manta Rays. They just swam on by."

"You weren't hurt at all?"

"As I recall, my swim shorts required some additional laundering attention."

Lynn laughed. "Did you keep surf fishing?"

"I transferred my fishing site to the State Park Pier a few miles away. I could get my bait farther out into the Gulf without having to look for bull sharks in the water."

"And why tell me this now?"

"This guy reminds me of a bull shark: silent, deadly, wants to kill and kill for the sake of killing. We never see him coming. The only time we know that he's been around is when we find another body part."

Trask's cell phone rang.

"Trask." He paused and listened. "Hi, Billy."

He listened again.

"I'll be there in thirty."

He looked at Lynn.

"Another severed leg just showed up on Ray Marsh's porch."

"You're kidding."

"I'm afraid not."

Trask walked to the closet to get a jacket.

She kissed him. "Be careful."

"I'm not in the water, and I'll stay on the pier."

He went to the garage and backed the Jeep out.

A shark is still a fish, and any fish will take the right bait if you're patient enough.

36

"You used me," Bishop said between sips of his coffee. They sat in a cafe outside the gaming floor at Harrah's North Kansas City Casino.

"Not at all," Trask said. "The tip I gave you was perfectly legitimate, and you wrote a perfectly legitimate story for your publication. As the facts were known at the time, everything I told you was accurate—still is, for that matter. The Chief *did* give Marsh a baton for the precise reasons I mentioned."

"But you knew they were wrong about the Gannons."

"No. I didn't *know* that. I *have suspected* it all along, and my hunch seems to have been correct."

"What tipped you off?"

"No, Jimmy, not yet. We've worked this the right way so far. I promise you'll be the first to get a call when we finally get to the bottom of this mess. I only know what I know, and—unlike some others—"

"Like Ray Marsh?"

"—you said it, I didn't—I try to recognize what I know and also what I don't know. I like to think that the method keeps me from prematurely arresting innocent folks—"

"And getting them shot in the process?"

"Are we still off the record?"

"Of course."

"Then, yes. And getting them shot in the process. Some wise old heads tried to train me to take care of all the details before I jump to conclusions, and not to get tunnel vision on any case. You know—coming to a conclusion before all the evidence is collected?"

"I try to do that as well."

"That's why your number is in my phone."

"Okay. I understand."

"Good. Understand something else, but don't worry about it unless I tell you to worry about it. Don't look at him, but the guy four tables behind me and watching us is named Dan Fuel. He works for Bonita Baylor and Ray Marsh. He specializes in screwing cops instead of criminals."

"What's that all about?"

"My guess is that Marsh—in his tortured mind—thinks we set him up. First you call him out on what he did to that poor Miller character in Dogpatch, then you write what he has come to believe is a Marc Antony speech praising him for taking down the Gannons. Now he sees us chatting."

"But I shouldn't be worried?"

"If he hauls you in for questioning or shows up at your door with a warrant, give me a call on the quiet. Inaccurate or out-of-control prosecutors can be dangerous animals. Ask the Duke Lacrosse Team, or the Gannons, or Sam Brown."

"Wish I could. Point taken."

"Do me a favor. Leave before I do. I want to see if Fuel follows you or waits for me to leave."

Trask made sure the Sig was in its pocket holster before he pulled the Jeep out of the courthouse's underground garage. He was at the Career Criminal Unit fifteen minutes later.

He found Foote, Graham, Suzuki, and Tommy Land in the conference room. Billy's event summaries were back up on the wall.

"We were trying to figure out what we missed," Tommy said as Trask sat down.

"Me, too. For weeks now. I just felt like it was out there."

"You were right," Billy said.

"*We* were right," Trask corrected him. "Everybody here doubted that the Gannons were the right targets."

"Then why the hell didn't any of you geniuses tell *us* about that?" an angry voice asked behind Trask.

He turned to see Ray Marsh and Dan Fuel in the doorway.

"I tried to, Ray," Foote said. "You were just hell-bent on winning some kind of race."

"Bullshit!" Marsh shouted. "The evidence all pointed to those truck-driving rednecks. Of course, you people were the ones collecting that evidence and putting it in front of us. I wouldn't put it past you finding that other leg and leaving it on my porch just to try and get me fired again!"

Trask kept his mouth shut.

John Foote didn't.

"Ray, you've just passed ridiculous, raced by sublime, and sped out to totally batshit crazy," Foote said.

"I agree," Tommy Land said, standing. "I won't have you making stupid accusations like that against my people. I don't care who you work for. Take your misguided dog and get out of my building. Now."

Land stood watching the door until Marsh and Fuel withdrew.

"Unbelievable," he said, shaking his head. "Sit tight for a few. I have to make some calls."

"Calls?" Foote asked after Land left the room.

"Chain of command," Billy said. "He's letting them know how far off the reservation Marsh and Fuel have gone. You remember the chain of command, right, John?"

"Oh yeah. That. It's been a while. Anyway, where were we? Ideas?"

"Just that someone set up the Gannons, and is laughing at us for taking the bait," Becky said.

"Bait is a good word," Trask said. *Let's throw some more in front of this shark.* "I was thinking. If this clown is so brazen to pull the same stunt on Marsh's porch again, there's nothing to say he won't be back to the track looking for more girls to cut up. What if we put some undercovers out there for him to find?"

"I like that idea," Becky said.

"Don't like it too much," Billy said to her. "*You're* not volunteering for that."

Becky didn't say anything. She frowned and sank back into her chair.

Uh, oh, Trask thought. *Trouble in paradise. Billy's going to hear about that tonight.*

"What the reverend *meant* to say, Beck, is that you're too valuable an asset to this team to risk at this point." Foote had noticed her reaction, too, and was trying to bail Billy out. "You have all our data systems under your fingers, and your corporate memory of the evidence we've gathered is probably only second to the human recording device sitting to my left." He pointed to Trask.

"I said that wrong," Billy admitted. "Sorry."

Tommy Land reappeared.

"I talked to the Captain and the Chief," he said. "They said they have our backs. Marsh and Fuel will not be operating out of this building in the future."

"Jeff has an idea," Foote said. "I like it, too."

37

"How many times do I have to apologize?" Billy asked her.

"I think that last one was sufficient," Becky replied, "just as long as you never do that again. I'm a cop like you. If the job requires going undercover, you would do it in a heartbeat. It's no different for me."

"I know. I know. Again, I'm sorry. You just can't blame me for loving you and wanting to protect you, even on the job."

"Not in front of other cops. That's very demeaning."

"I got it."

"Okay. Then we're good."

She kissed him and opened the door to her apartment.

"I'll see you tomorrow."

He turned and slowly walked to his car.

If we really were *good, I'd be inside with her right now.*

He opened the door and started the car. He began backing away from her building. His phone rang.

"I can't stay mad at you. Come back inside."

He re-parked and ran back to her door. He almost knocked, then stood there for a moment.

"It's open, silly," she said from the other side.

He pushed the door open. She was standing in the entryway in a robe. The depth of the open neckline indicated that there was nothing under it.

She walked to him and kissed him again.

"You were right. John was right. He just said it better. I'll be staying with the monitor team and not actually going under on the streets. You okay with that?"

"Absolutely."

She started unbuttoning his shirt.

"You still feel like you're wading in shark-infested waters?" Lynn asked Trask as he finished his dinner.

"Not now," he replied. "Now, we'll be putting bait out for him again, and I certainly won't be wading. I'll be on that nice, tall pier with several lines in the water. What that means is I'll be in the command van a few blocks away. Instead of dreading the shark making an appearance, we'll be inviting that appearance."

"How many ladies volunteered for the assignment?"

"Four. We're putting two on each end of Independence Avenue: Two on the west end, where Central Patrol will help with the support roles, and two on the east end, out toward Dogpatch. East patrol will help out there."

"Four lines in the water, huh?"

"Yeah. Looking for a shark who hands out business cards, and who cuts his food with a bone saw."

"Any ideas yet?"

"Plenty. I've run it all by you. Who are you thinking?"

"It has to be somebody in the enclave near Holt. Two—what did you call them?"

"Targets of opportunity."

"—right—targets of opportunity. The Brown girl and Gloomy. There's no other explanation for them disappearing in the same vicinity. Your shark has to have some connection with the area."

"Agreed," Trask said.

"And the shark has to have had some connection with the Gannons in order to frame them, right?"

"Agreed again. He at least had to know them. Even the business cards are carbon copies of the ones found in Gannon's desk. It could be someone else in a handicapped or deaf-mute circle in the vicinity. Someone had to have seen those cards before."

"That could include anyone who brought him a deer to butcher."

"Yeah, that's true. John Foote said that when the Gannons were being interviewed, he showed them a photo of one of the cards from the crime scenes. Gannon just kept saying, 'That's wrong,' or at least he was *signing* that—you know—making the signs that his wife was translating."

"What was he saying was wrong? The accusations? Something else? The cards?"

"John said he never got to ask that. He was about to when Ray Marsh jumped the shark—no pun intended here in our shark-fishing plan—and went ballistic. That's when the Gannons refused to answer any more questions."

"You think somebody changed the lock on that one door?"

"Yeah. Our shark. Approach from that side, cut the old padlock off with a pair of bolt cutters, leave the evidence to frame Gannon, sweep out your footprints on the dusty floor, and sweep the dirt outside that door as you leave. That again points to someone who not only had known the Gannons, but someone who had been in that shed before."

"We're back to anybody that ever brought him a deer. Did he keep any records?"

"Actually, yes. The search team that tossed his house found a whole stack of receipts going back several years. His wife appears to have done the bookkeeping, filed their taxes, all that. The receipts were fairly organized."

"How many customers?"

"Dozens. Becky Suzuki has been compiling a list at work, eliminating anyone who's died or moved out of the area."

"Is she one of the ones playing hooker?"

"No. I think she wanted to, but Billy pitched a fit in front of the rest of the team when she started trying to talk herself into it, and Foote immediately started talking her out of it. I don't think she'd fit the bill, anyway."

"Why do you say that?"

"I've met a lot of hookers doing this work. Very few of them are actually pretty, at least the ones who walk a track. That's another movie myth. You might have some pretty, high-priced call girls in some towns, but they're on call for big money. The poor ones walking the streets aren't going to make the covers of *Playboy* or *Vogue*."

"She could ugly-up some. We gals all know how to make ourselves look as good as possible. You just reverse that process."

"I'm sure that's what the vice team will be telling the volunteers tomorrow. They have the local experience and can brief the undercovers on how to ugly-up, and how and where to strut their stuff. If we get a bite, we'll be ready to roll. I guess I should say ready to *reel,* as in reel him in."

"Maybe he'll do something stupid and commit suicide by cop. That way, I won't have to deal with another three months of your trial-head."

Trask laughed. "A message I can't really pass on to the troops, even though it would be well-deserved and cheaper than a trial."

"What happens if the shark manages to grab one of the UCs?"

Trask did a double take.

"I hadn't considered that possibility. As wired and monitored as the undercovers will be—they have a new radio monitor they carry in their purses that looks just like a car's key fob—I don't see that happening. We'll have eyes on each of them as well. The minute we see a signal from them, the arrest team will be rolling."

"Reeling."

"Yeah. That, too. The girls will be briefed not to touch one of those cards if he offers them one."

"No vehicle description?"

"Just an older model pickup. That was from the patrol officer the first time the butcher tried to take Red Miller's friend, Sally. The cop wasn't close enough to get a make or model or plate. He thought he was just going to collar Sally for hooking again."

"Did anyone near the Gannons have a vehicle matching that description?"

Trask smiled.

"You're good. Always have been. Becky ran that possibility down. None of the Gannons' neighbors have any wheels like that. Not registered, anyway. The Gannons used to have an old pickup, but it seems to have disappeared. It wasn't at their house or the shed."

38

"THE BOSS SAID you could have one more week," Cam said. "I don't think you'd get that much time if it weren't for the facts that your target has done so much damage and Ray Marsh is so freakin' incompetent. We can still investigate the drug thing, but if and when you ID this scumbag—"

"I know," Trask said, resting his elbows on his desk, "it's still a county case for the murders. I should say it's a state case. I'm now thinking that the murders didn't even happen in Jackson County. The victims could have been snatched here, killed in another county—probably up near Holt—then had their body parts dumped here, there, everywhere. That's another reason why Tommy Land finally pushed back and threw Marsh and Fuel out of the building. We may be handing this off to a completely different county prosecutor. Marsh can file on abuse of a corpse or something like that."

"What's *your* next step?"

"Hooker decoys. I'm about to head out to the command center. We've got four spread out on Independence Avenue. By the way, tell J.P. I'll be dressing down for the week. Jeans and a polo shirt, like the cops. I'll be less likely to look like a federal prosecutor with a valid but marginal claim on jurisdiction in this mess."

"Okay. Approved."

Trask chuckled. "Sorry. I forgot that he delegated authority over such minor matters to you."

"Don't forget it again. I might be writing your report card soon," Cam said, smiling. "Thanks again for the promotion."

"With a little luck, that report card might include something about grabbing this creep. Gotta run. I'll call if anything pops up."

"Where'd you park the bus?" Trask asked Billy, speaking into the Bluetooth telephone connection in the Jeep.

Billy gave him the address.

Makes sense. Halfway out the Avenue. We could roll east or west depending on where we got a hit.

"Good. See you in about ten."

"By the way," Billy said, "it's called a Mobile Command Center, or 'MCC.' It's not a bus. The chief is proud of these things. He might show up, so—"

"—So, I won't call it a bus while he's around. Got it. Anything going down yet?"

"Becky had put out a BOLO for the old pickup truck registered to the Gannons. She got a call from the Holt Police Department when they saw the flag. The Gannons actually reported the truck stolen about five weeks ago. The cop in Holt said that they'd been working the case but hadn't put it in the system yet because of a backlog in filing."

"For *five weeks*!? I wonder what kind of case work that means. Forgetting about it, probably."

"Yeah, I had the same reaction at first, but we're talking a country town of 500 people and only about a dozen officers when they're fully staffed, and they've had some folks out on leave and sick. I think they're down a couple of bodies besides that. It's probably not unusual that their filing and system entries have stacked up; investigations probably got lost in the stacks as well."

"How does that report date fit the timeline the Gannons gave John with their logs?"

"The pickup went missing just before they went out on their last long haul."

"Even more proof the Gannons weren't good for the murders," Trask said.

"Exactly."

"I'll see you in a bit."

"Okay."

The big, white bus, otherwise known as the MCC, was parked in a supermarket lot about three blocks north of Independence Avenue.

Trask climbed the stairs and opened the door.

"Who is this casual dude?" John Foote asked, pointing a thumb at Trask as he entered.

"Just another undercover reporting for duty," Trask replied.

He looked toward the rear of the bus. The MCC was truly a command center, equipped with all manner of computer, telephonic, and radio communication gear. Each side was lined with fixed seats and worktables underneath all the communications equipment on the walls. Billy, Becky, John Foote, and Tommy Land were all monitoring various radio frequencies. Land motioned Trask toward an empty seat.

"Our girls are working two, four-hour shifts today," Land told him. "Afternoons from two to six, a break, and then eight to midnight. We're not doing typical vice arrests. If the guys who approach our gals aren't who we're looking for, the girls have been told to price them out of the game and send them on their way. We've got visual surveillance on all the undercovers in addition to their transmitters."

"Sounds good. I'm here for the duration." Trask looked around. "Got anything for me to do while we wait?"

"Just be ready to roll if something comes up. Billy told you about the pickup?"

"Yeah. The Gannons weren't our targets."

"I'm with you, and I feel even sorrier for Sam Brown. He loses his family, and then goes out killing two innocents himself."

"First nibble," Foote said a few feet away. "UC's transmitter is going on speaker."

"Hey, baby," the undercover's voice came across loud and clear. "What you doin' out here today?"

Good voice, in character, Trask thought. *Vice briefed the undercovers pretty well.*

"Just lookin' for some fun," the would-be john replied.

"Anything in particular?"

"Nothin' weird."

"That's good to hear. I got a rent to pay, baby. Can't do anything for under two-fifty today."

"*Two-fifty*!??" the man protested. "You ain't worth two-fifty, and I ain't got it."

"Come to think of it, I'd have to have five to put up with you, anyway. You ain't *all that*, and you could use a shower. Just move along, then, 'til you get a job that pays for something worth takin' home. Move on down the road, sonny boy."

"Bitch."

The sound of a car motor pulling away came over the speakers.

"Maybe somebody could at least stop that asshole for speeding," the UC said.

"Welcome to vice," Billy said to Becky. "The highest level of humanity."

Two hours passed before the next contact.

"It's still early in the day," Land explained to Trask. "We didn't want to pass up these hours because some of the working girls *are* out here. It does get busier after the sun goes down. More girls; more johns."

Trask nodded.

"I might want to take another run at that road in Holt while we have daylight, then," Trask said. "The one by the creek where Gloomy disappeared. Chat those folks up a little more, maybe look for places the pickup might be hiding. I'll be back for the night shift. Can you spare anybody?"

"Take John with you. Or he can take you. His car is burning CCU gasoline. You won't have to use yours."

Trask and Foote left the bus and got into Foote's Expedition.

"Thanks," Foote said. "I think we'd have heard that first contact replayed about seven times before dinner."

They drove east toward the interstate.

"You again," William Kirby said when he answered the door.

"Glad you remembered," Trask said. "This is John Foote. He's with the FBI."

"Federal case now, huh?" Kirby asked.

"Could be," Trask replied. "Mr. Kirby, I wanted to ask how well you knew the Gannons, the folks who had the deer processing shed up the road."

"Not well. It's not like I could talk to Butch, you know. I took one deer to him several years back before I started cutting up my own."

"You butcher deer, too?" Foote asked him.

"Not commercially. I just learned how to do my own so I wouldn't have to pay somebody else to do 'em. Save some money, you know?"

"Sure," Trask replied. "Where do you process yours when you get one?"

"I got an old shed a few yards behind the house. Keep my cutting gear and freezer back there."

"Is that the only other building on the property?" Trask asked him.

"No. Got a barn next to it for my tractor."

"Mind if we have a look?" Foote asked.

"Actually, I do. You got a warrant?"

"No," Foote replied. "Should we get one?"

"That's entirely up to you," Kirby said icily. "If you can. Actually, if you'd asked me when you folks were out here the first time, I probably woulda said, 'Go ahead,' but—seein' as how you seem to have got the Gannons shot for nothin'—I'd rather not have you guys crawlin' all over my place. You might arrest *me* for somethin' *I* didn't do. I can tell you one thing. I don't think the Gannons would hurt a fly."

"I think you're right, and we tried to stop the county authorities from arresting them," Trask said.

"But you didn't, did you?" Kirby shot back. "I think you should just leave now."

Trask nodded. He and Foote walked back to the Expedition.

"Can't say that I blame him," Trask said. "He actually had a point."

"But—" Foote began.

"Yeah, he's on the list now," Trask said. "Lives alone. Cuts up deer. Has the buildings in the back. Could hide a pickup in the barn. To the next stop up the road."

"The Hemeter place," Trask said as they pulled into the driveway. "Mom, dad, and teenage son Billy."

"If you say so," Foote replied. "I wasn't with you when you were up here before. It was just the Rev and the future Mrs. Rev."

"That's right. Maybe a fresh set of eyes and ears will help."

Billy answered the door again.

"Hello again," Trask said. "Remember me?"

"I think so. Police?"

"Close enough," Trask said. "Folks home today?"

"Not yet."

"Okay. We won't be long. Did you know the Gannons who had the deer processing shed up the road?"

"No, sir. I just knew he couldn't hear, from what my dad said."

"Is your dad a deer hunter, too?" Foote asked.

"Yes, sir, but he's not very good. I think he only killed one in the past four years. He usually uses Mr. Dewey, but I think he was busy the last time, so Dad had to go to Mr. Gannon to have it cut up."

"Did your dad ever use Mr. Kirby for that?"

The boy looked confused. He hesitated.

"No, I don't think so."

"That's okay," Trask said. "Do your folks have any sheds or barns out back?"

"Just a little tool shed," Billy replied. "You can see it over here. The lawn mower is in there, too."

They followed him to a side of the house.

"That's it," Billy said. "Right there."

Trask followed Billy's point and saw a wooden shed—about six by eight feet—a few yards to the rear of the house. There were no power lines leading to the structure.

"Thanks again for your time," Trask said.

He met Foote back at the Expedition.

"He didn't even know that Kirby did venison," Foote offered.

"I got that, too. Next stop is Thomas Leggett and family."

The Leggetts were home. Trask knocked, but got no answer at the front door. He heard voices at the rear of the house, so he walked to the side of the residence and looked toward the back. A large barn stood about sixty yards behind the house.

"Hello?" Trask called.

"Come on back," a man's voice responded.

Leggett, his wife, and two children, both girls, were playing with a dog in the back yard.

"More questions?" Leggett asked.

"Just a couple," Trask said. "Thanks in advance for a few more minutes of your time. Did you know the Gannons up the road to the north? Not a house, just a venison guy, to the north of Mr. Dewey."

"Never met them. Sorry."

"You a deer hunter?" Foote asked.

"Nope. Sorry."

"Livestock in the barn?" Trask inquired.

"Maybe a few mice. It's empty. We just wanted to get away from the city and bought the place about a year ago. I'm thinking of turning that barn into something useful when I get a few more bucks. It's too far back to use as a garage. Maybe a home gym or music studio or something. I play guitar; been thinking about doing some producing, too."

"It would make a nice studio," Foote observed. "You're far enough out so that any noise wouldn't disturb the neighbors."

"Yeah. We like it. Lots of room between the houses out here. Come take a look," Leggett invited.

They walked to the barn, and Leggett swung one of the front doors open. It was empty except for some remnants of piles of hay lying on the floors of stalls on the left side.

"Know any good contractors?" Leggett asked them.

"I may know a guy in town," Foote said. "If you like, I can have him give you a call."

"Sure. I'd like that." Leggett handed Foote a business card.

Trask thanked him again, and they returned to the Expedition.

"He's not on the list," Foote said.

"Agreed. Do you really know a guy?"

"I always know a guy."

"That card didn't say 'deaf-mute guitar player,' did it?"

"No. He's a banker. Next stop?"

Trask checked his watch.

"The bus. It's getting dark. By the time we get back, the night shift will be cranking up. Dewey's venison shed is the next place to the north, and we'd just be talking to a surveillance camera in the dark. He can wait for another trip."

39

"LET'S CALL IT A NIGHT," Land said. "We'll give it another shot tomorrow afternoon. Get some sleep, everybody. I'll drive the MCC back to our shop."

Trask joined Billy and Becky outside in the parking lot.

"So, no attempted kidnappings, no old pickups rolling by, no new missing persons reports, and no new severed limbs on Ray Marsh's porch," he said.

"That's an accurate summary," Billy replied. "It does, of course, leave out two arrests for simple assault after our UCs offended the egos of a couple of their amorous suitors."

"But neither one of them was carrying any dope, or deaf-mute cards," Becky added. "And one of them got the worst of the assault. Donna Myers whipped that dude's butt six ways to Sunday."

"She's not a small girl," Billy informed Trask, "and she really enjoyed the martial arts training at the academy."

"So, he goes to the hospital before he goes to jail," Trask observed. "It's injury to insult instead of the other way around. We'll see you tomorrow afternoon. I'm going to sleep in if the pups will let me."

"We're parking the bus at a convenience store south of the avenue tomorrow," Billy said. "We don't like to stage it at the same place for too long. It invites reporters and crowds."

"Just text me the address," Trask said.

He walked to the Jeep and got in. He saw Billy throw his arm around Becky and lead her to his car.

Young love; I remember it well.

He turned on the radio as he drove south. Perry Como's "Round and Round" was playing on the oldies station.

A number one hit during the hit parade days. 1957? I always thought that Perry was the smoothest of the crooners, a thousand percent better than Sinatra. He was just a Pennsylvania barber and didn't have the New York mob backing him for publicity, so he had to get by on talent instead of connections. There's a concept. Different kind of wheel, too. It takes you to the one you love.

The pups met him at the door when he got home, but Lynn was already asleep. He quietly undressed, and they all crawled into bed next to her.

He did not sleep in.

At six a.m. sharp, Trask was awakened by long, slow, Koko kisses. Each one had a stop in the middle before the tongue finished its wet journey across his cheek.

Who told these dogs how to tell time? Or does Koko have an alarm clock somewhere?

He slowly crawled out of bed, letting Lynn sleep. He threw on some clothes and a jacket and snapped the dogs into their harnesses and leashes.

"Okay, ladies, let's go."

They walked across the spillway where the water from Hidden Cove emptied into the main part of Raintree Lake, following the main road for a mile before they turned around.

"Here we are again, Koko. Up before the sun because you like the cold air. You are our pack leader, and Kodi and I are your sled. Don't pull too hard, please."

His mind was back at the farm road northeast of Holt.

Kirby? Too obvious after yesterday? Dewey? He's actually been helpful so far. Maybe we'll talk to him again today if the afternoon is slow. Someone else?

Where's the motive for any of these murders? For framing the Gannons? I can't make sense of something that has no reason behind it. Maybe there IS no motive. Maybe he IS a bull shark and just likes killing. Maybe we'll get lucky in the bus today.

He opened the door and let the dogs back into the house. Lynn was up and was waiting with breakfast for all three of them.

"Thanks for letting me sleep," she said.

"It was Koko's idea."

"I figured. What's on tap for today?"

"A quick check-in on the computer at the courthouse, then I'm back in the bus. Maybe another run to do interviews up in Holt."

"How many days left 'til J.P. pulls you back in?"

"One down, six to go."

"Jeans again today?"

"Yep. No tie. That's the good news. No perp. That's the bad."

"You'll get him."

He kissed her. "I appreciate your faith and optimism."

He headed for the shower.

Trask checked the text from Billy. As promised, the bus was parked on the side of a convenience store south of Independence Avenue. Trask saw that Billy, Becky, and Foote were at work when he climbed aboard.

"No Sarge today?" he asked.

"Tommy's back at CCU," Billy said. "Bank robbery. Our guy isn't the only crook on the street, and Tommy never learned how to turn down a request for help. We've got six people out with the FBI guys chasing down some leads."

"Anybody hurt?" Trask asked.

"No," Foote responded. "But the suspect may have some eye trouble pretty soon. The bills he got from the bank have a couple of nice, red, dye bombs buried in them, just waiting to go off in his face."

"How about here?" Trask opened his hands, motioning about the MCC.

"Quiet as a mouse," Billy replied. "The word has apparently gone out to all the horny men in KC that rampant inflation has struck the local chapter of the world's oldest profession. All our ladies are getting out there at the moment is blisters from their high heels."

"John?"

"Holt again?"

"Why not?"

"I think I know the way, now."

They reached the entrance to Dewey's road shortly after one o'clock.

"Just this one contact today?" Foote asked. "We could have called."

"We've never been able to get past the gate chain," Trask explained. "Only way to do that is to ask to see the place."

He got out and pushed the button.

"Yeah?" the familiar voice came over the intercom.

"Jeff Trask again, Mr. Dewey. I was here with the police officers before. I'm here today with an FBI agent. Are you home, or just monitoring your camera?"

"I'm actually out of town—in Saint Louis. Got a sister here who's going through a rough patch, so I came over to help her out. I'll be here a couple of days."

"Okay, understand," Trask said. "Just a couple of quick questions, then. Do you have any idea where the Gannons' pickup might be?"

"That old thing? No, why?"

"It's been reported stolen."

"Who the hell would want to steal that piece of junk? It barely ran!"

"I have no idea. Just wondered if you might have heard anything."

"Not a thing."

"How many other deer processors are around here?" Foote asked.

"Everybody up this way hunts, 'cept for city transplants like that Leggett guy next door there. 'Bout half of us know what we're doin' when we get one. The other half pay *us*. Don't exactly know the numbers."

"How about your taxidermy business?" Foote asked. "How many people do that in the area?"

"I might be the last one left," Dewey said. "There was another guy across town—Bobby Link—but he died a couple of years back. Why?"

"Just curious," Foote said. "Mr. Kirby down the road showed us a duck you did for him. Nice work."

"That's weird," Dewey said. "I do deer heads, but I don't do birds. Maybe Bobby did that for him and he got confused."

"Sorry to bother you again," Trask said.

"No bother at all."

As they drove back toward Kansas City, Trask turned the radio on.

"Mind if I change the station?" he asked Foote.

"Not at all. Don't like country?"

"Some of it's okay. Just in a different mood."

The Temptations' "Ball of Confusion" echoed through the Expedition.

"Of course," Trask said. "Why not?"

40

"Night shift is running slow again," Billy observed. "Maybe vice had our girls 'ugly up' too much."

"I think you had it right this morning," Trask replied. "The sudden rise in the price scale may be suppressing demand."

He turned to Becky.

"What was the make and model on that old pickup the Gannons reported stolen?"

She thumbed through some papers on the table in front of her.

"1979 Ford F150."

"Okay, thanks."

"What are you working on?" she asked Trask.

"Just doing some online searches on variables I hadn't run before."

"Like what?"

"The DMSO," Trask replied. "I realized I had just been going on my own experience with the stuff until now. Thought I'd see if I was overlooking anything."

"Did you?"

"Still checking."

He flicked the phone screen from article to article.

Yeah, super solvent, penetrates cell walls ... veterinary liniment for horses, topical use for treatment of arthritis ...

"I'll be damned," Trask exclaimed.

"Is that a question?" Foote asked.

"No!" Trask held up his phone. "This is an article on DMSO. Some taxidermists mounting birds use liquid DMSO solutions to rehydrate feathers that were damaged when the birds were frozen in storage. When we talked to William Kirby in Holt—not you and I, John, but when I was up there before with Billy and Becky—Kirby showed us a duck. He said Willard Dewey had mounted it for him, but when we asked Dewey about that today, he said he'd never done any birds for Kirby."

"And Kirby said that his duck had some damage on it from being frozen," Graham added.

"Do you think Kirby was lying about Dewey?" Becky asked Trask.

"More likely the other way around," Trask said. "Kirby's responses to Billy about that duck seemed spontaneous to me. It's not like he had time to plan that deception. Dewey said that Kirby may have had it done by another taxidermist and gotten confused. If Kirby wasn't confused, it almost has to be a lie by Dewey. I can't imagine that he would have forgotten mounting a duck for a neighbor."

"Does that get us a warrant?" Foote asked.

"Not even close," Trask said, shaking his head. "Just another needle in our haystack for now."

"Contact going on speaker," Becky said.

"What's up, handsome?" The undercover's voice came over the MCC's speaker system. "Want a date?"

"Only if you're a helluva lot cheaper than the skirt up the road."

"We takin' risks bein' out here at all tonight, baby. Ain't you heard there's a serial killer on the loose? Where there's risk, there's gotta be some reward, ya know?"

"Yeah, I heard, but that ain't me. I'm no killer."

"You could just be sayin' that."

"How much?"

"For what?"

"Straight sex."

"You a cop?" the undercover asked him.

"No, are you?"

"*HELL,* no! I just don't want to get arrested any more than I want to be cut in pieces."

"So, how much?"

"Probably the same you heard back that way. Two-fifty is the goin' rate tonight, baby."

"When did you girls form a union?"

She laughed. "That's funny, but it's still two-fifty. Interested?"

"Shit."

They could hear the car driving away.

"Maybe we drop the price back down tomorrow," Billy suggested.

Trask checked his watch. *Almost midnight.*

"We might have to," he said. "Of course, we might just start picking up johns if we do that. Doesn't seem like our guy is out here tonight."

"I have to drive the bus back to CCU," Billy said to Becky. "Your car's outside?"

"Yes."

"Okay, I'll see you back there in a few. I'll ride home from the shop with you."

"I just have to visit the ladies' room first," she said. "See you soon."

Trask stepped down from the MCC and walked to his Jeep. He was on I-435 southbound ten minutes later.

Have we been too visible in some way? Is the price the issue? NO. He wouldn't care about that if he's not paying anyway. The price is doing what it's supposed to do—clear the johns out of our hair. Maybe he's just being careful. Maybe he smells something.

Becky Suzuki washed her hands in the women's restroom of the convenience store. Before leaving the room, she checked her phone for messages. There were none. She dropped the phone back into the fanny pack around her waist and walked out the front door of the store.

He met her on the sidewalk.

"It's Detective Suzuki, right?"

"Yes. Oh, hello. I didn't recognize you at first. You're from Holt, aren't you?"

"That's right. This is really a coincidence. I found something earlier tonight on my property, and I thought I shouldn't waste any time bringing it down to you guys. I would have just called, but I lost that card the other officer left with me."

"What did you find?"

"It looks like somebody carved a fake gun out of a bar of soap. It was lying by the creek at the back of my land. I didn't know if it was important, but if it was, I didn't want to take too long, so I was going to drive it downtown to your headquarters. I just stopped here to get some gas, and I ran into you."

"That's okay, I can save you the trip downtown. Where is it?"

"In my car, over here." He pointed to a sedan on the side of the building.

"Did you get your gas already?" she asked.

"Yeah, I was coming inside to hit the head."

"Okay."

"It's in the trunk."

He popped the lid on the trunk and pointed inside.

Becky looked into the trunk and saw the soap gun lying on a towel.

She started to turn back toward him. "That's very good of you to bring this all the way—"

The hand-held taser in her back made her collapse as he pushed her into the trunk. The syringe he plunged into her neck made her pass out. He ripped the fanny pack from around her waist and opened it, seeing her phone and the gun. He put the card inside and dropped the pack to the pavement.

41

TRASK WAS HALFWAY to Lee's Summit when the song on the oldies station changed. He had just finished singing along to the Eagles' "Peaceful, Easy, Feeling" when Bobby Darin began his cover of "Mack the Knife." Trask shook his head, took an exit, crossed the interstate, and turned the car back northward.

"*When the shark bites, with his teeth, dear,*" ... *We missed something. The music never lies to me.*

He pulled back into the convenience store and saw Billy Graham and Tommy Land standing by one of the CCU's unmarked cars. He checked his watch.

I left forty minutes ago.

His cell phone vibrated as he got out of the Jeep.

"Don't bother with that," Land said. "It's me calling you. How'd you know to come back?"

"Just a feeling," Trask said. "What's up?"

"He's got Becky," Billy said, ashen-faced.

He held up the fanny pack. Trask glanced inside and saw the phone, and the card.

"I am a deaf mute," he read to himself.

He started to ask a question, but Billy answered it first.

"No surveillance camera. Wires were cut."

John Foote drove up in his Expedition and hopped out.

"I got your call, Tom. What's the plan, guys?"

"Holt. Now," Trask said. "We still don't have enough for a warrant, and by the time we do any super, by-the-book planning or operational staging, she could be gone for good. We leave now and she's got a chance. Tommy, you can alert the county guys or the state police up that way while we're rolling. He's got almost an hour head start on us."

"Who, Jeff?" Billy asked. "Which one?"

"The more I think about it, it has to be either Kirby or Dewey. One of them's lying and laughing at us, daring us to figure this out."

"John and I'll take Kirby," Land said. "John knows how to get there from his trips up with you, Jeff. Billy, are you okay to drive?"

"Yeah," Billy said emphatically. "Jeff and I've got Dewey. Let's go!"

Trask grabbed his range bag from the back of the Jeep and threw it behind the passenger seat of Billy's unmarked car. Billy left the parking lot first. He turned on his lights and siren. Trask glanced back and saw Foote's Expedition following them.

She came to slowly, groggy, her head pounding. Feeling the pain, she reached for the burn points on her back, but she found her hand restricted by the cage wall behind her. Hers eyes fluttered open. He was sitting on the floor, watching her.

She instinctively flinched and lurched backward, banging her head on the ceiling of the cage. He cackled.

"The shot wore off right on time," he said. "You know, you're special. The rest of 'em didn't hear me say a word. After all, I was pretending to be deaf and dumb, you know."

"We knew all that, Dewey. You should know that my squad is already on the way."

"Yeah, sure." He cackled again. "Like they wouldn't have been here already if they had a clue."

"That's why they were here earlier."

"Bullshit. They was just fishin' like before."

"Believe what you want. I'll enjoy watching them take you down, you sick little fuck."

"I don't like that talk from a woman, even a woman cop."

"I don't care what you like."

If I keep him talking, I buy time.

He shook off the anger and smiled at her.

"You're kinda lucky, you know. I mean, on top of me tellin' my story, you only get to spend *one* night in the cages."

"What are you talking about?"

Keep him talking. Seconds turn into minutes.

"Usually, I line you up in threes: one on the table, two in the cages. I got another cage in the garage outside. You skipped that one 'cause—with all you cops crawling all over my avenue—it was kinda slim pickin's the last couple of days. I was only able to grab one besides you."

He nodded to his left. She followed the nod, but she could only see the white wall outside her cage.

"That's a freezer," he explained. "So is the other one to your right. I got all kinda surprises stored up in those."

"We keep finding them."

"Yeah, when I want you to. I could just sink 'em deep in the river, and you'd never find 'em, but I let some of 'em just float on downstream. I know you get called out on those."

"We do." She nodded.

Minutes could turn into hours.

"And some, I left on that prosecutor's doorstep—the one with the big mouth. I *know* you got those."

"You're right. We did."

"Well, anyway, I got some more to make tonight, and you get a front row seat. Actually, you won't *see* all that much. You'll be able to *hear* all of it, though."

"I'll pass, thanks."

He laughed again, the hoarse, shallow cackle echoing through the building.

"No, you can't *pass*. She's right here on the table, waiting for me to finish up. I've already got a good start on her, but she ain't bled out yet. I made some mistakes on the first ones, hit the femoral artery too soon, but I learned how to work around that, so she should have a scream or two left in her for you to hear. I like to try and match the screams with my grinder, up there on the bench behind me. Can't do that with the moans while they're bleeding out, almost gone. By then, they don't have the strength to scream anymore."

He cackled some more.

"Now you know what all to expect, and it won't be a big surprise. I ain't tried that before. We'll have to see which is better—knowing or not knowing—won't we?"

He disappeared to his left. The screams that followed were unlike anything Becky had known were possible.

42

"You think it's Dewey, don't you?" Billy shouted over the siren as they raced northward on the interstate.

"That's my best guess. Could be either one, but the only reason Dewey would have to lie about that stuffed duck is the DMSO. Aside from that, it's an Occam's Razor situation, the simplest answer. His deer shed is just to the south of the Gannons' shed. He approaches the Gannon shed from the south—just where the footprints were swept out—cuts the lock off with bolt cutters, changes it, plants the DMSO and pink and that severed arm, and goes back the way he came."

Trask looked at the car's speedometer. They were doing 105 miles an hour.

"He seems to keep them a couple of days before he starts on them, Billy," Trask said. "We may have more time than we think."

"We may not."

Trask nodded.

I could ask him to slow down, but he wouldn't if I asked. I wouldn't if that bastard had Lynn right now.

"Can you switch on the radio for me?" Trask asked.

"It's on the CCU frequency. Tommy has a hand-held." Billy handed him the mic.

"Tommy, have you reached the county or highway patrol yet?" Trask yelled over the siren.

"Yeah, but it's like you said. They have their operational protocols. They're standing by, but they want to know which address to respond to before they roll. We don't have a warrant, and everybody's hinky about making a wrong decision after the Gannon fiasco."

"Here are the actual addresses," Trask said. He gave them to Land from memory. "If we don't see something at Dewey's place, we'll let you know. If you clear Kirby first, radio us. Whoever sees anything of our perp alerts the other team, and they call in the cavalry and medics. "

Trask clicked off the microphone but remembered something else.

"Billy, Dewey's place had that surveillance camera monitoring the entrance. I think we should go into the Gannons' old road and hit Dewey's place through the trees."

"Good idea," Billy said. "All of it."

He noticed that Trask was strapping on the tactical rig for the Sig Sauer.

"How much ammo you carrying?"

"Eight plus one in the gun, eight more rounds in a spare mag," Trask said. "Never thought I'd be wearing this for real. Let's go in on the road from the north," he suggested. "If we drove past Dewey's with the cam on the entrance, he might even see us passing his place. He's seen this car twice already. We go silent when we get close?"

"Yeah. Got it," Billy said.

They exited the highway and turned toward Holt.

"Siren's going off," Billy said.

Trask watched the Expedition turn off to their left as Billy kept moving northward.

They'll get to Kirby's place before we reach Dewey's. Maybe they can help out here.

Billy drove for another couple of minutes before turning left toward the road that paralleled the creek, the road they'd driven too many times in the past few weeks.

"The Gannons' old shed should be coming up on the right, pretty soon," Trask said. "There it is."

Billy pulled the car up to the chain blocking the road.

"Cut it or stay here?" Trask asked.

Billy didn't answer. He jumped out of the driver's side and ran to the metal pole holding the left side of the metal chain. He grabbed the pole, pulled it out of the ground, and tossed it to the other side of the road.

Adrenaline, Trask thought. *Amazing stuff.*

Billy jumped back in the car and pulled it forward. Seconds later, they stopped in front of the Gannons' shed. Billy popped the trunk and took out a shotgun.

"Ready?" he asked.

"I think so."

"I think she's gone," Dewey said, taking off the blood-soaked apron.

"Disappointing, really. Some of 'em seem to want to go out as soon as they can, once I get started. Others fight the end off as long as they can. I think you're a fighter. Are you?"

"Count on it."

With every fiber of my being, you sick bastard.

"Good, good. That's what I like to hear."

He held a hand to his ear and cocked his head skyward.

"Speaking of hearing, what I *don't* hear are your friends coming to save you. Ain't that a bitch?"

"Where's the Gannons' truck?"

He cackled again.

"Ain't that somethin'? You figured that part out, did ya? Smart girl. It's in the garage outside, where I keep that other cage I been tellin' ya about."

"How'd you get it?"

He's proud of all this. Keep him talking.

"Easy as pie. Just waited for 'em to fall asleep one night, crept into their kitchen, and grabbed the keys. She didn't hear me, and I know for a fact that *he* didn't hear me."

The cackle filled the building. Dewey loved his own joke.

He walked to a coat tree at the end of the workbench. He pulled on a Kansas City Royals hoodie.

"Recognize this?"

"Yeah. Tell me about Sally."

"She was a fighter, that one. Kept screamin' and cussin' me out a lot longer than I thought she would. Right up until the last breath, almost. Then—poof—she wasn't there."

"Why go back for her?"

"Couldn't risk that she might've recognized me. I know that my dope *can* make 'em forget some, but a couple woke up and remembered damn near everything. Had to watch for her to come out again on the avenue. Used my car instead of the old truck—just like I did with you tonight—had to follow her home and take her out there."

He pointed at the cage.

"She kinda left a little calling card, ya know?"

"What are you talking about?"

"Pull up the corner of that pad underneath you. You'll see. Excuse me; gotta sharpen up some tools."

She lifted the corner of the pad. She let it fall back into place, closing her eyes and saying a prayer.

Please hurry, Billy.

43

Trask followed Graham through the dark woods, heading south from the Gannon shed. Their pace—a careful, crouched jog—was not exactly silent, as they kept hitting beds of broken branches through uncleared brush under the trees. Billy suddenly stopped and motioned Trask down with an open hand.

"Garage, barn, something ahead. About forty yards."

Trask peered through the darkness. He could see the dark outline of the building through the trees. He nodded.

"I go left, you go right," Billy said. "We work our way around the outside until we get to a door. Keep your gun ready, just don't shoot *me*."

"Got it."

They slowed their approach to the building. Halfway around the right side, Trask found a window. Most of it was obstructed by something on the inside.

Is that cardboard? Plywood?

Trask did find a lower corner that he could see through.

"Billy!" he barked in kind of a shout-whisper.

"Don't do that again," Graham warned him as he appeared around the corner in front of Trask. "The wrong ears could hear you. What is it?"

Trask pointed to the corner of the window.

"Looks like a '79 Ford pickup," Billy said.

"That's what I was thinking," Trask said.

"There's a concrete block building a few feet the other side of this one," Billy whispered. "One door on this end. There's probably another way inside on another wall. You take the door on this end. Give me time to get to another door. Count to twenty, then we crash together. Watch your aim."

"Should I go back to the car and radio Tommy first?"

The sound of a high-pitched, metallic whir from inside the building interrupted them.

Bench grinder? Saw?

"No," Billy said. "We go now."

Trask nodded, and started counting.

At count sixteen, all hell broke loose.

Trask heard voices yelling a short distance from the front of the building.

"Trask, damn you! This is not your case! Where are you?"

That sounds like Ray Marsh!

"Ray, don't be stupid! Get behind some cover and shut up!"

That's Fuel. What the hell? This isn't even their county! How did they—they must have monitored the CCU radio frequency again. They probably pulled up in front of that damn camera!

Trask lunged to the corner of the building and looked toward the front. Two figures were silhouetted in the dark, backlit by the headlights of a car parked at the front of the dirt road. He started to shout his own warning, but the first tone of his voice was drowned out by the crack of a rifle shot. He saw the wider of the two shapes—the one that had been Ray Marsh—collapse. Fuel turned and tried to run back toward the car.

The headlights are still framing him!

A second rifle shot rang out, and Fuel lurched forward onto his face.

Trask froze for a second.

I lost count!

He strained to hear any other sounds.

Was that a door hinge?

He reached for the door handle on his end of the building, and quietly squeezed it.

Locked!

He hunched over to stay under any other windows, and circled around the back of the building, looking for Billy, looking for another way inside.

Roll your steps slowly, quietly. Keep the weapon ready. Don't shoot Billy. Check your six from time to time.

He heard his own heart pounding, his breathing shallow and frantic.

Deep breaths. Control. Be ready to take a punch, and then counterpunch if you have to.

He reached the far corner.

This is the other end. If there's a matching door to the locked one, it'll be on this side. Maybe Billy's inside already.

He risked a quick peek around the corner, then pulled his head back again.

There is a door, and someone's lying in the doorway!

He took another quick glance.

Those are Billy's shoes! He's down! Do I retreat, fall back to the car?

A scream from inside the building made his decision for him.

Becky?!

Trask cleared the corner of the doorway with the Sig at the ready.

He straddled Billy as he pointed the pistol toward the interior of the building. He was at the entrance to a small room. The door on the other side of the room was open. There was a long, metal table with the nude, half-dissected corpse of a young woman on it in the center of the far room. Trask saw a figure in a blue hoodie on the other side of the table pointing a rifle at something.

Trask fired.

The round struck the man in his right shoulder, sending the rifle crashing to the ground. The man disappeared below the end of the metal table.

Trask moved forward slowly, his pistol aimed and ready. In what seemed like a millisecond, the man rose from behind the end of the table, the rifle starting to level at him.

Trask fired again. Again. And again.

Dewey reeled backward toward the end of a workbench along the left wall. He collapsed backward, dropping the rifle again while the hood of his sweatshirt caught on one of the hooks of a coat tree. Dewey hung there upright, blood spurting from his open lips. Trask heard a gurgle as Dewey's lungs collapsed and he died.

"Jeff? Jeff!"

Trask holstered the Sig in his tac rig and turned to see Becky in the cage behind him.

Jesus! I thought that might have been her on the table.

"He was about to shoot me. Get me out of this goddam thing!" she cried.

Trask looked for a key to the padlock on the cage. He found a key ring sitting on the workbench.

She crawled out of the pen and pulled herself up on him, crying.

"Where's Billy?" she gasped between sobs.

"He's down, Beck. In the other room. We need to check on him."

Trask heard a growl from her that surprised him. He felt her drop. He started to look down at her, only to see her with his Sig in her hand. She fired the gun at Dewey's hanging body until the pistol would only make the clicking sound of an unloaded weapon.

"I think he's done," Trask said, gently taking the gun back from her.

He wiped the grip with the edge of his polo shirt, then gripped the gun again with his own hand before returning it to the holster.

"Let's check Billy."

He led her into the smaller room and reached down to check Billy's neck and nose.

"He's breathing and he has a pulse."

"Oh, thank God!"

They gently rolled him over.

"No wounds that I can see," Trask told her. "He does have quite a lump on his head. Probably got clocked with a rifle butt on his way in. EMTs should be on the way shortly."

She sat down and cradled Billy's head in her lap.

"Who was that bastard shooting at?"

"Marsh and Fuel tried to crash the party from the front. They're down outside."

Trask noticed a sink in the small room.

"You need to wash your hands, Beck."

"What?"

"Gunpowder residue. You guys have to face shooting review boards. I don't."

She nodded. "Yeah. Okay."

Billy groaned.

"I got him for a minute," Trask said, bending down to support Graham's head. "I'd look for some ice in those freezers—"

"You don't want to do that," she replied.

"Figured."

John Foote and Tommy Land appeared in the doorway, their guns at the ready.

"He's down and we're good, I think," Trask said. "Billy will need a trip to the ER. Head trauma."

"EMTs are right behind us," Land said. "We called 'em as soon as we cleared Kirby."

Land kept his weapon ready as he walked past them and into the main room.

"*Christ*! Who is—was—this?" he asked as he passed the table.

"Just another girl from the avenue," Becky said. "I never got a name."

He stopped and looked at Dewey's body sagging from the coat tree.

"Who got him?"

"I did," Trask said. "I think I emptied my nine into him."

"Yeah," Tommy said, taking another look at the body. "I'd say so. The rifle?"

"His. He was about to do Becky when I came in, then he pointed it at me. Did you see Marsh and Fuel out front?"

"Yeah. They're both dead."

A chorus of sirens began howling from the front.

"My head," Billy moaned.

Trask checked his watch as he put it on the nightstand.

Six forty-five.

He crawled into bed beside Lynn.

"You just now getting home?" she asked sleepily.

"Yeah. Long night."

"Everybody okay?"

"I'm okay."

"Okay." She rolled over and went back to sleep.

Trask put his head down. Five minutes later, Koko started licking his face.

44

"I DON'T HAVE to go through your public relations guy?" Jimmy Bishop asked.

"Not this time," Trask replied. "Mr. Barrett apparently thinks we can trust you to get this right, so—as long as we understand that some of it may be off-the-record—to be determined by me—we both get to do this without our babysitter."

"Did you find the drugs you were looking for?"

Trask chuckled. "Yeah, it kind of seems like an afterthought, but there was a lot of illegal dope in that shed. Pink, black market morphine, some fentanyl. He had a lot of DMSO, too. It's a solvent used to treat arthritis, but it can also be used to transfer other substances through the skin. Mr. Dewey would certainly have been arrested for that—as well as for the homicides—had he survived."

"What was in the freezers?"

Trask shook his head.

"The dismembered corpses of several unfortunates. The freezer to the right of the holding cage had arms, legs, and torsos. The one to the left—the CSI folks called it the "trophy case"—had all the heads in it."

"Were any mistakes made in the investigation?"

"Sure. I think I made one big mistake. The drug-soaked cards had a mistake on them that I didn't spot until after Dewey was killed. He had matched the cards used by Mr. Gannon in every aspect except one: he didn't include a hyphen between the words 'deaf' and 'mute.' Looking back, we should have seen that. In his interview, Mr. Gannon kept telling us that the cards were 'wrong.' As a lifelong deaf-mute, he knew the correct way to write the term. If we had recognized earlier that the killer wasn't a real deaf-mute, maybe the Gannons wouldn't have been arrested."

"That's a mistake the county prosecutors made, not you."

"You'll have to talk to them about that, Jimmy."

"One's not around anymore."

"Same response."

Bishop smiled. "Okay, I get that. I do have one question that really puzzles me. Why did this happen? What was Dewey's motive?"

It was Trask's turn to smile.

"Read a statute book sometime, Jim. I mean one of the criminal code books. With the narrow exception of a few hate crimes, you know what is usually *not* an element of the offense that we have to prove?"

"What's that?"

"Motive."

"Really? I never knew that."

"Oh, it's always something we look for—motive evidence—because it makes the rest of the crime easier to explain. The wife killed her husband to get his life insurance money; one neighbor shot another because the victim kicked his dog. We always *want* to have a motive, but they're not in the statutes."

"Why is that?"

"Because," Trask explained, "some of the wise old heads that wrote those laws recognized that there are times when evil doesn't need a reason. It's just there, kind of like a shark that just exists to bite things."

"How does it feel to be a hero?"

"I have no idea."

"You don't feel like one?"

"I was at the right place at the right time to do something, and I did it. Dewey didn't give me a choice to do anything different."

"You shot him in self-defense?"

"I did, and in defense of others. He had already killed several people, and he was trying to kill me and Detective Suzuki."

"How many times did you shoot him?"

"I can't remember."

Trask stood next to Billy as the organ began playing "Here Comes the Bride."

Billy bent over and whispered to him.

"Thanks for being the best man."

"This is the only time I'll wear that title," Trask whispered back. "Happy to do it."

"Becky told me what you did for her. Thanks."

"I don't know what you're talking about," Trask said. "I do know that secrets only stay secrets if no one tells them."

AUTHOR'S NOTE

I hope you have enjoyed reading *The Grinding Wheel.* You may find it interesting to know that both of the serial killer characters in the book, while fictional, are based upon real villains.

I worked as a federal prosecutor in Kansas City, Missouri, for twenty-five years. Although a beautiful city and a great place to live, the Kansas City metro area has had its share of serial killers. Robert Berdella is believed to have raped, tortured, and killed at least six men in the mid-1980s. He entered pleas of guilty, was sentenced to life imprisonment, and died at the Missouri State Penitentiary. John Edward Robinson lured women to their deaths in online chat rooms. He kept the bodies of some of his victims in large, metal chemical drums. He is currently on death row in Kansas. Terry Blair was convicted of killing seven women, with those murders occurring between 2003 and 2004. He is currently serving a life sentence in the Missouri state system.

The character of WaShaun "Gloomy" Stewart is loosely based upon Steve L. "Moody" Wright, Jr. I was the prosecutor in Wright's federal trial. Like the Stewart character, Wright killed several people before his eighteenth birthday, and at least one thereafter. He was one of the leaders of the 51st Street Crips, a drug-dealing street gang infamous for its violence. Wright claimed that he was innocent, but he was convicted at trial and sentenced to life without release. His case was investigated by the Career Criminal Unit of the Kansas City Police

Department. Wright's appeals have been rejected, and he is serving his sentence in the federal prison system. Those wanting to read the appellate opinions can find them online at https://caselaw.findlaw/us-8th-circuit/1478596.html, and https://casetext.com/case/wright-v-united-states-272. The latter opinion is also reported at 902 F.3d 868 (8th Cir. 2018) for all you attorneys.

The character of Willard Dewey is based—again, loosely—upon Gregory Breeden, who was suspected of murdering seven women in the Kansas City area. My wife was working as an investigator for the Jackson County Medical Examiner at the time, and she had the grim duty of retrieving one of the victim's severed legs after it floated downstream in the Missouri River to a neighboring county. Breeden was never convicted of any of the murders, but—while a suspect in the killings—he did serve a ten-year sentence on an unrelated bad check conviction. During his time in prison, the grisly murders stopped. Breeden continued to deny any connection to the killings until his death in 2014.

To the best of my knowledge, in real life, Steve Wright and Gregory Breeden never met.

WaShaun Stewart's escape in the book is also based upon a real incident, in which a bus--transporting prisoners from federal court in Kansas City to a confinement facility--was actually hijacked by a detainee who had carved a pistol out of a bar of soap.

As is unfortunately the case in many American cities today, those working in law enforcement in Kansas City are often under attack by the very systems of government they serve and protect. The Kansas City, Missouri police force is only about 80% manned today, and no new officers are being trained at the police academy. Some in the city and county government apparently believe that they get more political mileage out of attacking the police than they would out of supporting them. As is usually the case, when politicians lie about such matters, people die.

In my experience, the vast majority of police officers in this nation uphold their oaths to protect and serve all citizens. The very few who abuse their positions deserve our contempt; the rest do not. They deserve our admiration.

ACKNOWLEDGMENTS

My sincere thanks to my reading and editorial board: Lea, Alta, Mary Jo, Margie and Tania. They all bring a different perspective and set of eyes to the book. As usual, a heartfelt thanks to my daughter, Jennifer, my professional polish editor, who always sees things that others do not.

Thank-you to Margaret Daly of Rukia Publishing US for bringing the book to print and online, and for her excellent marketing service.

A final special thank-you to my readers. You are my driving force.

ALSO BY MARC RAINER

Capital Kill

Horns of the Devil

Death's White Horses

A Winter of Wolves

Death Votes Last

Mob Rules

Turn the page to learn more about each of the titles . . .

CAPITAL KILL

BOOK 1 IN THE JEFF TRASK CRIME DRAMA SERIES

A few short blocks from the safety of the museums and monuments on the National Mall, a ruthless killer prowls the streets of Washington, D.C. Federal prosecutor Jeff Trask joins a team of FBI agents and police detectives as they try and solve the series of brutal murders. As the body count rises, the investigation leads to a chilling confrontation with the leader of an international drug smuggling ring, and no one is safe, not even the police.

Capital Kill is a swirling thrill ride through the labyrinth of a major federal investigation and trial, with a gripping conclusion that no one will see coming.

Read Capital Kill

Editorial Reviews of *Capital Kill:*

"Lawyer Jeff Trask is just settling into his new job as an Assistant U.S. Attorney when he becomes embroiled in a high-stakes international case that could break an already-strapped legal system. Characters are well developed, and the elements are assembled so seamlessly that the story feels fresh. Rainer's attention to setting also shines through. The streets of Washington, D.C. come alive; those who have lived or worked in the nation's capital will recognize Rainer's cunning use of seedy locales to give the action in the book a realistic tone. The book's intense action, realistic tone and memorable characters will keep readers engrossed in this thriller with a superb payoff." - Kirkus Reviews.

"Marc Rainer has joined the ranks of trial attorneys turned fiction writers with Capital Kill, a legal thriller. Rainer introduces us to what may be the most diabolically inventive method of homicide since the south end of King Edward II met the north end of a red-hot poker. The climax is a blockbuster -it's as good as anything I've read in courtroom fiction." The Reporter

"The best crime drama I have read in a long time." - Editor, *EBookObsessed.*

"Mr. Rainer is capable of writing a hell of a good sentence. The writing is crisp, hard, nearly flawless. The love story woven in has a way of arriving with perfect pitch; it is warm and right. I can safely recommend Capital Kill to anyone who wants a thrill, scented with a world of truth." - Palmetto Reviews.

HORNS OF THE DEVIL

BOOK 2 IN THE JEFF TRASK CRIME DRAMA SERIES

The beheaded body of an ambassador's son is dumped on the curb in front of his father's embassy just blocks from the White House. Federal prosecutor Jeff Trask and an FBI task force are called upon to solve the murder. Their search for the killers leads to the MS-13, a hyper-violent gang from El Salvador, but Trask and his team soon learn that someone else is also tracking their suspects, and with deadly efficiency. When Trask himself becomes a target, he realizes that he is caught in a cross-fire between two of the most ruthless organizations in the western hemisphere.

Read Horns of the Devil

Editorial Reviews of *Horns of the Devil*:

"Federal prosecutor Jeff Trask returns to work on a case involving Salvadoran gang members. Trask is an engaging lead character: His extraordinary intelligence and eidetic memory are the same reasons he sometimes has trouble concentrating. Rainer also turns the spotlight on other, equally gripping characters. A well-paced mystery featuring an entertainingly complicated protagonist, supported by a robust cast." - Kirkus Reviews.

"Another great thriller by Marc Rainer. With an author who doesn't hesitate to harm a character, either major or minor, it keeps you on your toes wondering if the killers might just win this time. An intriguing story with great characters in real danger. Like any good thriller, it kept you guessing until the very end. If you love a good thriller, I recommend giving this new author a chance." - Editor, EBookObsessed.

"With Horns of the Devil, author Marc Rainer has given us another brilliant ride, a genuinely suspenseful book full of intrigue and action, the twists often leaving the reader in fear for the characters they've come to love. The command Mr. Rainer has over his material, the pure writing skill on view, not only keeps things flowing, but never lets it seem that any of what is going on is less than real. The story goes along in a thrilling way, right until the end, where there is one more twist waiting. The whole tale is unnerving and great fun. Highly recommend it." - Palmetto Reviews.

DEATH'S WHITE HORSES

BOOK 3 IN THE JEFF TRASK CRIME DRAMA SERIES

In *Capital Kill,* he went after a ruthless local serial killer. In *Horns of the Devil,* he faced some of the deadliest gangs in the western hemisphere. Now federal prosecutor Jeff Trask is back on the case, after a series of drug overdoses places investigators face to face with Los Zetas—the most dangerous of the Mexican drug cartels. What begins as an investigation of local heroin trafficking soon turns into something far more serious. The cartel will do anything to protect its cash flow–including a series of attacks against Trask's team that cement Los Zetas' status as one of the most ruthless criminal organizations of the century. Inspired by actual events from Mexico's cartel wars, *Death's White Horses* is Marc Rainer's third book featuring federal prosecutor Jeff Trask. While showcasing the challenges faced by law enforcement on both sides of the border, it also highlights the deadly consequences seen on either end of the US-Mexico drug trade.

Read Death's White Horses

Editorial Reviews of *Death's White Horses*:

"Death's White Horses is the third installment in author Marc Rainer's series featuring savvy prosecutor Jeff Trask. This fictionalized account of the Mexican drug cartel wars presents a dark, gripping and violent tale of barbarous criminals and the law enforcement officials on both sides of the border charged with fighting a bloody war. Many of the characters portrayed are taken from real life, such as drug kingpins Chapo Guzman and Heriberto Lazcano. Rainer has provided another unflinching, engrossing chronicle." - Palmetto Reviews.

"No one in the world is writing better than Marc Rainer, with pitch-perfect prose full of intrigue, a favorite in suspense, elegant by any literary standard!" - MCS Film Review Team.

"An invigorating thriller with an engaging protagonist surrounded by equally worthy characters." - Kirkus Reviews.

A WINTER OF WOLVES

BOOK 4 IN THE JEFF TRASK CRIME DRAMA SERIES

Federal prosecutor Jeff Trask is summoned to a murder scene. A Park Police officer has been brutally murdered at the Lincoln Memorial. As Trask and a team of local and federal investigators try to find the killer, more police officers are murdered. While attending the funeral for one of these victims, Trask and his team find themselves in a firefight with a cell of radical Islamic terrorists. Disqualified because of his involvement at the scene at Arlington National Cemetery, Trask is reassigned to Washington D.C.'s Joint Terrorism Task Force, where he discovers that the firefight at Arlington was only part of a bigger and much more sinister plot that threatens the entire Eastern Seaboard.

Read A Winter of Wolves

Editorial Reviews of *A Winter of Wolves*:

"The lawyer-hero remains, as always, resolute and razor-sharp . . . Plenty of backstory on the villains makes them both intriguing and intimidating . . . A riveting final act which delivers plenty of action." - Kirkus Reviews.

"A riveting suspense thriller of a novel from beginning to end, A Winter of Wolves reveals author Marc Rainer's impressive flair for creating a deftly crafted and memorable novel that will prove to be enduringly popular." - Midwest Book Review.

DEATH VOTES LAST

BOOK 5 IN THE JEFF TRASK CRIME DRAMA SERIES

With an evenly-divided United States Senate, the stakes are high for the nation's political power brokers. The leader of one party decides to change the numbers by arranging the elimination of one of the other party's senators. As the senator's death sends shock waves through the nation's capital, federal prosecutor Jeff Trask and a team of FBI agents and police officers must solve not only the senator's homicide, but the murder of one witness and the attempted murder of another. Further complicating their efforts is the fact that the trial of the killer must take place in the political swamp of Washington, D.C. As Trask and his team investigate the deaths and prepare for the trial of the century, the nation's political fate hangs in the balance.

Read Death Votes Last

Editorial Reviews of *Death Votes Last:*

"I love it when a series goes back to the basics of what made it great. Like Law & Order, this series gives us the best of both worlds as you follow the story from investigation to conclusion. The court drama was compelling, and the danger from up high felt palpable. I couldn't put it down. The story kept me intrigued, anxious and very much pissed off in what can only be seen as failings in our legislative system."- Editor, EBookObsessed.

"In Rainer's fifth thriller featuring federal prosecutor Jeff Trask, a U.S. senator's suspicious death may very well be a political assassination. Also, someone's trying to ensure that a key witness doesn't make it to the stand, which puts Trask, as a potential obstacle, in peril. Although the protagonist, a "former military guy," has spent preceding books largely engaged in action scenes, this story places him firmly back in the courtroom. It's a welcome return, as he shines during jury selection (what he calls "juror elimination") or while dealing with a judge tossing pertinent evidence. Along the way, Rainer adds charming touches, such as plot-relevant tunes: the Rolling Stones' 1966 song "Paint it Black" is on the radio at the morgue, and a cynical Trask gets Aerosmith's 2000 song "Jaded" in his head. A rousing, standout series entry." - Kirkus Reviews

"A gripping, intriguing, complex crime drama especially recommended for readers interested not just in being entertained, but in learning more about courtroom proceedings and the logic behind investigative routines." - D. Donovan, Senior Reviewer, Midwest Book Review

MOB RULES

BOOK 6 IN THE JEFF TRASK CRIME DRAMA SERIES

Assistant United States Attorney Jeff Trask moves from Washington, D.C., to Kansas City, where he begins an investigation into an international drug ring smuggling the deadly combination of fentanyl and heroin from the southern border to the Eastern Seaboard.

In this case, Trask is fighting a rival whose criminal genius matches Trask's own intellect, and—while Trask is bound by the legal code and his own set of morals—the mob boss on the other side of this battle is unencumbered by such restrictions. The investigation forces Trask to choose whether to operate within the legal system or to venture outside it to bring down the murderous kingpin. Marc Rainer again blends actual events from his career with a compelling plot line to add to a series of novels hailed by law enforcement professionals for their realism.

Read Mob Rules

Editorial reviews of *Mob Rules:*

"Packed with action, humor, and a few sad, sentimental moments, Mob Rules is a masterfully written thriller that left me longing for more." - Donald Richard, TopShelf Magazine.

"Former federal prosecutor Marc Rainer has a dynamic way of blending his true life trial experiences with the fictional world of Jeff Trask to amp up the excitement of a criminal investigation. These stories have an excellent mixture of the investigation and prosecution which details what truly goes into finding the criminals, determining guilt and then establishing that guilt in a way which would allow the prosecutors to obtain a verdict in a court of law." - Editor, ebookobsessed.

"Engrossing and educational, all at once ... a satisfying tension to the story line that keeps readers not just involved, but on their toes. Mystery, thriller, and intrigue readers will be delighted with Trask's many challenges, which operate on more than one level." - D. Donovan, Senior Reviewer, Midwest Book Review

"The bad guys in this tale are just as enthralling as the virtuous players. The story thrives on the attorney's legal fisticuffs. Secondary plot lines shine. The persistently entertaining lawyer leads a superb batch of characters and subplots." - Kirkus Reviews

ABOUT THE AUTHOR

Marc Rainer is the pen name for Charles "Chuck" Ambrose. He is a graduate of the United States Air Force Academy, a former Air Force JAG Circuit Prosecutor, and a former federal prosecutor in Washington, D.C.

In his more than thirty years of experience, he has tried hundreds of both military and federal (civilian) major cases, including prosecutions of homicide cases, federal conspiracy trials, and mafia and other organized crime cases.

He weaves scenes from his investigative and trial experiences into the plot lines of his novels, which have been hailed by those in the criminal justice fields for their realism. He has co-authored a manual on how to try murder cases, which was published by the American Bar Association's Criminal Law Section.

He lives in a suburb of a major northwestern city with his wife, a retired Special Agent of the Air Force's Office of Special Investigations (OSI), and their rescue mutts.

His web page may be found at www.marcrainer.com

Find & Follow Marc Rainer

The Grinding Wheel is a work of fiction.

Names, characters, places, and incidents either are the product of the author's imagination or are used fictitiously, and any resemblance to actual persons, living or dead, business establishments, events, or locales is purely coincidence and is unintentional.

ISBN: 978-0-578-91185-4
Library of Congress Control Number: 2021910332

Rukia Publishing US

Dansville, NY, USA

Publisher's Note:

Made in the USA
Monee, IL
04 November 2026

67383827R00167